SRTD

STUDIES IN RELIGION, THEOLOGY, AND DISABILITY

Accessible Atonement

Accessible Atonement

Disability, Theology, and the Cross of Christ

David McLachlan

BAYLOR UNIVERSITY PRESS

Cover design and typesetting by Kasey McBeath
Cover image: abstract painting, clivewa/Shutterstock.com

Library of Congress Cataloging-in-Publication Data

Names: McLachlan, David, 1963- author.
Title: Accessible atonement : disability, theology, and the cross of Christ / David McLachlan.
Other titles: Studies in religion, theology, and disability
Description: Waco : Baylor University, 2021. | Series: Studies in religion, theology, and disability | Includes bibliographical references and index. | Summary: "Engages systematic theology with pastoral concerns to expand our understanding of Christ's sacrifice so that persons with disabilities are more integrally included in our conceptions of soteriology and ecclesiology, especially liturgy"-- Provided by publisher.
Identifiers: LCCN 2020041147 (print) | LCCN 2020041148 (ebook) | ISBN 9781481313674 (hardcover) | ISBN 9781481314053 (pdf) | ISBN 9781481314046 (mobi) | ISBN 9781481313698 (epub)
Subjects: LCSH: Disabilities--Religious aspects--Christianity. | Church work with people with disabilities. | Atonement.
Classification: LCC BT732 .M35 2021 (print) | LCC BT732 (ebook) | DDC 234/.5--dc23
LC record available at https://lccn.loc.gov/2020041147
LC ebook record available at https://lccn.loc.gov/2020041148

Printed in the United States of America on acid-free paper with a minimum of thirty percent recycled content.

Series Introduction

Studies in Religion, Theology, and Disability brings newly established and emerging scholars together to explore issues at the intersection of religion, theology, and disability. The series editors encourage theoretical engagement with secular disability studies while supporting the reexamination of established religious doctrine and practice. The series fosters research that takes account of the voices of people with disabilities and the voices of their family and friends.

The volumes in the series address issues and concerns of the global religious studies/theological studies academy. Authors come from a variety of religious traditions with diverse perspectives to reflect on the intersection of the study of religion/theology and the human experience of disability. This series is intentional about seeking out and publishing books that engage with disability in dialogue with Jewish, Christian, Buddhist, or other religious and philosophical perspectives.

Themes explored include religious life, ethics, doctrine, proclamation, liturgical practices, physical space, spirituality, and the interpretation of sacred texts through the lens of disability. Authors in the series are aware of conversation in the field of disability studies and bring that discussion to bear methodologically and theoretically in their analyses at the intersection of religion and disability.

Studies in Religion, Theology, and Disability reflects the following developments in the field: First, the emergence of disability studies as an interdisciplinary endeavor that has impacted theological studies, broadly defined.

More and more scholars are deploying disability perspectives in their work, and this applies also to those working in the theological academy. Second, there is a growing need for critical reflection on disability in world religions. While books from a Christian standpoint have dominated the discussion at the interface of religion and disability so far, Jewish, Muslim, Buddhist, and Hindu scholars, among those from other religious traditions, have begun to resource their own religious traditions to rethink disability in the twenty-first century. Third, passage of the Americans with Disabilities Act in the United States has raised the consciousness of the general public about the importance of critical reflection on disability in religious communities. General and intelligent lay readers are looking for scholarly discussions of religion and disability as these bring together and address two of the most important existential aspects of human lives. Fourth, the work of activists in the disability rights movement has mandated fresh critical reflection by religious practitioners and theologians. Persons with disabilities remain the group most disaffected from religious organizations. Fifth, government representatives in several countries have prioritized the greater social inclusion of persons with disabilities. Disability policy often proceeds based on core cultural and worldview assumptions that are religiously informed. Work at the interface of religion and disability thus could have much broader purchase—that is, in social, economic, political, and legal domains.

Under the general topic of thoughtful reflection on the religious understanding of disability, Studies in Religion, Theology, and Disability includes shorter, crisply argued volumes that articulate a bold vision within a field; longer scholarly monographs, more fully developed and meticulously documented, with the same goal of engaging wider conversations; textbooks that provide a state of the discussion at this intersection and chart constructive ways forward; and select edited volumes that achieve one or more of the preceding goals.

Contents

Preface

DID GOD GIVE ME EPILEPSY? AND OTHER HARD QUESTIONS

Jamie came into the education reception area full of energy on a chilly late-autumn afternoon. In his usual disarming way, without any preamble and fully expecting an answer, he asked me a question that had probably occurred to him more than once: "Did God give me epilepsy?" He was not angrily throwing down a gauntlet, simply asking the question. Whether the answer was going to be "yes" or "no," or somewhere in between, I could sense the presence of a follow-up question hovering somewhere in the wings: ". . . and what is he going to do about it?" Jamie was a student at a campus near our village in Southeast England established to provide educational, medical, and residential facilities for young people with epilepsy and with other complex neurological conditions. I was the (very new) pastor of the local church, just joining the governing body at the campus, so there was no pretending that I was not the legitimate target for his question. Jamie was from a Christian family. He expected a Christian answer, probably involving Jesus.

Of course, Jamie might have put the question in other ways. He might have asked, instead, whether I thought God would heal him, and on the surface it sounded like that might be what he was getting at. But his actual question, although deceptively simple, was more penetrating by far. In the first place it asked about origins. It asked how his life had come to be the way it was and how God was involved or implicated in that. It also contained within it questions of purpose. It wanted to know what place Jamie and his friends, many of whom had far more disabling conditions, had in God's plans for the world. It contained questions of response. It wanted to know what God, and Jesus in whom Jamie and his family trusted, thought about the value of his life and where they should look to find God's response to their struggles. And yes, in there somewhere were questions of healing and hope and destination. It wanted to know what God might (or ought to) heal or transform in this present life and what Jamie's body and brain chemistry might be like come the resurrection, the life to come, the new creation.

Whatever inadequate and rambling answer I gave to Jamie all those years ago I mercifully cannot now recall, and perhaps neither can he. But the question he asked endures, and it demands a meaningful response. Few people will go through life without asking it at some point for themselves or for others. That brief conversation in the reception area was certainly not the end of the matter at the time. Several of the young people from the campus, together with those charged with their care, attended services at our village church from time to time. The fellowship of the church, to their great credit, were warm and welcoming. Indeed, there was a sense of being privileged that these young people would choose to join them. Discussion soon turned to matters of the physical accessibility of the building and whether our facilities were adequate. Then there was discussion about the shape and content of our worship services and how we could make better provision for the students to feel at home and take part. We discussed the need for freedom and ease of movement in and out of the services at any moment, as might be needed. Although prayer for healing had become part of the regular fare in the church, no one at that point had yet asked what we should do about suggesting prayer for healing for these young people.

That was all very positive but, as Jamie's thoughtful and disconcerting enquiry about his epilepsy had demonstrated so very well, we seemed to be running ahead of (or perhaps more accurately, stepping around) a much deeper, harder conversation. As the one tasked, week by week, with offering to the church an account of the Christian gospel, there seemed to be a number of unsettling prior questions to do with disability, or long-term disabling conditions, and our faith that needed to be faced up to before we would really be equipped to answer those practical ones about accessible spaces and services. Those prior questions surely included the following: What place is there in this gospel we are sharing for mental and physical disability?[1] Does what we call "disability" naturally have a place in that gospel, or is it always to be added later as a "special case"? How do we understand the existence and experience of disability and God's part in it? Given a Christian understanding of God, what should our hopes be for lives lived with disability right now, or come the resurrection, and where do ideas of healing fit in? Not only that, but how do we relate all of this to Jesus, and to his cross and resurrection, which seem to stand at the center of it all?

The response of our local church, asking itself questions about inclusion, was prompted both by a genuine compassion and desire to do well, and by the awareness that rights of access and inclusion are an important and positive part of contemporary culture. This is what we ought to do, and rightly so. But it nonetheless leaves a sense of unease or superficiality. It is true that those with disabilities have found themselves on the margins of church life because, among other things, difficulties of physical access or the effects of visual or auditory impairment have been widely overlooked. It is also true that thoughtful practical changes can and should overcome much of that marginalization. What is more worrying, however, is that those with disabilities should find themselves marginal to the very gospel itself. There is little that is distinctively Christian about simply arguing for inclusion. The deeper question is whether the argument for inclusion, and the very conviction of its rightness, is built upon the foundation stones of the gospel that is shared week by week, on Jesus, his incarnation, cross, and resurrection. If people with disabilities were to find that they are inherently central, not marginal, to that gospel, that would seem a far more confident place for the argument for inclusion to begin.

If, then, all of those questions prompted by Jamie's asking whether God gave him epilepsy could find a sound theological foundation that starts with the central tenets of our faith in Jesus Christ, that might give us confidence to explore whether our discussion about access to the church and to worship is really mostly about ramps and the width of the doors, or whether it is part of something much, much deeper out of which all of us might grow in our faith. In our small local church, with its limited space and resources, it might give us a better starting point for working out what welcome, access, worship, and the grace and joy of the gospel might look like with Jamie and his friends as a vital part of the fellowship. It should also give us a firmer grasp of what we are really doing when we offer to pray for healing in a world that contains a complicated mixture of disability and variety, illness and vitality, sadness and joy, distress and hope.

Acknowledgments

Many have contributed, some unwittingly, to this book reaching its final form. I am particularly grateful to colleagues and students at Spurgeons College in London for letting me try out various proposals on them; also to Professor Peter Scott from Manchester for his good humor and his keen eye for fruitful lines of inquiry. As the ideas in the book have taken shape, they have been kept grounded by the dedication and wisdom of the staff and students at Young Epilepsy. At the same time they have been inspired and spurred on by conversations at the Summer Institute on Theology and Disability when I have been able to attend. When it came to marshaling all of that into book form, invaluable help and advice were provided by Cade Jarrell and his colleagues at Baylor.

Of course, those who have put up with the odd rhythms of research and writing for what must seem like the longest time are my wife and family, Mary, Lachlan, Jacob, Joel, and Mercy. Their love and encouragement are a constant and indispensable joy.

Introduction

THE PROBLEM OF DISABILITY, SIN, AND THE CROSS

A distinctively Christian theology of disability and inclusion must do business with the cross of Jesus Christ, since in Christianity the cross tests everything.[1] But if the cross is to be the source of a theology of disability and inclusion we must be honest and admit that it has also been a problem. Bringing together disability, sin, the cross, healing, and salvation has an awkward history. In some places the Bible seems to link disability and sin, or indicate that salvation through the cross is tied up with the "healing" of bodies we would label disabled, conforming them to what we consider to be "typical" bodies. Healing ministries have at times compounded the problem, particularly where an impairment persists, leaving people with disabilities wondering where they fit into this salvation narrative.

Thinking about the cross brings us to the heart of the problem. Christians believe that salvation and new creation come through the cross of Jesus Christ and the resurrection to which it leads. The cross is where God addresses the whole human condition. But if the cross is all about and only expressed as dealing with sin, then for God to address through the cross all the challenges and suffering that situations of disability can cause, it follows that disability must also be a matter of sin. Because sin is a moral issue, a turning away from God, that seems to make disability also a moral issue, something "wrong." The relatively young and developing field of study that is usually called disability theology has taken on the task of giving a positive Christian theological account of disability. Much excellent ground has been covered and sharp challenges have been raised, but there is a conspicuously thin patch in the tapestry that disability theology has been weaving. It is at the place where there should be a deep discussion of disability and the cross, and it is most likely this awkward history that has made us wary of tackling such a discussion.

And yet Christians are fully convinced that the good news of the kingdom of God, which is announced for all people, is a drama of redemption that finds its very source and climax in the person of Jesus, his incarnation and most profoundly his death on that cross, and the resurrection that followed. At the cross we encounter what we can call God's great action of atonement. There, the character of God, his purposes, and his relationship with humanity and with all creation are most vividly revealed. If we are looking for a distinctively Christian theology of disability and distinctively Christian answers to the questions that disability raises, then that theology and those answers must surely find their foundations in the drama that reaches its crucial moment on the cross. The cross is the place where God, in the person of Jesus, addresses our whole condition and opens up the way for resurrection, new creation, and the fulfillment of all things. As the apostle Paul puts it, this is the place where "in Christ God was reconciling the world to himself" (2 Cor 5:19). If that is so, then this should be the place to which we carry our hard questions about disability. If we do not, then our friends and family members who have disabilities will forever find themselves on the margins of the story, and inevitably on the margins of the church, whatever claims we make about inclusion.

The shorthand of the title of this book, *Accessible Atonement*, tries to condense the challenge into just two words. If God's action of atonement through Jesus at the cross is the cornerstone of Christian faith that gives access through the curtain to the Holy of Holies, to resurrection and the outpouring of the Holy Spirit, that is preached in church week by week and revisited whenever the church baptizes or shares the Lord's Supper, and that shapes how we see the world and how we live, then what does that atonement at the cross have to say about disability? Attempting a response necessarily entails approaching the knotty problem of how disability is related not only to sin and salvation but also to healing, given, as mentioned, the often awkward juxtaposition of these things, both in theology and in the text of the Bible. Although the question of healing is not always the first to be raised when a church finds itself grappling with disability and inclusion, it must at some point become a significant part of the mix. It is hardly difficult to open the Bible and find Jesus, and later his disciples, healing people both of diseases such as leprosy and of what we would typically call disabilities, such as being deaf, blind, or paralyzed. And many of those who are healed become his followers. We will have to ask how we should read those passages and interpret them in our own times, as well as asking who gets to say what counts as "healing" in the first place. Added to all of this, if within that same gospel, to be "saved" involves being expected to "repent, and believe in the good news" (Mark 1:15), something requiring agency and cognition, we cannot avoid the question of what that means for people with significant intellectual impairment or with nontypical brain chemistry.

Importantly, to ask these questions is absolutely not to seek out or try to construct a sort of special-interest theology, or a special reading of Scripture, which only applies to, or "works" for, those particularly concerned with disability. That is to be resisted with utmost vigor. In addressing the questions emerging here, there is no attempt to find a niche or specialized presentation or expression of the atonement, a way of speaking about the cross, that happens to address particular disability concerns in a special-interest debate. To do so would be to leave those with disabilities still as outsiders, admitted to the gospel only by extension or concession. The objective is entirely different. It is to ask in what way our main Christian account of the cross and the atonement might allow itself to be disrupted and reformed, encompassing from its roots upward all of humanity, inclusive of disability.

If the field of disability theology has been tentative in its engagement with the cross and the atonement, it is even more evident that scholarship on the cross and the atonement has engaged hardly at all with the existence and experience of disability. Atonement theology has certainly had much to say about humanity, but little about a humanity that explicitly includes disability in all its variety.[2] It has had much to say about the suffering of Jesus and human suffering, but little about the complex mixture of challenges and joys entailed in the very broad range of situations that we label as "disability." The task in redressing that balance is not to assess any one historic contribution to atonement theology in the light of disability considerations. Instead, it is to ask how the whole field of atonement theology as currently debated and preached should be shaped by, and should shape, our theological approach to disability.

If that can be achieved, it has significant implications. One is the possibility of arriving at a way of understanding the atonement that enables the cross, the cornerstone of Christian faith and life, to be a true foundation for disability theology and a place from which to answer the hard questions highlighted here, rather than a source of awkwardness to be skirted around when disability is discussed. The desire is to build a theology of disability on the central tenets of Christian faith, but to do so by allowing those central tenets to be critiqued by insights that arise out of a disability frame of reference.

Another implication is that if God's action at the cross were inherently inclusive of all humanity in all its variety, that would bring people with disabilities to the center of the gospel. The argument for inclusion in church and worship would then stand on the much firmer ground of finding that people with disabilities are already "within the camp," included in the central work of Jesus Christ, and critical to our understanding of God and the gospel.

A third implication concerns healing. A reading of the healing narratives in the Gospels and the later New Testament that assumes a direct link between moral sin and anything we label as "disability" has long been unhelpful and a stumbling block for many. Maintaining the crucial assertion that at the cross God, in Christ, deals with sin is essential. However, allowing the insights of disability theology to open up a more fruitful conversation about the existence of disability as part of humanity holds out the prospect of opening up a differentiated response to healing, sin, and forgiveness, and a deeper reflection on the whole human condition addressed by God at the cross.

NAVIGATING A MAZE OF IDEAS

Questions about disability and the cross may be theological, but they are certainly not just theoretical or academic. They arise in the context of Christian ministry and of Christians working out what it means to live each day as followers of Jesus Christ. Therefore, if answers are to be discovered, they also have to make sense in the midst of the practice of Christian living. That will mean seeking out a foundation for a Christian theology of disability that starts in that same place. It will mean beginning with the gospel that is shared in churches week by week, that is our main account of the "big story" of Scripture, the great redemption drama of God.

That drama incorporates all of creation. It includes the fall, the call of Abraham and Israel, the Exodus, covenant, exile, Jesus, Pentecost, the church, and the fulfillment of all things in the new creation. However, it is also true that the pivot on which that great account of God's work of reconciliation and redemption turns is Jesus Christ, his incarnation, ministry, death, resurrection, ascension, and promised return. Even within that there is the sense of a particular turning point, the very fulcrum of the whole story: the death of the man Jesus Christ from Nazareth, who is also fully God, on a cross outside the city of Jerusalem on the Friday of the Passover festival in a year around AD 33. That event cannot be detached from the rest of the drama, and yet there is a sense that it is after the cross that nothing is the same.[3] For that reason, the language and ideas used to describe that event will be vitally important in this discussion. There will be powerful ideas of sacrifice, justice, and victory to come to terms with, ideas with long tradition whose roots lie deep in both Old and New Testaments.

This is why a theology of disability must do business with the person of Jesus Christ and with God's action of atonement at the cross. These are central doctrines of the gospel. If discussion of disability were to remain on the periphery of such doctrines, dipping in from time to time, and with its own interpretations, its own ideas for its own context, then little would have been done to help the body of Christ as a whole to move closer to our sisters and brothers with disabilities, and perhaps all that would have been created would be a sort of theological ghetto for disability.

It quickly becomes clear that the task ahead will involve taking the questions that have been raised above and navigating them through something of a maze of theological ideas about both disability and the cross. First, this will involve looking across the field of disability theology, identifying the objectives it has been pursuing and the themes it has been exploring. The purpose in doing so is to discover to what extent it is already interacting with the atonement, the gospel drama centered on Jesus and the cross. It will not be sufficient just to find references to the cross or the atonement, or a lack of them. What is sought is both where ideas about the cross are directly referred to or made use of, and where concepts about the cross or the atonement appear to influence or shape a proposed theological understanding of disability.

Second, it will involve a careful look at the current debate around the atonement. This is a challenge, since there are so many possible threads to that debate. Models and theories abound. There is also something of a movement against the idea of having theories or models of the atonement at all, that such doctrinal discussion becomes sterile and disconnected from the actual drama of reconciliation. However, it is essential that this sometimes unwieldy collection of arguments and tensions be marshaled into a usable framework of ideas so that the present task can make progress. The purpose there will be to discover whether the existing ideas of what God is doing at the cross, and the powerful language in which they are expressed, provide the resources for the cross to speak fundamentally into a theology of disability. To the extent they do not, the task will be to make use of the insights emerging from disability theology to disrupt and re-form an understanding of the atonement, developing one that is inherently inclusive of all humanity, including those with disabilities, and that can act as a foundation for the continuing pursuit of the objectives of disability theology.

In finding a way through all of this, it would be easy to become rather vague about what kind of atonement, what kind of action of God, is in mind. When ways of expressing the atonement (models, theories, and so on) are considered, what is it about the death of Jesus on the cross that we want them to convey? Similarly, when the insights of disability scholars are examined, what is it about the cross that we are interested to find included in, or informing, their arguments? Not only does that sort of interrogation need to be kept on track, it must also be consistent and fair. What is needed, then, is to be clear about the measure by which these things will be assessed. Such a measure is sometimes called a "hermeneutical key," by which is meant a test that is consistently applied to weigh up texts and arguments.

An effective measure or key for discussions about the atonement is the challenge lying at the heart of the central claim that Christianity makes about the cross. That claim is that what we might call the "Christ event," especially the death of Jesus on the cross, is a particular event in history that brings about a universal ontological change which is effective for all time. Following that event, things are not as they were. Most importantly, it was not just that there was, or is, a change in how things are perceived by us or by God. Rather, the effects of sin are dealt with effectively. This goes beyond sin being just ritually addressed and declared to be nullified or forgiven. Sin's hold on creation and humanity is actually and effectively confronted and broken. It also goes beyond claiming that the cross illustrates in a unique way some eternal truth about God or his character, although it may indeed very much do so. Rather, the event of the cross itself constitutes a universal reconciliation. Through this event God is working to reconcile all of creation, including humanity, to himself, instigating a cosmic renewal. This means that somehow this particular event reaches into every part of time and space and has an impact on all aspects of the universe, even in those times and spaces where current experience and evidence indicate that the effects of sin and nonreconciliation continue.

This is a bold and comprehensive claim, but that is what makes it a useful hermeneutical key or measure for the work. It is best seen as made up of two essential component parts, the universal and the particular. The change that is brought about is universal, a cosmic reconciliation, and yet it turns not on a general movement of people or events but on the very particular person of Jesus and the very particular event of his death on the cross that Friday afternoon, to be followed by his resurrection on the third day. It is a large claim, balanced on a narrow pivot.[4] Maintaining this central claim about the cross and the atonement, with its universal and particular parts, is not necessarily easy. It could seem a very different matter to talk of universal reconciliation in the present compared to New Testament times. In the Greco-Roman world of Jesus and the apostle Paul, the human concept and experience of the cosmos and the scale of the world was, we assume, different. In our present world, with so many people on our planet and our awareness not just of them but of the vastness of the physical universe and the length of human and geological history, together with the realization that the majority of people and places never encounter the gospel, this claim for the atonement having universal scope may seem to have become more of a stretch. Yet that is the claim about the cross, and it remains so.

Similarly, it can feel uncomfortable to claim that this one particular event could have such universal impact. Such discomfort can lead us to diminish the claim. At the extreme end of that movement, some theological writing has drawn away from the event of Jesus Christ, from his birth to his ascension, as being in any way necessary for salvation. Instead, salvation becomes a much less specific matter, with Jesus demonstrating for us certain things about God but the cross becoming no more unique than any other historic event.[5] More subtly, there can be a mere change of emphasis. The claim that the cross is constitutive of salvation can be omitted in favor of an emphasis on its power to reveal the nature of salvation and the nature of God's character. This change might arise out of a laudable desire to connect with the humanity of Jesus and an instinct for demythologizing the language of the Bible. Whatever the motivation, Jesus and the cross can easily become just a supreme example of a faithful life and death, filled with the Holy Spirit. The challenge taken up here, and to be used as the measure of each contribution from disability theology and atonement theology, is to insist on asking what each contribution says both about an actual universal reconciliation and about the particular event of the cross that constitutes it.

Before taking a deep breath and diving in, it is worth noticing that even at the outset there is encouragement to be had, from both the universal and the particular of the atonement that have been emphasized so strenuously here. First, in its dependence on the particular death of Jesus Christ on the cross, the atonement focuses on a specific, concrete body and on the specific lived experience of that body, including the experience of being despised, disfigured, and ultimately broken. This is fitting for disability theology, which demands an emphasis not on abstract doctrines but on concrete bodies and on lived experiences. It challenges the perception that theology should be conducted principally with "normal" or "typical" bodies in mind. The acknowledgment of the particular embodied experience of Jesus demands that all bodies, including nontypical ones, should be thought of as a resource for thinking theologically.[6] It asks directly how the claims of the gospel, and claims about the cross that lie at its heart, can be said to have meaning for people who are most likely very aware of nontypical bodies and of an embodied experience, much of which is very demanding.

Taking particularity a step further, the focus of the atonement on the concrete body and experience of Jesus continues through the appearance of Jesus as a physical body following the resurrection. The universal cosmic renewal wrought by the atonement has become embodied in this risen, albeit in some way transformed, body. There is both continuity and discontinuity with the body that went to the cross, not least in its bearing visible wounds from crucifixion. It prompts us to make space for those with what might be considered nontypical bodies to ask what sort of continuity and discontinuity is entailed for them, and by extension for all of us, in this great work of God.

Second, the universal claim of cosmic reconciliation is a matter of the scope and nature of change. Christians claim that the atonement is in some way God's answer to the problems of the world, perhaps especially problems of injustice and oppression. Disability theology in its present form, which has its roots firmly in the disability rights movement and disability studies, is addressing a group of particular "problems" in the world, those of the existence and experience of impairment and of the oppression of those with disabilities. Insisting on the universal aspect of the atonement provides the discipline of insisting that this is not a special-interest discussion but one that is looking for an understanding of the atonement that is inherently inclusive of all.

All People and This Person

In a discussion that claims to be about disability, there is a danger of becoming vague about who or what situations of disability that discussion is about. Our own lives and the lives of those who surround us reveal the great diversity of situations that tend to be grouped under the heading of "disability," despite the obvious fact that many of these life situations bear little or no relation to one another. A child born with Down syndrome, a war veteran who has lost a limb in combat, and an elderly person living with dementia might all be said to have a disability. We might want our theology of disability to encompass all three, but we also want it to recognize how little their situations have in common. That sheer diversity of life experiences seems to press for a step-by-step or group-by-group theological approach. Perhaps we should answer our questions for one category of disability and then test how what we find might extend into others. Confining ourselves to, say, physical disability or intellectual disability might be the way to make progress. On the other hand, to do so seems simply to have picked up the inclusion/exclusion barrier, full of good intentions, only to discover later on that all we have done is move it a little way down the road, and that we have failed to come to grips with that underlying question of how God addresses humanity as a whole.

Deciding whether all or just some disabilities should be in view certainly entails recognizing that there are important clinical differences from situation to situation.[7] It also entails recognizing that other factors may be at least as significant as clinical distinctions, such as duration (some disabilities being permanent and others either temporary or intermittent) or the impact on aspects of lived experience, such as mobility, engagement in education, or the need for personal carers. Furthermore, it calls for a recognition that much of the experience of disability arises from encounters with a society unwilling to change its behavior to allow for the flourishing of those whose bodies or brains lie outside a range broadly regarded as "typical." If nothing else, such considerations should be a note of caution in thinking that boundaries can easily be drawn or categories of disability easily defined.[8] Within a Christian frame of reference there is a strong instinct to argue that all people are human, all made in the image of God, and that at the cross God addresses all of humanity. However, it is equally certain that at the cross God does not just address us all, and the human condition universally, he also addresses "you" and "me" and our situations in particular.

It seems essential, then, in discovering useful responses to these questions about disability and the cross that they should both apply to all people and yet make sense without sounding glib in the context of the individual. The way to achieve this is to keep two strands of thinking moving along together. First, it is to embark on the task with all of humanity, including all of its variety of ability and disability in mind, not restricting that discussion to any discrete subset of disabilities. Second, or as simultaneously as possible, it is to keep asking whether the answers proposed remain relevant to particular situations of disability. The first strand of this approach should avoid generating answers that apply only to a certain category of people, perpetuating the theological invisibility of others. At the same time, the second strand should ensure that what is said does not fall into the trap of being so general that it becomes disconnected from real lives.

Achieving this second strand requires some discussion of those real lives. Across disability theology literature there is considerable helpful testimony and theological reflection from people with disabilities and from those who live closely with them, and this will be kept in mind. As the discussion proceeds, it will be open to the voices of some of my own friends and acquaintances in similar situations, who have given permission for their thoughts on these hard questions to be shared.[9] This or any limited group of individual people cannot claim to cover all possibilities exhaustively. New friends with their own circumstances will always be found. Christians who have disabilities, or who have friends or family with disabilities, and anyone asking these questions about God, Jesus, the gospel, and disability are warmly encouraged to keep testing and refining what is explored here. Having said that, those mentioned here can nonetheless begin to represent the various ways in which the theological discussion connects with the particularity of actual lived experience.

I

CURRENT INTERACTIONS

1

Disability Theology and the Cross

THEMES AND OBJECTIVES IN DISABILITY THEOLOGY

Disability is practical, lived, and experienced. My friend Martin does not have multiple sclerosis in theory. When he and his wife, Eve, arrive at church on a Sunday morning, their worship and prayers and how they hear the word of God are shaped by the practical experience of the hours of intricate physical and emotional exertion through which they have traveled together, from waking to being physically present among us. Any theologizing about disability must begin with listening to and reflecting on experiences like theirs. If the insights arising out of that listening and reflecting really are going to disrupt and re-form how we think about the cross and the atonement, it is essential to identify the avenues of thought that they invite us to explore.[1] Disability theology is the name generally given to the growing field of work that has taken up that challenge. It has set itself the objective of a positive and rigorous theological response to the existence and experience of disability, as well as giving a disability perspective greater visibility and voice within Christian theological scholarship and ecclesial practice.[2] The question here is whether that work has engaged with the challenges that disability raises for how we think about the cross. That, in turn, might indicate whether such work is already contributing to a distinctively Christian account of disability, rooted in a gospel of which the cornerstone is the cross of Jesus Christ.

Disability theology has already covered much ground, following certain lines of inquiry and asking searching questions. It has asked, for example, what it means to be human and whether our ideas of humanity being made in the image of God contain unexamined presumptions about the typical human body or mind. That has also led it to ask whether our approach to prayer for healing might contain presumptions about some sort of typical body or mind or emotional condition that God would "obviously" want us to have. In turn it has asked about the effect of disability on our ideas of salvation and the resurrection body. It has raised theological questions about access and whether we have designed our churches and our experiences of worship around presumptions about our senses of sight and hearing and the ability to sit still, stand, read, or speak, not to mention to recognize when we are expected to do these things. It has challenged the way we read the Bible and whether in our reading we have ignored both our own presumptions about disability and those prevalent in the cultures of the times in which it was written and its events occurred.

This network of challenges can usefully be grouped into four main themes or areas of exploration: theological anthropology (who we are in the sight of God), a theology of access (our ability to be present and participate in worship), hermeneutics (how we read the Bible, particularly accounts of healing), and soteriology (how we understand salvation). The point of grouping them in this way is to facilitate two things. The first is asking how the insights emerging from each theme should affect how we understand the cross of Jesus Christ, the Word made flesh. The second is identifying the main objectives within each theme and asking whether the cross and the atonement, as God's putative answer to the state of creation and the whole human condition, might be the best place from which to pursue those objectives and argue their case. The first part of that work is asking what business each theme is already doing with the cross. This is not simply looking for direct references to the cross or atonement but finding the ways in which the universal claim and the particularity of the cross already appear in, or seem to have shaped, the insights being developed in each of these themes of disability theology. Just as important is identifying the questions that disability theology might be raising that our accounts of the atonement have not sufficiently addressed to date. In doing this, keeping in mind the hermeneutical key is important. Asking at each point how both the large claim of universal reconciliation and the narrow pivot of the cross on which it is balanced are involved should keep the investigation on track.

Interpreting these major themes of disability theology also involves recognizing the context in which disability theology itself has arisen and how that context has shaped it. The field has emerged as a theological response, or corollary, to the disability rights movement and the wider discipline of disability studies to which that movement has given rise. That inheritance is what has given disability theology its distinctive air of advocacy. One of the most significant contributions of the disability rights movement has been its reaction against what became known as the "medical model" of disability. This term came to be used to describe an approach to disability that classified it principally in terms of loss of function. Such loss of function was viewed as a personal tragedy to be addressed, and in some way "fixed" or "improved," through medical intervention. Within the disability rights movement (at least in the UK, where the analysis has had something of a political edge to it), the medical model was considered to have arisen historically from a combination of the rise in status of the medical profession, in diagnosis and treatment, and the rise of capitalism. The emphasis of capitalist economic thinking on the value of the individual in terms of what he or she could contribute to the productivity of an increasingly urbanized society correspondingly devalued those with disabilities. It was then the task of the medical profession to intervene to make that life more productive.[3]

In contrast to that way of thinking, the disability rights movement has developed a "social model" of disability to replace the medical model. The idea of the social model arose from the argument that people with disabilities needed to discover and write or tell their own histories, as black people and women had, rather than merely accepting an interpretation dictated to them by others.[4] This involved challenging unexamined presumptions about what it is to have a "typical" or "normal" body or mind (so-called normate presumptions). It also challenged the idea that anyone lying outside those presumed norms of function or productivity would inevitably want to be brought within them. An important distinction has emerged from these twin challenges: on the one hand there is impairment, which is to be lacking part or all of a limb, or to have a defective limb, organ, or other function; on the other hand there is disability, which is the restriction of activity caused by society taking insufficient account of those with impairments, the effect of which is to exclude them from the mainstream of activities and prevent their flourishing. The social model is therefore in large part a constructionist approach to disability. It is rooted in the experience of those with impairments and characterized by its recognition both of their voices and of the political and social structures that either support or oppress them. There is clearly a balance to be struck between the extent to which the experience of disability is a social construct in this way, the product of unhelpful systems, and the extent to which it arises from the "brute facts" of our varied bodies and minds.[5] Nonetheless, it is fair to say that the social model has become the dominant interpretative concept within disability studies as a whole.[6]

This is the wider context within which the relatively young field of disability theology has emerged and developed. Indeed, disability theology is in many ways a theological response to similar concerns. It similarly challenges unexamined normate theological presumptions, as indicated by the four major themes being investigated here. Those themes are also shaped by wrestling with ideas of the "typical" or "normal" and theological versions of the assumptions lying behind the medical and social models of disability, as will become evident. The question here is where the cross, where God was in Christ, reconciling the world to himself, features within this and whether it is in fact the best place from which to begin.

WHO WE ARE: THEOLOGICAL ANTHROPOLOGY

Of the four major themes, disability-perspective theological anthropology (who we are in the sight of God) has probably received the widest attention. This is perhaps to be expected, since it goes straight to the heart of what it is to be a human being made in the image of God, and it intersects significantly with the objectives of the disability rights movement on questions of equality and inclusion. Contributions have often come from those writing theologically from their own experience of disability, or of being closely involved with people with disabilities, and what that experience has revealed to them about our understanding of humanity in the sight of God. This theme also extends into questions of eschatology, what might be called an anthropology of the new creation, as well as questions of medical ethics and genetics, since those again are questions of what we think humanity is or should be. The theological responses that have emerged run along a number of lines, and those interact with the cross and the atonement in different ways.

Humanity Made in the Image of God: The Cross as Revelation

This is not so much a matter of asking whether humanity holds a unique place within God's created order as whether we regard those with disabilities as being of equal worth, in our own eyes as well as in God's eyes, as those who by our assessment do not have disabilities. That brings in what it means to be made in the image of God, both as that term arises in the Bible and as it has been interpreted historically.

One place to start is to reconsider what our image of God himself might be. Nancy Eiesland's book *The Disabled God* is a first port of call for many who are getting to grips with disability theology as a whole. In it Eiesland addresses this question of our image of God in a creative way. Her challenge is whether we would find it possible to picture God in a sip-puff wheelchair. This is a type of wheelchair used by people who, owing to paralysis, control the movement of the chair through air pressure, inhaling and exhaling through a tube, sometimes called a "wand."[7] Eiesland's suggestion is arresting because, while we might habitually picture God as elderly (the Ancient of Days), rarely in our mind's eye would we think of him as disabled. Yet it disrupts our typical *imago Dei* and presses uncomfortably the possibility of God's identifying fully and directly (not sentimentally or condescendingly) with those with disabilities.

While the idea of an *imago Dei* that incorporates disability to that extent might on the face of it appear extreme or unnecessary, it seems less so in light of the risen Christ bearing the wounds of crucifixion in his hands, feet, and side (for example, Luke 24:39-40 and John 20:27). The argument would be that the risen, wounded Christ, who bears the marks of his experience of becoming disabled on the cross, is perhaps the most complete and profound revelation of the *imago Dei*, and that the same risen, wounded Christ is the fullest revelation of the flesh which the Word took on at the incarnation.[8] Combining these considerations points to a solidarity with those with disabilities, which is also presaged by Jesus' emphasis on being intentionally present to those with disabilities and disabling conditions during his ministry.

Building an argument along these lines inevitably leaves some questions open. For example, the physicality of the visible wounds of the risen Jesus might seem to favor those with visible physical disabilities with a special identification with the *imago Dei*, which is not so clearly held out to those with less visible disabilities.[9] Would we be as willing to accept the idea of God with intellectual or emotional impairment, and if so, where is he to be found?

Another part of generating an inclusive theological anthropology has been to challenge concepts of the *imago Dei* that are based in reason and agency. There have been various approaches historically to identifying what makes human beings distinctively human, or what gives special worth to human lives. These have been based on criteria of rationality or self-awareness, on ideas of having and recognizing purpose, or on the ability to set and achieve life goals. However, introducing into that discussion the very challenging case of people with profound intellectual impairments has the effect of making all of those approaches look increasingly inadequate. This is because we want to assert, quite rightly, that people with profound intellectual impairment are fully human, like all of us. But when assessed against the criteria of those historical approaches, all of which involve a measure of agency or self-awareness, people who do not meet those criteria will inevitably be regarded as less than human, or at best as humans of less worth.

For all of us, including those with profound intellectual impairments, to be regarded as equally human and equally made in God's image, the measure of that humanity cannot therefore be intrinsic, self-generated, or dependent on the human being. It must be extrinsic to us and unconditional. One suggestion is that being made in the image of God is fundamentally an expression of the worth of the human being. The measure of such worth begins with God and comprises two elements. The first is an inherent element, found in God's gift of life itself. The second has to do with the purpose or goal of life, sometimes called a teleological element. This purpose is found (adopting Roman Catholic terminology) in the gift of eternal communion with Father, Son, and Holy Spirit. Expressed in another way, this second element of human worth lies in the gift of resurrection life and a place in God's new creation. The meaning of being human in the first place, therefore, is grounded not in ourselves but in God's love, his friendship toward us, and his good intentions for us.[10] We might say that that love is most clearly shown to us through the cross, but that aspect of this argument has yet to be developed.

The impetus behind these approaches to the *imago Dei* is the desire to challenge unexamined normate views of what it is to be human and what the image of God encompasses. Those presumptions have measured what it is to be human in terms of individualism, reason, and consumption, which is oppressive to those unable to reason or consume or express their individuality in the expected manner.[11] A disability-perspective theological anthropology has in its sights a different approach, one that sees disability as only one of many factors involved in living as finite beings. It is part of a universe that is open and unpredictable.[12]

When our hermeneutical key (the particular event of the cross and its claim of universal impact) is held up against these arguments, it is clear that they do, at least in part, draw on aspects of the cross. While the large claim of a universal ontological change brought about by the cross may not feature, the suffering and death of Jesus on the cross and the concrete embodiment of the atonement in the person of Jesus are significant in terms of identification and revelation. The revelation is that God identifies fully and eternally with human impairment and the experience of it. The role of that revelation in terms of the objectives of a theology of disability lies in changing our perception of our relationship with God and with each other. That change should arise out of the recognition that the *imago Dei* does not just allow for the possibility of disability but incorporates it fundamentally: there is no true expression of the *imago Dei* that does not incorporate disability. Such a change in perception ought to function to dispel noninclusive normate ideas of the *imago Dei* and lead to positive changes in the behavior of the church and society toward people with disabilities.

Disability as Revelation

As well as the cross acting as a source of revelation, a further suggestion within this theme of theological anthropology is that disability itself reveals what it means to be human and how human life might be understood and lived. Interaction with the cross is less apparent, but the points raised are significant. In the words of my friend Diane, reflecting on the experience of bringing up her son, Paul, who has been diagnosed with quite severe autism, she and her husband "*know a different stream of parenthood–one that can rejoice in things other parents don't even notice; one that is fiercely protective as well as proud of the small steps; one that reverses the order of things and provides a contrast with the aims our society expects parents to have for their children (academic achievement; independence; job and financial security). In many ways Paul's autism has been our 'healing.' We are more rounded, whole people because of him.*"

Diane's experience is echoed in testimony emerging from other contexts, such as the L'Arche Christian communities, established by Jean Vanier, which serve people with severe learning disabilities in many places around the world. Within L'Arche, people with disabilities are seen as the core of a community where the objective is for those who assist them to become their friends rather than simply their carers.[13] Again, the testimony that emerges is that disability of whatever sort reveals to us what it truly means to be human, which is that we are vulnerable and dependent, something those without disabilities have simply learned to hide.[14] Indeed, disability shows up the vanity and illusion of humanity's pretense to power and success.[15]

It is also possible, with some care, to suggest that disability acts to reveal an element of God's judgment. Given the sensitivity around any suggestion that disability is somehow a consequence of sin, it is crucial to make it clear that this is not God's judgment in terms of punishment but in terms of testing. Society is tested by how it treats those with disabilities and what this test tends to show is that the response of our society is ambiguous at best.[16] As a result, disability acts not only to reveal vulnerability and dependence as fundamental to the human condition but to reveal through our response to disability our need for a redemption of some sort.

This line of argument about what God reveals through disability has to come with something of a theological health warning. There is a clear danger of moving from an argument that disability is revelatory to the conclusion that it is therefore somehow necessary for humanity as a whole that some people live with disabilities.[17] We should be cautious about insisting that we can identify the "contribution" of those with disabilities in that way. Doing so falls into the trap of functionalizing or valorizing disability, rendering some disabilities more "useful" or "showing more courage" than others. It also potentially misconstrues the motivation of those caring for people with disabilities as being to gain the benefit of that contribution.[18] The idea that disability is revelatory or that it tests society is therefore instructive, but it is incidental to the existence of disability as part of the variety of humanity.

However, recognizing that note of caution, it is possible to go on to argue that disability also reveals something of our calling as human beings, and especially as the church, to respond and to be willing to be with those who are vulnerable. This might pick up on Jesus' words in Matthew 25 about welcoming the stranger, clothing the naked, and visiting those in prison. Jesus puts into the mouth of the king in his parable the words "just as you did it to one of the least of these who are members of my family, you did it to me" (verse 40). The interpretation is that we encounter Jesus himself in those who are most vulnerable, in this case those with disabilities. The calling of the church is to learn to be with and to love them every day as part of a calling to be with and to love God.[19]

That calling in turn points to another aspect of humanity revealed in particular by those with profound intellectual impairment. Their involvement in most aspects of daily life is enabled by others, especially those caring for them. Their participation is therefore by nature corporate, not individual. To recognize those sisters and brothers of ours as part of the body of Christ or of any community is to recognize the inherently corporate, interdependent nature of that body and of what it means to be made in the image of God. The body of Christ is a corporate image, rather than an individualistic one, and it is incomplete unless it incorporates all of its diverse elements, including disability. Indeed, both the original Adam and Christ are corporate figures: we were all in Adam, and we are fully in God's image when, together, we are in Christ.[20]

Exploring these ideas of revelation again draws out some of the theological significance of disability. The focus in doing so has not been on connecting that significance to an account of the cross or the atonement, and so those have not particularly featured in the discussion, apart from the suggestion that some need for redemption can be glimpsed in society's response to those who are different through disability. However, there is an implied link at work behind this discussion. If disability provides a deeper revelation of humanity as a whole, then it is a deeper revelation of the sort of flesh that the Word assumed at the incarnation, and of the sort of flesh that the particular person of Jesus represented on the cross.

Eschatological Questions

A disability perspective on eschatology raises its head here, as well as under the theme of soteriology (how we understand salvation) that is discussed below. The general question is what place there is in the new creation for what we consider to be the disabled body or mind. This has not yet been developed as extensively as other areas, perhaps because any discussion of the form of the resurrection body and mind is inevitably speculative. However, there are normate assumptions about the anthropology of the new creation that can be challenged. One biblical text through which this has been done is Jesus' parable of the great banquet in Luke 14:15-24. The insistence by the host that "the poor, the crippled, the blind, and the lame" are to be gathered into his feast allows for the argument that those with impairments are included in the kingdom of God just as they are. Inclusion is not conditional on their impairments being in some way "fixed."[21] That argument is supported by references to Old Testament prophecies of the restoration of the people of God, interpreting that restoration eschatologically. Luke seems to be consistent with Jeremiah 31:8-9, Micah 4:6-7, and Zephaniah 3:19b-20, in which visions of the restoration of Israel typically include the blind and the lame among those who are gathered. A connection might also be drawn between this argument and the discussion above of Jesus' wounds. The marks of Christ's disabling by the cross, still present in his resurrected body, could indicate not only solidarity with humanity inclusive of disability but the anticipation of a continuing diversity of able-bodiedness and disability in the post-resurrection new creation.

The point here is not to critique in detail the exegetical legitimacy of these readings of the various texts but to discover how those readings interact with the atonement and disability. The main area of engagement has been a resistance to the presumption that God's eschatological vision for humanity includes the homogenization of human bodies and minds, bringing them all into conformation with a notional perfect form, in line with criteria set by whatever happen to be current ideas of able-bodiedness.[22] Resisting that presumption is certainly useful. However, doing so has not addressed the relationship between an eschatological vision that allows for disability and what is happening at the cross, which is the event that opens up that eschatological future. It also raises but does not answer the thorny question of the relationship between the atonement, disability, and healing, whether now or at the resurrection.

Genetics and Medical Ethics

Genetic testing of fetuses and the ethics surrounding it has also been explored within this anthropological theme. Our response to such testing capabilities says something very sharp about what it means to be human and what sort of humanity we aspire to. A disability perspective questions what the practice of testing indicates about attitudes to the development of personhood in the womb. It also asks what assumptions are being made about the types of persons who are acceptable in the world. Again, the discussion is not theoretical; it revolves around the experiences of pregnant women being encouraged to consider terminating a pregnancy if there is evidence that the fetus is likely to have a disability at birth, such as Down syndrome, tested for though amniocentesis or more recently through noninvasive testing.[23] The ethical objection is to an approach that seeks to eliminate certain categories of people from the (future) population, suggesting they are less qualified as humans than the rest.[24] Theologically, much of this again revolves around our concept of humanity made in the image of God. The part played in the debate by an account of the atonement, or its impact on how we should interpret the atonement, has not yet been explored explicitly. It would perhaps be possible to discern the outlines of a soteriological discussion if the medical approach were interpreted as succumbing to a temptation to offer a form of salvation, the achieving of an idealized, homogenous form of humanity.[25] Failing to recognize that temptation might contribute to an unexamined theological presumption of the homogenization of bodies and minds come the resurrection.

WHO IS IN OR OUT: THEOLOGY OF ACCESS

A second major theme is a theology of access, exploring questions of how people with disabilities are able to be present and participate in the life of church and society. As a practical matter, questions of physical access to places of worship (sometimes under the requirements of disability discrimination legislation) are often the first point at which a church encounters the concept of disability theology and its connection with disability advocacy. However, a theology of access goes beyond the enabling of physical presence in worship services, important though that is. It addresses a range of barriers to the full participation of those with disabilities in ecclesial life. Thinking again of my friend Diane, it is often hard to see how Paul, with his autism, is to be involved in worship when the ways in which Scripture, liturgy, and tradition are usually used are simply not accessible to him.[26] Within our concept of what constitutes worship and sacrament, there are potential barriers of language, sight, hearing, ritual, physical practices, intellectual comprehension, and expected response. Again, the question here is what responses have arisen and how they might relate to a theology of disability grounded in the cross.

Theological arguments for full inclusion and access have so far approached their target from both christological and pneumatological directions.[27] On the christological front, Jesus Christ is God's gift for all humanity, in which case all humanity should have access to respond to him in worship. That is emphasized not least by Jesus' deliberate identification with the outsider and the marginalized, in this case the person who experiences exclusion because of disability. Jesus is the one who gives the outsider the right to become an insider. Often this line of argument stops there, with what might be called the inclusivity of the incarnation. However, it seems important to extend it to say that it is affirmed most fully and precisely by the cross, the "particularity" dimension of our hermeneutical key. The cross not only demonstrated the extent of Jesus' willingness to identify with outsiders by becoming the ultimate outsider, the one unjustly executed, but the cross and resurrection incorporated disability into God (or at least revealed it there) in the wounds of the risen Christ. This surely offers those with disabilities a clear invitation to full participation in worship as humanity's response to God's gift of Christ.

A second christological element focuses on the pattern of Jesus' ministry as recorded in the Gospels and his willingness to be present and to devote attention to those with disabilities, particularly in the healing narratives. Rather than relying on those with disabilities exercising their rights of access, this calls for a theology of access that, particularly in the case of those with profound disabilities, inspires those who are temporarily able-bodied to move toward those with disabilities out of an appreciation of their sameness of humanity.[28]

On the pneumatological front, one approach recognizes that historically in the life of the church the Holy Spirit has been the least prominent member of the Trinity. In a sense he has been marginalized.[29] This is again useful as a point of identification for those who experience marginalization as a result of disability. Another connection is the role of the Holy Spirit as advocate and the particular resonance of that term within the disability rights movement.

However, the role of the Holy Spirit in a theology of access has been developed more extensively in an inclusive understanding of the nature of the church. The emphasis is on the church as an inclusive fellowship of the Holy Spirit.[30] This inclusive fellowship emerges from the experience at Pentecost of the Holy Spirit poured out on all flesh, including those with disabilities. It grows through the apostle Paul's metaphorical body of Christ in 1 Corinthians 12, within which "the members of the body that seem to be weaker are indispensable" (verse 22). This is the hospitable body constituted by the Holy

Spirit, interpreting people with disabilities as falling within Paul's category of the weaker members. Although Paul's rebuke in that letter was to the elite who were not sharing their material or spiritual blessings with others, and is not directed at disability, the argument does seem consistent with Paul's rhetoric.[31] Indeed, pressing the point further suggests that unless the church has the most vulnerable and marginalized at its core, it may simply not represent the body of Christ at all.[32]

Stepping back and applying our hermeneutical key to these various arguments around a theology of access, it is clear that they interact little with the universality or the particularity of the atonement. They are based, rather, on the inclusiveness of the incarnation, Jesus' ministry, and the work of the Holy Spirit in forming the church in a response of friendship and the recognition of vulnerability. At the same time, however, something about the cross is at work in the background. It is noticeable that a common reflection on the practical outworking of a theology of access is on access to the celebration of the Eucharist.[33] Who is present and able to take part fully in at the Lord's Table and who is not goes to the heart of inclusion in worship.[34] There is no suggestion that somehow nonparticipation in the Eucharist by those with disabilities denies them the benefits of the atonement, or that in some sense they do not require those benefits, albeit that this has not yet been explored adequately. However, this emphasis on Communion seems to imply something, perhaps rather subtle, about unexamined attitudes within the church at large to the relevance of the atonement to the lived experience of disability. It also seems to speak of the significance to those with disabilities of the intimate connection with the embodied particularity of the atonement that the Eucharistic celebration affords.[35]

TROUBLE WITH SCRIPTURE: HERMENEUTICS AND HEALING

The third major theme of disability theology identified above is hermeneutics: how we read the Bible from a disability frame of reference. Reading Scripture without an awareness of normate bias can prove oppressive to people with disabilities in several ways. It can denigrate disability as being in some way indicative of moral failure in the person with the disability or in their family; it can trivialize it by rendering those with disabilities nothing more than an illustrative cipher for the better understanding of the gospel by those without disabilities; it can present those with disabilities either as the grateful recipients of goodwill or as valiant sufferers. However, the task of redressing the balance and arriving at a reading of the Bible that avoids such pitfalls faces substantial challenges. Not least among these is that we cannot assume that either in biblical times or throughout much of the history of the church there has been an understanding of disability similar to that of today.[36]

Another challenge is that Scripture presents something of a mixed message on disability. Two comparisons illustrate this. In the Exodus account, God makes it clear to Moses that God himself is the source of disability and ability alike (Exod 4:11), implying perhaps that neither should be denigrated, and yet soon after we read that those with various impairments are barred by the Torah from the honor of presenting the priestly offering by fire (Lev 21:16-23). Skipping forward to the New Testament, John's Gospel finds Jesus warning the man healed by the pool of Bethesda not to sin lest something worse happen to him (5:14), seeming to link sin to the lameness from which the man has been cured. Yet later, in the case of the man blind from birth, Jesus explicitly dissociates his blindness from sin (9:2-3). The biblical account has Jesus seeming at various times both to support and to contradict a causal link between sin and disability. These examples from John also raise what has probably been the most awkward and contentious aspect of reading Scripture from a disability perspective, how to read the healing accounts. The way we understand the accounts of Jesus seeming to heal most of the people he encounters who have illnesses or disabilities, and how we interpret and apply these in the life of the church are among the great bones of contention in Christian theology and ministry.

Some helpful and constructive hermeneutical tools have emerged that can guide the reading of Scripture in general from a disability perspective. One three-part guide is to read on the basis that (i) people with disabilities are created in the image of God, (ii) people with disabilities are people first and are not defined by their disability, and (iii) disability is neither evil nor necessarily to be eliminated.[37] This last point is particularly relevant in situations where the condition regarded as a disability is intimately bound up in a person's identity. A clear example is Down syndrome, which is a chromosomal condition and therefore part of a person's genetic makeup. To eliminate the condition of Down syndrome would seem to eliminate the person. Armed with hermeneutical principles of this sort, it is possible to revisit passages of Scripture containing people with disabilities with a view to rediscovering them as complex characters of narrative depth and importance.

There is a useful distinction to be drawn within this work between the search for a positive way of reading Scripture from a disability perspective, and the connection between disability studies and biblical studies. In pursuing the former, the latter is essential as it is seeking to understand the way that disability was perceived by the biblical authors themselves. That involves discerning how ideas about disability and illness in the ancient Near

East, its time, geography, and culture, have influenced what and how those authors have written.[38] The hermeneutical challenge is to use those insights from biblical studies to make sense of the biblical narrative from a present-day disability perspective.

Having made these observations, something can be said about how these disability-perspective hermeneutical strategies relate to the cross and ideas of atonement. The two main links are with the passion of Jesus and the various healing narratives. Taking the passion first, a disability-perspective reading of the Gospel accounts of the crucifixion, resurrection, and post-resurrection appearances of Jesus follow very much the "disabled God" approach. The theological focus is on a revelation of solidarity rather than on how the universal ontological change brought about by the atonement opens the way for the forgiveness and transformation of all humanity, including those with disabilities.

Particular details can be highlighted within that reading. For example, John Hull, a theologian who became blind during his lifetime, points out a part of the passion that many readers might miss and that adds to the picture of solidarity. Hull suggests that when, in the approach to the crucifixion, Jesus was blindfolded by his tormentors (Luke 22:64) he entered the condition of blindness, enabling people who are blind to identify with the passion of Jesus.[39] Another such detail could be the fact that through the process of crucifixion, several of Jesus' joints would have been irreparably damaged. While this approach is undoubtedly pastorally helpful to many in their personal reflection on Jesus' passion, others raise a note of hermeneutical caution. There can be a temptation to manipulate particular facts in Jesus' life and experience to create a special identification with particular groups, with the danger of leaving others out in the cold.[40] Jesus lived his own limited life in a particular place and time. His death was a particular death through one method of execution. However, Jesus should be seen as representative of all humanity through his incarnation and the embodied nature of the atonement at the cross. What is needed is a way of reading his life, death, and resurrection such that those detailed observations become illustrative of something of deeper and all-encompassing significance.

The second intersection with the atonement lies in reading the healing narratives in the Gospels. In those accounts it is not uncommon for Jesus to appear to link healing with faith and salvation. A comparison from Luke illustrates the point. In Luke 7:50 Jesus says to a woman who had led a dissolute life but demonstrates repentance, "Your faith has saved you," which seems to join up easily with the saving power of God through the cross. In Luke 18:42 Jesus speaks the very same phrase to a blind beggar whose sight he has restored. In that second context the Greek word σέσωκέν is often translated as "healed."[41] The use of the same phrase or formula in the two situations appears deliberate in Luke, and it goes to the heart of the conundrum. It appears on the face of it that the same faith in God, who was in Christ at the cross, has the power both to save and to heal from a whole range of diseases and disabilities. That juxtaposition of saving and healing can, on the face of it, appear to link illness, disability, and sin in ways that have proven oppressive to people with disabilities or chronic conditions. It might also be possible to infer, unhelpfully, that if God is to be glorified in healing, he is not glorified in disability, suggesting in turn that only able-bodied people can be true followers of Jesus.[42]

A disability-perspective reading of these healing accounts has argued against any such causal connection between sin and either disability or sickness (what might be called a "sin model of disability"). It has instead drawn a distinction between the curing of sickness and the holistic healing and restoration of the whole person. This also involves eliminating, or at least reducing, the connection that Jesus might appear to be making between the healing he was instigating in the present and the benefits of the atonement he would soon enact. The maneuver undertaken to date has been to play down the emphasis on curing of medical conditions or disabilities and to claim that the gospel emphasis is on holistic restoration and the reintegration of the individual into the community.

Broadly, two things emerge when our hermeneutical key is drawn alongside current disability-perspective hermeneutics. One is that the reading of the particularity of the cross and resurrection narratives emphasizes the bodily disabling of Jesus and its revelatory power, much as observed in relation to theological anthropology above. The other is that, to the extent that the gospel healing narratives point forward to the atonement, current disability perspective reading avoids the universal element, which would identify a miraculous cure as presaging ontological change to be brought about by the atonement. Instead, it identifies in those narratives a more subjective outworking in the restoring of the individual's sense of self and acceptance in society. This in turn is linked to the purpose of the atonement being regarded, as noted above, as the creation (certainly eschatologically, but also at least in part in the present) of a truly hospitable community as a work of the Holy Spirit, through the renewing of attitudes in response to the Christ event as a whole.

HOW WE ARE SAVED: DISABILITY-PERSPECTIVE SOTERIOLOGY

The last of the four major themes of disability theology concerns what is meant by salvation. Through Jesus, God has wrought some sort of salvation. We can speak of being saved. The question is how that is interpreted from a disability point of view, including not so much who is saved but what is saved, preserved, transformed, or healed through this initiative of God's. Clearly this asks something very direct about the relationship between the cross and disability theology. Four existing ways of responding to the question are reviewed here to see what they reveal. Each has its origin in the testimony of a particular experience of disability.

Salvation as Worth

As with much of our account of God, profound disability prompts some rethinking. David Pailin writes in the light of his encounter with the life of a young child, Alex, who was born with a range of severely disabling conditions and whose life was short as a result. In Alex's context, ideas of being "saved from" something by a savior whose action requires our comprehension and acknowledgment seemed to make little sense. Pailin concludes that for Alex, and by extension for anyone, salvation is perhaps more meaningful if it is experienced through one's worth and significance being demonstrated by others.[43] One of the implications of this is that the valuing of others becomes a prime calling of the church, which is called to value all people, including someone like Alex.

Applying our hermeneutical key, this approach has moved quite deliberately away from any account of an objective universal reconciliation achieved by the atonement, focusing instead on the subjective changes in perceptions and behaviors brought about by what God reveals to us through disability. Also, although the embodied facts of disability play a crucial role here, they are not linked explicitly to the embodiment of God's initiative in the particularity of Jesus' crucified or resurrected body.

Salvation as Pneumatological Transformation

Another approach is to talk more directly of salvation involving a combination of Jesus and the work of the Holy Spirit. Here the redemptive power of the life, death, and resurrection of Jesus is located in their revelation of God and of his identification with human vulnerability. The lived experience of disability has its own revelatory role in enabling us to grasp that significance. Beyond that point, however, salvation is a pneumatological accomplishment.

It is the work of the Holy Spirit, bringing transformation into all areas of human life and moving us away from sin and alienation toward reconciliation and peace.[44] Amos Yong writes about this, reflecting on growing up with his brother, Mark, who has Down syndrome. Following that line of thought, salvation ought to emerge in all aspects of life: embodied, social, political, geographical, and interrelational. It should be accessible to all and should involve body, mind, will, and habits. As a work of God, salvation must involve all of these elements but is not something reducible to, or somehow contained within, any subset of them.[45]

There is much richness in this approach. Again, it incorporates a critique of the intellectualization of access to the benefits of this salvation in terms of "believing and confessing," which otherwise seems to put it beyond the reach of many. The pneumatological salvation proposed can be experienced subjectively in the present by people anywhere on a spectrum of ability. For many, part of what lies behind this way of talking of salvation is questioning what the atonement means for someone with intellectual impairment. It may be difficult to identify occasions when they have intentionally done what they know to be wrong, but that leaves us wary of suggesting that they are innocent in the sense of not needing some aspect of the atonement. To do so would seem to smuggle in by the back door a subtle suggestion that, being unable to sin in a conventional sense, someone with intellectual impairment is not fully human.[46]

Although the cross is more clearly in view here, the soteriological weight of Yong's argument again leans away from the large claim of a universal objective ontological change wrought there, toward salvation as an experienced change in attitudes and behaviors.

Salvation as God's Double Reparation

A rather different way of skinning the soteriological cat involves insisting that whatever the answer is, it must be found at the cross. Frances Young does this, bringing to it the testimony of life with her profoundly disabled son, Arthur. That experience has demonstrated to her that there is a pattern in life, also deeply embedded in Scripture, of the need for hope within despair. If the cross and the atonement are central, then whatever they achieve, they must surely render that pattern, and particularly the hope within it, credible.[47] With that in mind, there are perhaps two things happening at the same time, a kind of "double reparation" at the cross. On one side of this reparation, the person of Jesus, as our representative, makes a perfect sacrifice of obedience, of which we can take advantage. That sacrifice deals with sin and restores relationships with God. Just as importantly, however, on the other side of this reparation God is present and willing to take responsibility for the "gone-wrongness" of creation.[48] This broad gone-wrongness exists because creation is not perfect as God is perfect. That difference allows for the existence of a world full of imperfection and fragility, including accidents and disability. For all of this God allows himself to be held accountable by being present at the cross. This double reparation, objectively dealing with sin and God being present, perhaps does makes hope credible. It also has a subjective side, calling for a human response of welcoming acceptance of people, particularly into the body of Christ.[49] That is how salvation would most readily appear to someone like Arthur.

Connecting this line of argument with the difficulties of interpreting the Gospel accounts of healing and saving, salvation here is more about hope than about "fixing." That hope does not depend on an insistence on disabilities being eliminated as a result of the atonement, because they are part of who we are and who Jesus represents on the cross.

Applying the hermeneutical key here, there is a focus on the particularity of the cross as well as a sense that Jesus' sacrifice is of universal significance. This approach also adds the idea that, at the cross, not only is the sin for which we are accountable being dealt with, but God himself is somehow present and accountable for the way the world is and the variety and disability it contains.

Salvation and the Elimination of Disability

These lines of argument from a disability perspective clearly move away from any link between disability and sin as well as away from the idea that God's intention is ultimately that human beings should be normalized, in line with a "typical" embodiment. Not everyone agrees with this, however. For example, James Barton Gould, drawing on his experience of living with his son, David, who has significant cognitive impairment, takes a very different line. What might be called the "elimination" view of salvation[50] is that all disabilities are healed or eliminated "in heaven." This will mean all people ultimately having typical mental and physical functionality as part of God's restoration of all things. The reasoning behind this view of what salvation must entail is that disability is one of the various effects of the fall of humankind recorded in Genesis 3. It is therefore a direct result of sin, though not of the sin of the person with the disability. When sin and death are defeated by God in Christ, disability must be eliminated, otherwise evil would remain eternally alongside God.[51]

Relating these theological assertions to the realities of life, the argument is that those with disabilities have been denied many of life's objective goods.

Those goods include full interpersonal relationships, productivity, and independence.[52] By that measure, if a life enabled by such things is objectively good, then disabilities which work against them are objectively bad and as such are to be eliminated in the age to come. The fact that someone with a disability is content could not be considered a sufficient argument against this. Instead, it would be maintained that the person (as they should be absent the effects of the fall) can be conceived of separately from the condition in making the assessment.

In a more eschatological sense, whether one has a relatively static idea of "heaven" (the contemplation of God found in Thomas Aquinas, for example) or an active view where there is a joining in with the activity of God and constant new discovery (found in Gregory of Nyssa's idea of *epektasis* and more recently in N. T. Wright), in order to participate in it we must have typical function, particularly intellectual function.[53] The response to the objection that this could render an individual unrecognizably different from the person who has lived this life is the suggestion that post-resurrection there might be a gradual developing, or filling in, of these functions. There is no space within this approach for the possibility that "typical" functionality might be measured at a corporate level and thus include a wide range of ability within what is typical for a broad group of people.

Applying the hermeneutical key again, an elimination soteriology as Gould presents it reflects very strongly an objective, effective dealing with sin secured at the cross. It does so because of a conviction that disability stems from the fall and is therefore bound up with sin. The focus is very much on that universal claim and is not so dependent on the particularities of the event of the cross and resurrection. Indeed, the suggestion that the disabling of Jesus through his passion, and the wounds on his resurrected body, should be interpreted as a revelation of God's solidarity with humanity inclusive of impairment would be counterproductive to this approach.[54]

CONCLUSION: CONNECTIONS AND OPPORTUNITIES

These four major themes being pursued across the field of disability theology—exploring what it is to be human, what accessibility is really about, how we read the Bible, and what it means to talk of healing and salvation—all display great creativity and energy. They demonstrate a keen ear for the testimony of people living with disability and respond with compassion and insight. The inquiry here is asking, within all of that, what business they are also doing with the cross, that cornerstone of Christian faith and life. It is asking in what way those themes are shaped by the cross as they pursue their objectives, or what challenges they are raising for how we understand the cross and God's initiative of atonement there.

This involves considering both the universal claim that God has brought about a cosmic reconciliation and the particular claim that this has come through the cross and resurrection of the man Jesus. It is fairly clear that the first of these currently plays a far more distant role than the second. It is perhaps not surprising that disability theology finds itself drawn to the particularity of Jesus and the cross, since as a discipline it is concerned with connecting theology with lived, embodied human experience. Jesus' own particular experience of bodily frailty and vulnerability, culminating in his being disabled to the point of death through the process of the passion and crucifixion, emerges accordingly as a revelation of God's identification and solidarity with all of humanity and humanity's impairments. That can in turn be linked to observations that disability itself reveals vulnerability and dependence on God as the true state of humanity, despite our pretensions to independence. The wounds that remain on Jesus' resurrected body also open the way for challenging the idea of salvation as the homogenization, or "normalization," of bodies and minds in conformity to a "typical" pattern.

On a broader canvas, subjective aspects of the atonement as an experience of transformed attitudes and as a call for the lowering of social barriers to participation has certainly resonated with the concerns of disability theology. But there is much less engagement with the universal claim of an objective change in the relationship between God and creation and of God's dealing effectively with sin. The caution around embracing that objective atonement is most clearly visible (and perhaps has its origins) in discomfort around finding convincing disability-perspective readings of the healing narratives in the Gospels. This is where the awkwardness of the apparent link between disability and sin is most keenly felt. The distinct preference in disability-perspective readings to date has been to emphasize the holistic and societal restoration of the individual and almost to reject an interpretation of those events as miraculous cures which presage an objective universal change soon to be wrought through the cross and resurrection.

But that observation in itself is revealing. This discomfort over the healing narratives and the way the themes of disability theology interact with the atonement as a whole begin to point toward the challenges that disability should be raising for an account of the atonement. While it might be said that the more subjective emphasis in disability theology arises just from not wanting to place the words "sin" and "disability" in close proximity, as it stands this seems inadequate as an explanation. What really underlies it is the sense that there is much in the experience of life that is not as we would like it to be and that we would look to the God of grace and mercy, who is also the judge of all the earth, to address in his great work of reconciliation and redemption. That includes some aspects of disability, not least society's often questionable response to it. However, saying that all of this is dealt with at the cross is troubling if the cross, which we believe changes everything, is essentially a matter of dealing with the moral failure of sin. That would mean that the whole of the phenomenon and the lived experience of disability is a matter of sin. What the theological work being pursued from a disability theology frame of reference demonstrates is that a way of approaching and understanding the atonement that does not make this simple equation has not yet been found but is essential if the cross is to be the foundation of a distinctively Christian theology of disability.

2

Making Sense of the Atonement

Models, Theories, and Metaphor

DEBATING THE CROSS: TYPOLOGY, THEORIES, AND TRUTH CLAIMS

While disability theology is a relatively young field, that of studying and interpreting the cross and the atonement certainly is not. It has a long and rich history winding all the way back down the road to Golgotha. Yet for all that, looking into existing atonement theology for a response to disability does not yield much. Little has emerged from studies of the atonement that speaks directly into situations of disability or that engages with the objectives identified above under the main themes of disability theology. What atonement theology demonstrates is that although the cross was a single event, what happened there is multifaceted. It is unlikely that there is one aspect of the cross that will provide a simple response to the experience of disability. Bringing its various dimensions to bear on disability will take some effort and care if not to prove superficial. There is no quick, obvious answer here, but if the cross, and the atonement wrought there by God in Christ, is to become the foundation for a Christian theology of disability, it is essential to discover what it is about the cross that makes it so.

The event of the cross is history. Much of the New Testament from the Acts of the Apostles onward involves the interpretation of that history of Jesus' death, his resurrection on the third day, and what God has achieved through it. The discussion in the New Testament began with puzzling over how what God has done through the cross could possibly apply to those who were not ethnically part of Israel, how it could be that this saving act of God really was for all people, even Gentiles. The debate has continued and grown ever since and is currently as lively as ever, certainly in Western (perhaps mainly Protestant) churches and theological circles. It has not, however, produced a creedal statement, emerging out of the councils of the early church, defining the boundaries of orthodoxy for the relationship between the death and resurrection of Jesus and the salvation they bring. There is no parallel to, say, the Chalcedonian definition of the person of Jesus.[1] That is important, because it has left the field open and required that each generation apply itself to the discipline of wrestling afresh with the meaning of the cross.[2]

As the church has done so, language has played a crucial role in mapping the contours of each facet of the atonement. There have been powerful metaphors of sacrifice, justice, and victory at work, mostly drawing on existing theological ideas from the Old and New Testaments. This has given rise to a variety of theories or models of atonement that say something both about what objective change the death and resurrection of Jesus achieved and about how, subjectively, that change might be experienced in this life. A survey of these models or theories can seem to present a convoluted and unwieldy collection of proposals, preferences, and tensions around how we speak of the cross. But bringing some order to that picture will be critical if a meaningful interaction between the atonement and disability theology is to be made possible. It will inevitably entail visiting what have variously been called models, metaphors, or theories of atonement. That sounds terribly dry and abstract, but if these can be marshalled in a way that brings them to life and that allows them to bring the drama of the cross to bear on lives lived with disability, the effort will be worthwhile.

It is clear from the ground covered so far that disability theology has not strongly adopted any one of the more commonly mentioned atonement models or theories considered here. That observation in itself hints at an uneasiness with what those models or theories might seem to communicate. It will make it important to consider openly whether, and if so how, any of them can function as an explanation of the cross that applies to the whole of humanity, inclusive of the full range of ability and disability. Any of those models or theories comprises both the idea or ideas behind it and the language it employs to communicate those ideas. Both aspects will have to be assessed carefully. That will involve drawing on scholarship in the realm of metaphorical language and how such language conveys meaning. But the first question is what sort of thing it is that we have been trying to say about the cross.

Typologies, Theories, and Truth Claims

A common starting point in setting out how the cross has been understood is what has come to be called the "threefold typology." This was described by Gustaf Aulén in his 1931 book *Christus Victor*. Aulén made it clear that he saw his task as reestablishing an understanding of the atonement as the victory of Christ over evil powers in the world as the one preeminent understanding, true to the early church, what he called the "classic" idea of the atonement.[3] Along the way, he argued that three main types of the idea of the atonement had developed over time. His classic idea, emerging as Christianity took shape, was the victory of Christ. That was, he claimed, usurped in the Middle Ages by the "objective" idea, attributed to Anselm of Canterbury, though building on earlier ideas from Tertullian and Cyprian. This was the legal idea of the atonement as Christ's offering of satisfaction in legal terms for the guilt of human sin, which has dishonored God. The leaders of the Reformation, many of whom were lawyers, introduced a more contractual sense of the law and the courts from their own era but retained the sense of an objective forensic accomplishment, which Aulén so disliked. Alongside these was the "subjective" idea of the atonement. Here the cross was a demonstration of the love of God that engenders, by its profound example, a response of change in the hearts of humankind. Though Aulén related the subjective type to the work of Anselm's contemporary Peter Abelard, he attributed it as much to the influence of the Enlightenment and liberal Protestantism.[4] These objective, subjective, and victory accounts have come to be referred to as Aulén's "threefold typology," which has continued to influence many a more recent discussion of the cross.

However, a brief review of Old and New Testament texts wherein God addresses sin and the human predicament quickly uncovers a much wider range of images, language, and ideas than can readily be accommodated by just those three types. They include concepts of liberation, ransom, redemption, salvation, sacrifice, propitiation, justification, expiation, atonement, reconciliation, victory, penalty, forgiveness, satisfaction, new covenant, and example, to name a few. That list in itself indicates something about the work that these different words are doing when they are used to describe the atonement. They are not all operating at the same level or performing the same function. For example, the term "sacrifice" represents a whole system of activity, drawn from Old Testament practices that provided an objective atonement for sin and reconciliation of the relationship between the individual and God or between the company of worshippers and God. Sacrifice in that sense provides a broad context for thinking about the death of Christ on the cross. In contrast, using the word "reconciliation" or "forgiveness" seems to speak not so much of a broad context as of a particular outcome that Christ's death achieves. It is therefore insufficient to assume that each image or idea encountered in the Bible contributes a whole separate model or theory of the atonement which can simply be added to Aulén's list of three.

Before trying to fit all of these ideas into possible theories of what is happening at the cross, other dimensions of what theories like these might be trying to communicate are worth bearing in mind. One dimension is context, whether theologians have been led by their own context to champion a particular theory. For example, the context of the twentieth-century world wars provided fertile ground for the reception of Aulén's emphasis on the cross as the victory of Christ. This is significant because while each such theory can present an internally coherent explanation of the cross and resurrection, each might also have more immediate relevance in some circumstances than in others.[5] A declaration of liberation, for example, might communicate more to a person laboring under a sense of oppressive evil than a declaration that the honor of God has been satisfied. Emphasizing context in discerning why one or another theory might be preferred raises an important question for the conversation with disability theology. There is a danger of reinforcing a view that disability, in all its variety, is a special case outside of "typical" humanity. The task could easily become one of finding which model or theory particularly appeals, or seems to "work," in the context of particular disability, rather than asking the much deeper question of whether our main account of the atonement (which each of the models or theories partly describes) is capable of encompassing all of humanity, inclusive of disability.

Another dimension concerns what sort of truth claim we are expecting a theory of the atonement to make, particularly whether such a claim is objective or subjective. Over the past century or so, there have been some debilitating effects on Christian confidence in claiming that the atonement is objective, involving an actual change in the relationship between God and humanity. On the one hand, there has been skepticism over claims that the sort of pictorial or metaphorical language used in the Bible to talk of the cross can convey any actual truth at all. On the other hand, the idea of the need for any atonement or salvation at all in a Christian sense has also come under attack. This latter has had its roots in, for example, Immanuel Kant's suggestion that God has become not the source of human freedom but a threat to the freedom of the individual, or even its enemy. On that account, what is called salvation in Christian terms has become something alien, something imposed unwanted on humanity from outside.[6]

In the face of these movements in thinking, some theological responses from a more liberal standpoint have retreated from the idea of an actual, objective atonement. Such responses prefer to speak of the accomplishments of the cross in purely subjective terms of inner transformation.[7] A slightly more positive response has been not to deny an objective atonement but to draw out parallels with aspects or patterns found in human life such as tragedy, self-giving, temptation, or heroism and to argue that the cross gives these greater meaning. The focus there is on demonstrating how the cross addresses the depth and breadth of concerns and hopes that already arise in human experience, as a kind of ultimate analogy, rendering talk of the cross and the atonement reasonable and relevant in any age.[8] Over the same period a more conservative response has often been to insist absolutely on an objective atonement and on penal substitution as the only acceptable, legitimate, orthodox way of describing or explaining it.[9] It is not surprising that in the midst of these tensions and this mixture of thinking it has been difficult to know how to bring talk of the cross, atonement, sin, and salvation to bear on the daily lived experience of disability.[10]

A More Constructive Approach

Disability as an integral part of humanity highlights the need for a response that is more constructive than this, one that does business with both the objective and the subjective truth claims swirling around the cross. It demands to know what it is that God has actually done through the atonement and what change that has brought about in a world that contains both the phenomenon and the often very difficult experience of impairment. It demands to know what change that has brought about in a world where our behavior toward others can promote goodness and flourishing but also evil and degradation. And it demands to know how that has come through the particularity of the cross. But disability also demands to know about the subjective, about how whatever it was God achieved through Jesus on the cross can have actual purchase on a life now. And it demands to know how all of this should draw on the resources of language and thought found in the Bible and on the theological work those resources seem to be doing there.

LANGUAGE MATTERS: METAPHORS AND MODELS

Each model or theory of atonement championed over the years has been striving to say something about how the great claim of a universal reconciliation finds it source and meaning in the particular event of the death of a man called Jesus of Nazareth on a cross outside Jerusalem in the first century AD, as attested to by the Gospel accounts. Bringing some order to how they do so cannot start with any one model or theory but has to start by unpacking the way in which the language they use operates to convey that meaning. Not least of that is deciding what is meant by terms like "model," "theory," or "metaphor" and what work they are expected to do, given that theologians have often used these terms loosely or interchangeably.

Metaphorical Language

An opening retort might be to ask whether it is really necessary to speak about the logic and achievements of the cross in the indirect terms of models and metaphors at all. Surely it must be possible to present the workings of the atonement in plain, literal terms rather than resorting to the illustrative "picture" language of the Bible. If a literal presentation were sufficiently full and accurate, it could presumably also rapidly make clear how disability did or did not fit into the atonement, or at least fit into a particular way of describing or explaining it.

However, this demand for literal language is misplaced. It is part of the shriveling of our thinking brought on by less helpful aspects of the Enlightenment. The idea that real meaning is conveyed only by a sort of mechanical, literal use of words is a misunderstanding of how language works. In fact indirect, metaphorical language is essential since all of our knowledge of the world, and certainly of God, involves interpretation and is indirect.[11] This is the case in any field, including scientific advance, since advances in knowledge rely on changes in the meaning of words and the use of figures of speech to describe what was not previously known but has now been discovered or is being theorized. What matters is whether the language used is successful in enabling a truthful human interaction with reality.[12] All such advances and expressions proceed by way of some form of comparison, which will tend to be called simile if explicit or metaphor if implicit. The use of imagery in making these comparisons as a means of describing and explaining what has been discovered is the principle way of opening a path to what was hitherto unknown.[13] That is the case whether the imagery in question arises in the Bible or elsewhere. No special pleading is being made for religious language, as if somehow only religious metaphorical expressions are irreducible, incapable of being replaced by literal language. Indeed, there is an element of irreducibility in all metaphors, since any replacement with supposedly literal language always involves some loss or shrinking of available meanings and associations.[14] Given that this is how language is typically used to express and explore the depth of meaning in new discoveries, it is not surprising that our understanding of the large claim of the atonement and its narrow pivot of the cross has also come to us in this way.

How This Language Operates

If indirect, metaphorical language is necessary, how does it operate, both generally and in relation to talk of the atonement?[15] That can most readily be explored with a working example, in this case the notion of calling the atonement a sacrifice. There is no widely accepted definition of what a metaphor is, but a useful and practical one is that "*metaphor is that figure of speech whereby we speak about one thing in terms which are seen to be suggestive of another.*"[16] For example, referring to Jesus as "the lamb that was slain" is applying a metaphor in this way. The metaphor conveys meaning by drawing together two, possibly quite different, sets of associations. In our case there is a set of associations around the person of Jesus, including what we know of his life, teaching, ministry, relationships, death, and resurrection. At the same time there is a set of associations around the slaughter of a lamb, which includes its presumed innocence and meekness, the unavoidable violence in the shedding of its blood by another, its resulting death, and the reasons for that death.

Crucially, the metaphor does not operate to dumb down a complicated idea, using another to make it accessible to the less sophisticated mind. Instead, deeper insight comes as the two sets of associations are presented together.[17] Indeed, this richness of meaning is contributed by the very tensions that exist within the comparison.[18] There is tension inherent in the choice of subjects: Jesus is not a lamb and was not slaughtered in the way that a lamb would be. There is tension between the literal and metaphorical interpretations of the expression: we could take the comparison literally, which would make little sense beyond the fact that both have been killed, or metaphorically, which might reveal something more meaningful. Then there is tension in the level of correspondence between the subjects and their circumstances: Jesus may not be a lamb, but there is correspondence between the lamb and Jesus' nonresistance, the shedding of his blood and the fact of his death, that opens up possibilities for deeper meaning and purpose to be discovered in that death.

An important point for atonement language emerges here, which is to recognize the extent and limits of the correspondence between the metaphor, in the present case the slain lamb, and the subject, Jesus.[19] Recognizing those limits ensures that the metaphor is not used inappropriately, but it also raises potentially fruitful questions about what lies beyond those limits. The fact that Jesus, unlike a sacrificial lamb, could have chosen to avoid that particular death prompts fresh questions about the significance of his death as a sacrifice. Such a limit of correspondence also helps to indicate where some images or terms need to leave off and allow others to take over the descriptive work.

The flow of meaning that takes place in the use of indirect language is not a one-way street. When a metaphor is effective in describing an event such as the cross, it can affect the meaning of the metaphor in other usage.[20] To talk of the death of Jesus in terms of the slaying of a lamb, drawing out associations with Old Testament sacrifice, affects how we go on to speak of sacrifice elsewhere. Because we have drawn together sacrifice (something done to a lamb) with Jesus' self-giving on the cross, the meaning of sacrifice might become extended to include not just the offering of an animal but the giving of ourselves. Indeed, it has been suggested that this can go further and that, ironically, if a metaphor is too successful, the metaphorical use becomes literal. It would be hard to prove, but it is possible that that was what happened in the past with the word "orange,"[21] where perhaps using a fruit to describe a color was so successful as to become the name of the color. Although that seems to be drifting into speculation, it does point toward an inevitable danger surrounding the language used for the atonement. If the metaphors used to speak of the cross are particularly powerful and successful, we might begin to mistake that metaphorical language for a literal description of exactly, and only, what God was achieving there.

From Metaphors to Models

A further step is required to enable full interaction with biblical descriptions of the atonement. This is from metaphors, which in a sense are momentary figures of speech that capture single ideas, to models, which are traditions that have been developed more fully over time. Such models are fuller, more systematic, in the resources they provide for describing, explaining, and evaluating their subject.[22] Something should also then be said about whether talk of "theories" of the atonement means anything different.

The term "model" again requires some definition. There are different levels, or types, of models, which are quite distinct and not all of which are relevant to the present discussion. Typically three types of models are recognized.[23] First, there is the scale model, which renders something which is otherwise too small or large intelligible at our own size. An example is a model train. Here some features will not correspond, but some, especially proportions, will. Second, there is the analogue model, where a structure or operation of interest corresponds to a greater and more complex whole, but where many other features of the whole are not represented. An example might be the operation of the water cycle as an analogue model of an ecosystem. Third, there is the theoretical model, which comprises a whole system or object with a high degree of correspondence to the features of the subject, but with which one is more familiar. That high degree of correspondence means that the theoretical model offers rich resources for developing connections and hypotheses. This is because a theoretical model allows us freedom to explore the more challenging subject and its relationships using the language of the described model. A scientific example might be the Bohr model for the structure of the atom as a notional solar system with its "orbiting" electrons.[24] Care is of course needed to ensure that we do not overstep the limits of correspondence between such a model and the subject and claim insights that are not valid.

It is this third type, what is called the theoretical model, that can be applied most usefully to discussions of the cross and atonement. Applying it to the working example of sacrifice, the whole structure of activity and belief that makes up the Old Testament practice of sacrifice becomes a theoretical model for describing the atonement. There are areas of high correspondence, such as the sacrifice being efficacious for the forgiveness of sin, in the manner of the sin offering described in Leviticus 4, or the slaughter of the Passover lamb of Exodus 12, the blood of which protected the people of God in the face of divine judgment, or the scapegoat of the Day of Atonement in Leviticus 16, which carried away the sin of the community. This correspondence allows the New Testament writers to explore the meaning of the death of Jesus using the language of sacrifice and drawing on that whole system of meaning. For a model, however, as for a single metaphor, there are limits to that correspondence. For example, if we were to insist that, to function properly as a sacrifice, Jesus must have been offered up by someone, we run the risk of claiming that the Father has offered up the Son in a way that unhelpfully separates the persons of the Trinity. At that point the limits of correspondence of the model become useful in making us consider carefully the relationship between Father and Son at the moment of Jesus' death and how the insights of other models might be needed to address that.

It is worth at this point acknowledging that it is fairly common for theologians and others writing on the atonement to complain about the use of abstract "theories" or models. The complaint is that they obscure the true drama of the gospel narratives.[25] However, the witness of the New Testament remains that there was more to be said about the event of the cross than just recounting a story of the tragedy of human violence, that somehow God was present and active within it. The New Testament witness does so by drawing widely on metaphorical resources, such as those provided by the sacrifice example used here. Such language seems unavoidable if the deeper implications of the events of Good Friday are to be articulated.[26] Having said that, one source of confusion has been that some writers use the terms "theory" and "model" interchangeably. Others use one or the other consistently, but few examine what sort of language it is. Because of this, and because the word "theory" has perhaps more often been associated with ideas of atonement mechanisms or arrangements rather abstracted from the biblical narrative, from here on only models of the atonement, not theories, will be discussed.[27]

Models and the Cross

From here on, then, when the phrase "model of atonement" is used in grappling with the cross and its relationship with disability, it will mean a theoretical model in the specific sense described above. In this inquiry, a "model" is therefore a whole system of thought or realm of activity that provides a way of exploring what happened at the cross. The resources of language that each model provides and that are used in applying that model will be referred to as metaphor, or metaphorical language. This discipline of working with language and meaning allows the field of atonement theology as a whole, not just individual ideas from it, to be brought into a detailed conversation with questions of disability without that conversation losing its way or becoming vague.

Taking this approach, the three such theoretical models that have proven to be the most enduring and useful are sacrifice, victory, and justice.[28] Each of these three draws on a wide arena of life and provides a cache of metaphorical images and terms that can be brought alongside the cross and used to explore its mysteries and significance.[29] Because they function in that way, they also helpfully encompass or gather in most of the ideas found in longer lists of biblical terms that point in one way or another to the cross and God's work of salvation. These three can be regarded as the "prevailing" theoretical models, and they will need to be explored in some detail, not only to see clearly how each one operates but to test whether they will continue to operate effectively as models of an atonement that is fully inclusive of all humanity.[30]

In practice of course these three models do not form watertight compartments, and some metaphorical language and meaning might well leak from one to another. The term "salvation," for example, may well arise under all three, since one might be saved from the blight of sin by sacrifice, or saved from the clutches of Satan and death by victory, or saved from condemnation when Jesus stands with us as advocate before the judgment of God. However, these three theoretical models as set out here provide an orderly and manageable structure within which to bring understandings of the atonement into constructive conversation with disability theology.

Models and Relationships

The last part in completing this language picture is to consider how these three models of the atonement are related not just through language but in a logical sense to each other and to the death of Jesus. The importance of this lies in affirming that the models can be used as a coherent system of understanding, rather than as entirely separate, isolated ideas or patterns. The relationships involved can be called relationships of analogy in two senses.[31] Firstly, the models are related to one another and to the death of Jesus by analogy of attribution: the models are all "salvific" (can be said to shed light on salvation) because they are all related to the death of Christ. That event has the attribute of being salvific in the ultimate sense and the purpose of each of the models is, in its own way, to describe that event. Secondly, they are related to the death of Jesus by analogy of proportionality: in the sense of "a is to b, as c is to d." Using again the example of sacrifice, it can be said that the death of Christ is to a sinner as the sacrifice of an animal was to Old Testament Israel.

The coherence of these three models also stems from the fact that they, like the metaphors and models used in all areas of Christian thinking, emerge out of Old Testament events, practices, and testimony, out of which Christian belief itself arose.[32] In other words, these models are related to the death of Jesus precisely through their source being in the Old Testament, which is foundational to our whole understanding of Jesus. In the present case we find that this statement, while true, is double edged. It provides a firm anchor for the three prevailing models, but it raises a possible difficulty regarding disability. Since it would be incorrect to assume that in biblical times there was a similar understanding of disability to that in our own time, the challenge of finding theological space for a present-day understanding of disability in such biblical models of the atonement is heightened. Having said that, however, this difficulty is what provides the impetus for reengaging with these biblical models in creative ways.

THE PREVAILING MODELS: SACRIFICE, JUSTICE, AND VICTORY

Sacrifice, justice, and victory: each opens a window onto a whole realm of life, full of personal, communal, and cultural meaning and possibilities. Each offers a host of associations that speak to our own experiences. Ideas related to justice (fairness, judgment, mercy, guilt, innocence) and to victory (conflict, struggle, overcoming, freedom) either relate directly to things that have happened in our lives and in the lives of those around us or can be used indirectly to put into words what we want to say about them. Sacrifice does not perhaps feel quite as close to modern living. The self-sacrifice of a parent or a public servant might make an immediate connection, but sacrifice as part of daily religious life seems more distant, more ancient. Yet we know that it is one of the most powerful threads that runs through the Bible. What is of interest here, though, is how each of these rich sources of meaning, applied as a model in the way that has been described, functions when it is used to describe and explain the event that changed the world forever and that remains relevant to every life, the cross of Christ. Exploring that will prepare the ground for bringing those ways of talking about the cross, with all their long heritage, alongside the insights of disability theology to discover how each might disrupt and reform the other.

An initial general observation is that all three models convey a strong sense of both substitution and representation. Jesus is both substitute and representative. He goes as our substitute where we cannot go, to achieve what we cannot achieve. However, he also acts as our representative so that by following him we also can come before God. It is true that not everyone agrees that the two roles are quite so balanced. Those who heavily favor a penal substitution interpretation of the cross, for example, prefer that the role of substitute should take precedence.[33] Those who see the atonement as being much more about restoring relationships, and who perhaps prefer the language of sacrifice as a result, more strongly favor Jesus' representative role.[34] However, what the models taken together demonstrate is that both dimensions, arising as they do out of the metaphorical resources of the Scriptures, speak of equally important aspects of what happened on the cross.

Sacrifice

Much has been hinted at already through the sacrifice model having been used as a working example in the discussion of metaphorical language. This model draws on the Old Testament system of sacrifice. While there was certainly widespread use of sacrifice across the ancient Near East, the model has in view the particular system instigated by YHWH, beginning at Israel's encounter with him at Sinai in Exodus and considerably fleshed out in Leviticus and the rest of the Torah. When the New Testament speaks of the cross, it often draws on ideas from that sacrificial system to do so. An example from Paul would be his description of the Christ event in Romans 3:24-25: "Christ Jesus, whom God put forward as a sacrifice of atonement by his blood, effective through faith." To that one could add the statement in 1 John 2:2 that "he is the atoning sacrifice for our sins, and not for ours only, but also for the sins of the whole world," as well as the extended discussion of the cross in sacrificial and priestly language in the letter to the Hebrews.

The purpose of Israel's sacrificial system was broad, including offerings not only for sin but also for thanksgiving and well-being, and to reinforce the covenant with YHWH. The system therefore had to do with relationships. The sacrifices to atone for sin—for example in Leviticus 4 (personal sin) and Leviticus 16 (Day of Atonement for Israel as a community)—effected a purification from sin and the restoring of the relationship between the individual and God, or the community and God, which had been disrupted by sin. That purification or cleansing from the pollution of sin was closely related to the shed blood of the sacrificial victim, the blood having been provided by God for the purpose of atonement (Lev 17:11) and being symbolically sprinkled as part of the sacrifice ritual.

The writer to the Hebrews presses the Levitical correspondence of the model a bit further. In Day of Atonement terms, the letter describes Jesus as our high priest (Heb 4:14–5:10). It explores the priestly similarity of Jesus' role as mediator and his identification with our fallible humanity through the incarnation. It also emphasizes the crucial difference that the sacrifice he makes is not to be repeated year after year, as it would be by the high priest but is once for all. Pressing the model even further, the letter goes on to ascribe to Jesus the simultaneous roles of both the sacrifice being made and the high priest making it, since "this he did once for all when he offered himself" (Heb 7:27).[35]

To speak of sacrifice is not, of course, to speak only of the Levitical system. It is hard to miss the fact that the timing and language of the Gospel accounts of the crucifixion link it strongly with the sacrifice of the Passover lamb. In terms of metaphorical resources, the Passover sacrifice provides Exodus concepts of freedom from slavery, a covering over of sin in the face of God's judgment, and pilgrimage to a promised land. That "new Passover" interpretation can be found in Paul (for example, 1 Cor 5:7: "Clean out the old yeast . . . For our paschal lamb, Christ, has been sacrificed") and was popular in the early church.[36] Taken as a whole, then, what the New Testament use of sacrifice references really achieves is a powerful mixture of both Passover release from slavery and Day of Atonement forgiveness of sins.

At this point it is also valuable to say something of the limits of correspondence of the sacrifice model. For example, while we use the language of Jesus being offered as a sacrifice, of course he was in fact killed through the combined efforts of the all-too-human Roman and Jewish authorities. In that sense it was not a sacrifice under the Old Testament system at all but an execution under imperial law. The way the model operates is by suggesting that God has taken that actual slaying and attributed to it the meanings of sacrifice in such a way that the benefits of Old Testament sacrifice, in terms of sin, covering, cleansing, setting free, and restoring relationships, are made available to all of humanity. A second example of a limit of correspondence is that Levitical sacrifice was for unintentional sin. For deliberate, "high handed" sin one could go to God and ask for forgiveness, but the only ritual remedy was to be cut off from the people (Num 15:30-31). At the cross this raises fresh questions about how the model is being extended to speak of Jesus' death being effective for the cleansing of all sin. As with any theoretical model, the greatest benefit comes from recognizing in what ways the cross was like Old Testament sacrifice and, equally instructively, in what ways it was not.

Justice

The idea of justice as a model for the atonement has considerable breadth. There is also some diversity of opinion as to how the model should operate and what constitute the boundaries of its legitimate correspondences with the death of Jesus. One of the strengths of justice as a model is that it seems to go beyond Christian discourse and express a universal, deep-seated human response to the world.[37] Another strength is that the model of the law court is put to work in the Bible in several ways. Often this is with God as judge, defending the weak or oppressed, but sometimes it even has the sense of God himself being called to account.[38] Examples would include David calling on the Lord to act as judge between him and Saul, who is persecuting him (1 Sam 24:12-15), the psalmist's reliance on the Lord to defend the cause of the poor (Ps 140:12), or Job's desire for a court hearing to plead his case against God (Job 23:1-7 or 31:5-40). Commentary in the New Testament on the death of Jesus certainly picks up the theme, particularly through the language of justification used by Paul. A single example could be Romans 5:9: "Now that we have been justified by his blood, we will be saved through him from the wrath of God."

As is the case in deploying any model, it is worth acknowledging that talk of law and justice is capable of dragging unexamined assumptions in its wake. The atonement through the cross is not a legal transaction but an act of grace, which this model enables us to describe and explore using legal metaphorical language.[39] In this regard, the justice model might most usefully be thought of as containing within it at least four concepts of justice. The first is the Old Testament concept of law, which primarily concerned the keeping of the covenant with YHWH.[40] The covenant was not only a basis for ordering life and resolving disputes, but something that gave shape to the identity of the people and their relationship with God.

The second concept of justice is that of satisfaction, associated with St. Anselm of Canterbury and mentioned briefly in the earlier review of the atonement debate. Anselm's argument, which may sound odd in the present day, has its roots in the feudal legal system of the eleventh century in which he lived. In his *Cur Deus Homo*, Anselm explores how we dishonor God when our will and actions are not in accord with his: "He who does not render this honor which is due to God, robs God of his own and dishonors him; and this is sin."[41] Because God's honor is infinite, the debt of guilt for this dishonor is beyond any human being to satisfy, and yet it is a human debt. Hence, says Anselm, only a God-man can pay it. The atonement offered by Jesus, who is without sin and is both human and divine, pays this debt of satisfaction, removing our guilt. Anselm tends to draw broad principles from Scripture rather than the direct textual references some would prefer. However, his instinct that a functioning justice system ought to have correspondence with an effective and fitting atonement for sin seems sound, even if his feudal language strays beyond what is found in the Bible.[42]

The third, more abstract, transactional or contractual concept of the law court is usually attributed to the influence of the Western church fathers and the leaders of the Reformation, some of the latter being lawyers. Here the focus is rather more on forensic guilt or innocence and, making much use of Paul's justification language, on atonement as the means by which the sinner is declared innocent, just as he or she would be if acquitted at trial. Penal substitution is one way of applying a forensic view, which has had much attention.[43] John Calvin is often credited with developing this strong sense of the necessity of a penalty being incurred for sin, with God actually passing sentence as at a trial and applying that penalty, but the sentence and penalty being borne by Jesus on the cross. It is probably fair to say that this approach received such a boost at the time of the Reformation because its focus on the once-for-all substitutionary punishment of Jesus was a way of counteracting both the postmortem punishment of purgatory and the need to keep witnessing the Mass, where Jesus was in some way resacrificed.[44]

A fourth concept within the justice model can be described as "transactions governed by law or custom." This brings in the language of ransom or redemption, each of which has to do with being released from claims of ownership or control. Such concepts draw on images from the marketplace, where a debt or an item given as security is redeemed, or where a redemption price is paid to release a person sold into slavery. Ransom or redemption can also refer to satisfying the obligations of the "kinsman redeemer" or *goel* of Leviticus 25:51 to buy a relative out of debt. A simpler, direct fit is also found in the declaration of trust in God who, for example, "will ransom my soul from the power of Sheol" in Psalm 49:15.[45] Used that way, ransom brings echoes of the economics of warfare, whereby prisoners of war were (and sometimes still are) ransomed back to their nation as a means of raising funds.

These various facets of the justice model illustrate the importance of recognizing not only limits of correspondence but also the influence of our own experience and preferences as interpreters in applying any of the models of atonement. Indeed, the range of metaphorical language to which we claim access in applying any of the three prevailing models might vary considerably depending on whether, to use this justice example, our own personal notion of justice is fundamentally one of covenant, satisfaction, trial, retribution, punishment, restitution, rehabilitation, transaction, or penalty.[46]

Victory

Discussion of victory as a model for the atonement often tends to revolve around Aulén's insistence that Christus Victor, as he formulates it, represents the church's original, classical view of the atonement. Certainly one of its strengths is that it presents the atonement not as a transaction or arrangement but as a drama. It is a drama initiated by God that does not just involve a penalty being paid or debt settled but that changes the nature of the relationship between the world and God. Scriptural references for the conflict include Colossians 2:15, referring to Jesus' triumph over "the rulers and authorities" on the cross, as well as much of the martial language of Revelation (for example, in Rev 6:2, the rider on the white horse who "came out conquering and to conquer"). Equally important, however, are the healing narratives in the Gospels, particularly those demonstrating Jesus' sovereignty and authority over the unclean spirits.

What is achieved by the atonement under this model is the vanquishing by Jesus Christ of the "tyrants" that oppress humanity. Typically these are labeled as sin, the law, death, and Satan.[47] The law refers to an oppressive, legalistic approach to the Torah. Satan is identified as the personification of evil and the wielder of the other three. That personification also gathers in Paul's references to the principalities and powers that are defeated by Christ. The outcome of the victory is freedom for oppressed humanity from any such tyrants. That victory is secured on the cross, but its promise of freedom is ultimately fulfilled when, as 1 Corinthians 15:24 describes it, Jesus "hands over the kingdom to God the Father after he has destroyed every ruler and every authority and power." It is noticeable that when the victory model is deployed, it usually has a distinct New Testament focus. While in the Old Testament YHWH is also presented as defeating his enemies and those of his people, use of this model mostly draws on New Testament descriptions of the victory of the cross. The main Old Testament connection is generally Satan's identification as the instigator of the fall in the early chapters of Genesis.

The victory of Christ is a positive and energetic model of the atonement. At the same time, use of its metaphorical resources needs to be approached with care. One area for such care is that attempts to identify a mechanism for Christ's victory should be alert to where the limits of correspondence lie. For example, reviews of atonement theology often point to the idea from Gregory of Nyssa that Satan was somehow defeated by deception.[48] As Gregory put it, it was as if the flesh of Jesus acted as bait to Satan, with which he swallowed the hidden fishhook of Jesus' divinity, by which he was then defeated. Gregory was no doubt using colorful, illustrative language to pique the interest of his congregation and, if pressed too hard, what he suggests raises questions about the morality of a God who would use deception to prevail. However, it does highlight that this cannot be a victory or defeat following the all-too-well-worn paths of worldly conflict. Perhaps the most significant aspect of victory being used as a model for the atonement has to be that it is achieved not through weapons that look more powerful or deceptive from a worldly point of view but through vulnerability and the apparent defeat of Jesus' obedience to death on the cross. It is those limits of correspondence that point to some of the deepest insights of what happened on the cross.

Another area for caution is that metaphorical language of spiritual conflict can run into the twin risks of either (i) being seen as merely a description of a psychological conflict that takes place within the mind of the individual, or (ii) being taken too far as a myth of a battle between transcendent beings, taking place in a realm which is abstracted from the realities of life. Keeping a right connection between this model and our own lived experience is important. Indeed, doing so provides resources for exploring something of the mystery of actual human encounters with temptation, sin, and healing, and how the cross relates to those. We avoid the atonement becoming remote and theoretical by not losing sight of the fact that the victory of Jesus was not just something that took place in a spiritual realm. Alongside the supernatural, cosmic victory, the human Jesus was involved in successfully resisting temptation, challenging evil, and remaining faithful all the way to the cross.[49]

The Prevailing Models and Disability

Any review of these prevailing models for the purpose of engaging with disability has to admit that direct discussion about how they relate to the theological questions that disability raises has been conspicuous by its almost total absence, at least as far as sacrifice and justice are concerned. The victory model has been used in one area, forming the theological background for some charismatic healing ministries. In that case, as discussed further below, testimony from those with disabilities indicates that the way that model has been deployed there has often been unhelpful and needs to be revisited. Beyond that, the work remains to be done.

THE IMPORTANCE OF THE SUBJECTIVE: MORAL INFLUENCE AND CONNECTION

These three prevailing models all speak powerfully about the nature of the objective cosmic reconciliation wrought by God through the cross. This in turn invites the subjective question of how the single past event of the crucifixion, however we talk about it or understand it, can bring about salvation, and indeed transformation, in the here and now. While the atonement does need to deal with the sin and brokenness of the world in a universal, objective sense, it also must have some purchase on the blight of sin and suffering in people's lives and bring an experience of transformation in the present.[50]

A typical approach to this subjective question has been to suggest that there exists a separate, wholly subjective "moral influence" model or theory of the atonement. Like Aulén, this has usually referenced Peter Abelard. It has associated him with a purely exemplarist view of the atonement, that the purity of Jesus' life and his self-sacrificial death inspire a transformed way of living in his followers. In that form Abelard, together with the notion of such a "subjective theory," has often been rejected either as being too vague on matters of substitution and sin,[51] or on the basis that human response, however deeply felt, can never be salvific.[52] However, that impression of Abelard is something of a caricature. The strongly exemplarist proposal was in fact an Enlightenment maneuver seeking a human-centric interpretation of the crucifixion and resurrection. It was adopted in nineteenth-century liberal Protestantism and tended to cite Abelard as its source or champion. In fact, read more carefully, Abelard does provide a crucial insight. His point in his own writing was not that we are redeemed by Christ's example at all, but that because Christ has redeemed us and we have come to recognize that, its impact in the here and now is evidenced precisely in our desire to imitate him.[53]

Abelard regarded the alienation between God and humanity as objectively real and the atonement as equally objectively real. He did steer away from models of victory and satisfaction, but that was not because they were objective. It was because the way they were being expressed at the time seemed to him to impose on God some sort of higher, alien principle under which God was constrained to act. God's objective action must surely be his initiative alone and a manifestation of his own character of love.[54] The result of encountering that love is that the individual is more fully bound to God, and the objective reconciliation wrought by the atonement takes root and manifests itself in the transformation of how a life is lived.[55]

That much deeper and more fruitful response, which establishes the objective achievement of the cross as the source of the subjective experience of salvation, allows the atonement to be spoken of not only as sacrifice, justice, or victory, but also as a healing act of love.[56] An encounter with this expression of God's love, whether at the time or through the sharing of the story or of personal testimony, particularly at baptism or the Eucharist, is capable of bringing real change and restoration.[57] This opens the way for the cross to speak into a pervading sense of alienation in modern human society and ought to provide a connection between the more objective models of the cross and many of the concerns raised so effectively within disability theology.

The point that emerges here is that tackling the subjective question does not give rise to a separate subjective, or moral influence, model of the atonement. Instead, this discussion shows that whichever of the prevailing models is deployed, and whatever proposal is made about the atonement and disability, it must also be capable of addressing this subjective dimension of connecting actual lives with what God has achieved through the cross of Christ.

CONCLUSION: A CLEARER, MORE USABLE PICTURE

What God has done through the cross of Jesus Christ cannot be contained in a single expression or a single thought or idea. In striving to map out the sheer scale of the universal claim of the atonement and how it flows from the events of the first Good Friday, the New Testament and the church have applied their richest treasures of language and imagery. That creativity has opened up new depths of meaning and significance that a single description never could. However, along the way this has also given rise to what can be a confusing picture of seemingly competing claims and emphases. It has been unclear whether one way of describing or explaining the atonement, one model or theory, should take precedence and whether or not what we are trying to do is to describe what "literally" happened on the cross.

Much of that confusion has arisen from a lack of attention to how metaphorical language operates, its way of applying words and ideas from the familiar to open up and explore the unfamiliar. Taking that into account, however, has provided a way of marshaling these descriptions and images into three main groups of ideas, or models, of the atonement. These three are sacrifice, justice, and victory. Alongside them sits the equally important requirement to make room for the subjective dimension of how such an atonement has purchase on lives in the present. This is not simply to say that each such model, in its own way, has strengths and weaknesses but to say that together they encompass the ways the church has spoken of the cross. Each has much to say, but each reaches its limits of correspondence with the event of the cross and from there must allow another model to take over the work and fill in further meaning. These are the powerful ideas, with their roots deep in the biblical narrative, that have shaped and continue to shape the way the cross has been shared, week by week, in the life of the church. It is when they are ordered in this way that these models allow the atonement as a whole to be brought into a creative conversation with the challenges and insights of disability theology. This is critical work, as it has become clear that this conversation has largely yet to begin in earnest.

3

Seeking Connections

First Steps in a Response

METAPHORS AND IDEAS, SHARED AND OTHERWISE

Two fields of thought lie side by side. On the one hand lies the atonement, the great cosmic reconciliation achieved by God in Christ at the cross. It is described and explained using models of sacrifice, justice, and victory, and the resources of metaphor they provide. On the other hand lies disability theology, with all its creativity and new thinking that opens up possibilities for seeing disability not just in a positive light but as a hitherto neglected source of deep theological insight. The challenge taken up here is to bridge the gap between the two, so that the hard questions that come from asking about the interaction of sin, disability, healing, the cross, and salvation can find a response that is neither oppressive nor evasive.

Although atonement theology has had very little indeed to say about disability to date, and although disability theology has drawn only on certain particular features of Jesus' crucifixion and resurrection, it is possible that between them these two fields might already contain the elements of such a response. After all, that is what metaphor is supposed to enable ideas to do, to cross between subjects and allow one to draw out meaning in the other. An example might be the metaphor of vulnerability. Disability theology has explored the vulnerability of those with disabilities and what that reveals of the truth that all human beings are vulnerable and dependent. From the atonement side, the sacrifice model speaks of Jesus' extreme vulnerability at the crucifixion in a way that reflects the extreme vulnerability of the Levitical sacrificial victim, through whose innocent blood God declares that sin has been dealt with and relationships restored.

The possibility that building up a picture of shared metaphors and meaning in this way might provide a means of bridging the gap has to be taken seriously. Either it will provide an adequate response, or, if not, it might indicate where else such a response should be sought. Each of the prevailing models of sacrifice, justice, and victory can be tested in this way to see what it yields. What that testing turns up is a number of tantalizing connections but ultimately the need to tackle a deeper question.

DISABILITY THEOLOGY AND SACRIFICE, JUSTICE, OR VICTORY

Sacrifice Language

Picking up that example of vulnerability, although the metaphor appears in each field, as it stands the link it provides between the two is only partial because it is being put to work in different ways. Disability theology is making more of an anthropological point, the common human condition of vulnerability, rather than making a connection with God in Christ, who chooses to become vulnerable through the self-giving of sacrifice to effect atonement. However, raising vulnerability does lead to another possible shared idea: that of identification.

The disability-perspective exploration of the image of God develops a strong argument that both Jesus' vulnerability, and his body disabled by the process of execution and still carrying the marks of the wounds after the resurrection, point to God's eternal identification with humanity inclusive of impairment. Identification is also significant in the sacrificial system. The individual or community in need of atonement is encouraged to identify with the sacrificial victim. An individual does this by laying his or her hand on the animal's head (Lev 1, 3, and 4). In the case of the community as a whole, on the Day of Atonement the high priest lays both of his hands on the scapegoat and confesses the sins of the community (Lev 16:21). The scapegoat is not then killed but permanently removed from the camp, so not a sacrifice in quite the same way but part of the same system.[1] The New Testament picks up on this idea of our identification with Jesus in these sacrificial terms, for example in Paul's declaration that "therefore we have been buried with him by baptism into death, so that, just as Christ was raised from the dead by the glory of the Father, so we too might walk in newness of life" (Rom 6:4).[2] Again, however, although the metaphor of identification is shared, it is difficult to connect its use in the two fields. The disability theology emphasis is on identification as a crucial affirmation of the individual, impairments and all, made in the image of God and acceptable to God. The sacrifice use is very different, being our identification as those in need of forgiveness with Jesus' body as a sacrifice of atonement which carries the burden of our sin.

A third metaphor, also linked to these two and playing an important role in both fields, is embodiment. Sacrifice as part of Old Testament worship could be described as embodied theology. God was in some sense encountered and interacted with, and the relationship between the individual and God, or the community and God, was repaired and developed through the medium of the body offered as a sacrifice.[3] Similarly, the atonement, with all its implications of cosmic reconciliation, is embodied emphatically in the person of Jesus (the hermeneutical key). That seems to resonate with the call in disability theology for theological insight to be grounded in actual, possibly impaired, bodies. However, the emphasis is again not quite the same. The important insight there is that of locating a source of theological discussion in real bodies and lived experience, particularly in tackling what it means to talk of humanity made in the image of God, rather than an embodied theology of God's dealing with sin.

Trouble with Sacrifice

Examining sacrifice language also means facing some concerns it can raise in the context of disability. One of these comes from the disability theology critique of normate assumptions about what is "normal" or "perfect" in a person. The emphasis on the bodily perfection of the atoning sacrifice in the Old Testament, typically "a male without blemish" (Lev 1:3, for example), potentially muddies the waters in matters of identification. Disability theology emphasizes identification with Christ disabled by crucifixion and retaining the marks of that disablement in his risen body. The sacrifice model, although coopting the idea of perfection metaphorically in terms of sinlessness, perhaps inadvertently suggests identification with a Jesus claimed unhelpfully to be blemish-free in all respects. Some careful distinction is needed there. A second concern lies in the suggestion that Jesus is most clearly identified with humanity, incorporating all disability, at the point when he is most disabled by the cross. As that is also the point at which he most fully bears the burden of human sin, there is a danger that the sacrifice model does little to dispel the equation of disability with sin and the fall.

Justice Language

Given the important and necessary vein of advocacy running through disability theology, it would be surprising if it did not share metaphors with a model of the atonement based on ideas of justice. However, where those appear they tend to be emphasizing different sides of the justice equation. Whether the justice model of the atonement is approached in terms of a broken covenant or in the more transactional terms of the law court, at its heart lies the problem of dealing with guilt for sin before God. Through the atoning work of Christ, the individual, against all the odds and the evidence, is declared innocent and set free, or the covenant is restored. Justice metaphors in disability theology focus less on Jesus' substitutionary death that deals with guilt and sin, and more on calling society and individuals to account before God for their poor response to "the other." This leads to the call for a transforming work of the Holy Spirit, bringing about a lowering of barriers to full participation, to be experienced in this life. That concept of justice in the form of inclusion, fairness, and the removal of prejudice shapes much of disability-perspective theological anthropology, the theology of access, soteriology, and also parts of disability hermeneutics. For example, the emphasis drawn from the healing narratives in the Gospels is the overturning of exclusion and the reintegration of the healed person into the community. Justice is highly significant here in terms of societal accountability and transformation, but that is quite different from its use as an atonement metaphor of Jesus standing as our substitute or advocate before God's judgment on our sin.

A closer connection might be discernible through a narrower focus on the language of vindication as part of the wider idea of justice. In the justice model of the atonement, Jesus is vindicated by the resurrection. His innocence of the charges brought against him, his claim that he will defeat death, and claims that he is the Son of God are all shown to be true. A comparison is possible with the disability-perspective challenge to what it means to be human, made in the image of God. It seeks an interpretation whereby any person, however profound their disability, is vindicated in their claim to be fully human (and, by extension here, in their claim to be represented by Jesus on the cross). Although these thoughts on vindication start from different directions, something about them does therefore come together at the cross.

Trouble with Guilt

As with sacrifice, the language of the justice model is not free from potential trouble. Perhaps the main difficulty lies in matters of guilt over sin. Where the justice model is expressed in the metaphorical language of a legal transaction, or case, it appears to demand an appreciation of accountability and guilt over sin on the part of the one atoned for. Justification is a setting free from this guilt through being declared innocent. This raises the question of how the model would operate in the case of those with profound intellectual impairment. To require a sense of accountability and guilt over sin seems inappropriate there. And yet to suggest a lack of such, and therefore an absence of the need for atonement, seems to suggest, perhaps in a subtle way, that the individual is somehow not quite human in the way that others are.

Victory Language

The victory model of the atonement makes for an interesting comparison. The metaphors it shares with disability theology prove to be in some ways strong and positive and in others particularly awkward. A significant shared metaphor is that of oppression (often interchangeable here with enslavement), both the acknowledgment of it and the demand for release from it. The victory model speaks of the oppression of humanity by sin, death, Satan, and the (Old Testament) law. The overcoming of these oppressive powers by Jesus Christ through the cross and resurrection, and the ongoing struggle with them in the life of the believer, are expressed in dramatic metaphors of spiritual warfare. To borrow Aulén's own summary: "God is pictured as in Christ carrying through a victorious conflict against powers of evil which are hostile to His will."[4]

A form of that argument is echoed in disability theology, which clearly identifies oppressive traits within society and its institutions, evident in normate views and behavior, within the church as well as more generally. Those traits may not be personified in quite the same way as in the language of Christus Victor, but we might identify at least some parallel with the "authorities" and "powers" which Paul mentions (for example in Rom 8:38 or Eph 6:12) and which feature in the language of the victory model. Flowing from metaphors of oppression and release are those of freedom. The victory model envisages the human being set free from the bondage of demonic spiritual forces. Disability theology speaks just as powerfully of freedom from an overmedicalized view of disability, freedom from prejudice, and the freedom of access and full participation in society and ecclesial life. Vulnerability also features in this comparison, although its work is different in the two fields. While vulnerability acts in disability theology mostly as a revelation of God's solidarity with humanity and of humanity's true condition, in the victory model it is through embracing vulnerability that Jesus secures his victory over Satan.

Trouble with Triumph, Vulnerability, and Healing

Other metaphors emerging from a victory model comparison are more problematic. With the introduction of ideas such as the disabled God, disability theology has made us rightly suspicious of the metaphors of Jesus as triumphant captain and conquering Lord, somehow overcoming human frailty along with the evil forces in the world.[5] When by extension those saved are considered conquerors themselves, the implied emphasis on agency and achievement makes the task of identification with Christ more difficult in the context of severe impairment.

The use of the victory model and its language of spiritual warfare in charismatic theologies of healing has also attracted criticism for some time. A detailed review of charismatic healing theologies is not set out here, but John Wimber could be taken as a significant and representative exponent of such an approach. Wimber describes all sickness (undifferentiated and including disabilities) as originating in Satan's kingdom.[6] Within such a scheme, prayer for divine healing is engagement in the conflict between Satan's kingdom and the kingdom of God, which he describes as "a warship, navigating in enemy territory."[7] When healing occurs it is a victory in this conflict and a demonstration of the truth of the gospel. There is great energy behind this and encouragement to the church to get out and engage in prayer for healing. However, from a disability perspective, by coopting the victory model's metaphorical language in this way, such an approach to healing seems unwittingly to have adopted a spiritual version of a strongly medical model of disability. Disability again becomes a personal tragedy that ought to be put right by intervention, in this case through prayer. If it is not put right, that intervention has failed. By seeming to focus only on a Christus Victor understanding of the cross, this approach to healing ministry seems to leave little room for a more holistic theological understanding of healing that perhaps is more like a parallel to a social model concept of disability.

DISABILITY THEOLOGY AND MORAL INFLUENCE

A comparison of shared ideas and metaphors should also ask what happens when we turn to the subjective dimension of the atonement, its connection with present lives. The themes of disability theology make theological calls for changes in attitude and behavior and for transformation that can be experienced, subjectively, in present lives. For example, the purpose of exploring Jesus' identification with humanity inclusive of its range of impairments, through his crucified and resurrected body, is to bring about a change in normate "us and them" attitudes and oppressive behaviors, moving toward a fuller appreciation and inclusion of those with disabilities. The same can be said of the argument that the vulnerability of those with disabilities reveals the true state of all humanity. The earlier description of salvation as primarily a transformative work of the Holy Spirit, creating a new, hospitable community, picks up that emphasis.

A purely exemplarist moral influence explanation of the atonement might on the face of it seem to align neatly with those sorts of concerns. The example of Jesus' self-giving on behalf of others as a motivation for leading a better life seems to fit. However, two objections immediately clamor for attention. One is that the existing work in disability theology seems to stake out its claims for where changes are needed perfectly well without the need to add that exemplarist view of the cross. The cross seen in that way is not really adding anything to what is already being said.

The second is that a purely exemplarist view of the cross has not been found convincing in any case. The far more robust view is that it is an encounter with the actual objective achievement of God through the cross, taking upon himself the consequences of the sin and brokenness of the world, that leads to a subjective experience of forgiveness and transformation in present lives. That subjective experience certainly should encompass the changes called for across the themes of disability theology. The important point, though, is that it still leaves open the question of what it is about the cross and about what God actually did there that renders the atonement wholly inclusive of all humanity, and that then enables it to act as the source and foundation for those more subjective concerns that disability theology so rightly and effectively puts its finger on.

INTERPRETING THE COMPARISON: A DEEPER QUESTION

This comparison of language and ideas at work in the two fields has thrown into sharper relief that question of where a response might lie to the interaction of disability, sin, healing, the cross, and salvation. There are clearly a number of terms, ideas, and metaphors where similar language is being used in both fields, whichever model of the atonement is in view. However, examining them more closely has shown that those metaphors, whether vulnerability, vindication, oppression, or others, are mostly doing quite different work when used to speak theologically about disability or about the cross. Many seem promising but then seem to "speak past" one another rather than connecting strongly, and some metaphorical components of the models are left, as things stand, sounding awkward in a disability context.

The fact that there are some similarities of language is at least encouraging. It affirms that the two fields are not somehow estranged from one another or contradictory, and that these different emphases are worth pursuing further. But the fact that the existing connections are often partial, and glancing suggests that the solution to bringing disability theology and the cross together convincingly will not stem directly from developing the existing language of either disability theology or the prevailing atonement models. That solution, it seems, will involve exploring a deeper, prior question about the nature of the atonement itself. It will entail going back and asking what sort of thing God's initiative at the cross is. It entails asking more fundamentally what sort of thing it is that these models of sacrifice, justice, and victory are describing, and understanding how that initiative of God's at the cross can be inherently inclusive of the whole of humanity, with all its variety and disability.

REAL LIVES, THE CROSS, AND A DIVERSITY OF HOPES

Stepping back and asking this prior question about the nature of God's initiative of atonement carries with it a danger that the whole discussion could become too general or theoretical to be of relevance to actual lives, lived at various times with or without disabilities. It was said at the outset that two strands of thought have to run in parallel in this whole enterprise. The first asks about the cross with all of humanity in mind, including all of its variety, not restricting that discussion to any discrete subset of disabilities. The second asks whether any answers proposed remain relevant to particular lives. That second strand is best served by asking what sort of questions those real lives seem to raise about the nature of God's atonement initiative and the transformation it achieves. Any account of the cross is expected to say how it addresses a sinfulness and brokenness that is common to all people. But each life experience will also bring its own questions to the foot of the cross, so to speak, and those have to be listened to carefully without presuming that our existing account of the cross provides a meaningful response. In conversations with people living with disability, the power of the cross is not theoretical. It plays out in wrestling with the whole business of healing and of how individuals and society respond to disability.

Disability theology has consistently challenged the presumption of those currently without disabilities that they know what those who are living with disabilities would, or should, look to God to change, whether in this life or come the resurrection. It is the idea that, when Jesus in Luke 18:41 asks of the blind man: "What do you want me to do for you?" those who are fully sighted already know the answer. But listening to people who are living with disability disrupts that presumption.

Martin and his wife, Eve, have lived for years with Martin's multiple sclerosis. Without hesitation they look to God for release and healing, through the power of the cross. As Martin puts it, "*My pain is everywhere*" and "*I look forward to my death and the release that I will have at that point, freeing myself from this heavy body that I push around every day will be a joy.*" And yet they both hold what that healing might be as an open question. Although they have had prayer for healing on many occasions, they are not demanding that Martin's MS be fixed in this life. And their resurrection hope is that such healing and release would not eliminate any of the good things they have experienced through it. They have seen the Holy Spirit powerfully at work when others have helped them and when their marriage has been tested but strengthened by what they have faced together. Their hope rests in God and the power of the cross, but it is not a simple formula.

We might also listen to Fern, reflecting on life with her daughter, Ruth. Fern has seen God touch people deeply when they have been healed in response to prayer. She has also seen God touch people through their responses to Ruth, whose brain injury at birth and its complex implications have not been healed in that way. This is not least when Ruth speaks of her own faith, although (and perhaps because) her words come slowly, spoken through a communication aid. Fern is reticent to say what God ought to do with Ruth's body and the effects of her brain injury either now or come the resurrection. Having said that, she trusts God, who has shown himself to be trustworthy through hard times. In his new creation there will in some way be freedom of movement, complete participation, and release from the sheer weight of the effort that Ruth's disability entails for now, but Fern and Ruth will trust God for how that will look.

Such hopes can sometimes become more polarized. Amos Yong, seeing his brother Mark's involvement in worship and prayers and ministry to others, suggests that people with Down syndrome are not in need of healing from their genetic makeup, either now or eschatologically. To do so would seem to eliminate that person. Indeed, to insist that such healing can be God's only response to what we call disability can seem almost like idolatry.[8] By contrast, James Barton Gould, mentioned earlier, insists that such healing of his son, David, bringing him in line with a typical body and mind, is an objectively good thing to be expected of God. In his view, the way for that has been opened through the cross and resurrection.

Situations of profound intellectual impairment have a particular way of putting much of our theological thinking to the test and do so again here. My friend Diane, again, relates her and her family's life with her son, Paul, who has severe autism. There are aspects of Paul's character and personality that seem to be as much part of who he is, as might be said to be part of his autism. Diane would always want to preserve the joy Paul takes in nature, his selflessness, and a simple contentment that seem to bring her and her husband closer to God's priorities than would otherwise be possible. There is a sense that this is Paul's ministry. As Diane puts it, "*You could say perhaps that Paul's autism brings healing to the world with its crooked perceptions*." And yet it is hard to separate that from the desire, in terms of looking to God for healing, for Paul to leave behind his terrors, "*when his anxieties are so very hard that he could not walk outside the house, or get his cutlery to his mouth, or play alongside any friend*," not to mention a deep longing for a future with the joy of free communication. Within all of that, discerning what Paul's own hopes are and whether or how they are located in or connected with God, Jesus, or the cross adds another layer of complication. An understanding of hope and fulfillment that demands that Paul engage in an intellectually typical way with the atonement, evidenced by a response of "repent and believe," seems to fall short, to say the very least, when most of the ways that church life and worship are conducted are barely accessible to him.

These are mere snapshots, but what gradually emerges from listening as people wrestle with what it means to speak of God bringing transformation through the power of the cross is not a single, one-dimensional answer. Instead it is what might be called a "diversity of hopes." That is not simply to say we do not know what God will do. It is to acknowledge explicitly that there is no one description of what constitutes a good, healed, complete, fulfilling, restored, and grace-filled life. It recognizes that what is good begins with God, and experience shows that the good is revealed in extraordinarily diverse ways and outcomes.

The implications of this are significant, as they demand that an account of the atonement that is genuinely inclusive of the variety of disability must be willing to embrace this idea of a diversity of hopes. It must also be an account that moves away from only seeing apprehension of and response to the atonement as an intellectual thing. And, crucially, it must be an account of the cross that does not stumble over healing but that recognizes the complexity of disability and healing and does not unhelpfully conflate disability and sin.

FIRST STEPS IN A RESPONSE

A useful starting point in discovering such an account is with the work of Frances Young. Young has written about her understanding of the cross, but like the conversations reflected above, she approaches much of her theology through her experience of bringing up her son, Arthur, who was born with very significant mental and physical disabilities. Her writing is therefore deeply informed by the sorts of concerns raised by disability itself, and within disability theology, that have already been explored.[9]

Grappling with Theodicy

For Young, the years of caring for Arthur call for the world to be dealt with as it is, taking into account from the outset its full range of ambiguity and suffering that arise from a broad mixture of apparent evils. Those evils certainly include sin in the sense of moral choice, but they also encompass experiences of pain (recognizing that sometimes it can act as a warning); the suffering that results from natural processes like storms, floods, and volcanic eruptions; and the more personal things that often appear to be accidental such as genetic mutation, infant malformation, and even death.

In the light of this, she finds that many approaches to the theodicy question (how we can speak of a good God in a world that contains such things) assume too readily that they can identify the nature, sources, and purpose of evil and suffering. Those approaches include ideas of suffering as soul-making or a clear split between moral and natural evil. Experience with Arthur has challenged these solutions as too easy and convenient.[10] Any account of theodicy, and indeed of the atonement, must instead address the suffering caused by what Young calls a deep and complex "gone-wrongness"[11] of the world. That includes a moral gone-wrongness which incorporates intentional choice but which equally includes the habits of living that accrue to individuals and to society along the way and in which all are caught up.[12] Taking Arthur as an example, the effects of this moral gone-wrongness befall him not least through society's often ambivalent response to how he is. That part of the moral realm may not reflect conscious individual moral decisions, but culpability for it and for its effects remains. The deep gone-wrongness also includes the contingent nature of life: things such as accident, variety, or disability that befall us, as they have befallen Arthur, though it seems they need not have done so. The question is whether God should in some way be called to account for the fact that life as we experience it is, as a result of all of this, chaotic and fragile, as prone to grief as it is to joy.

To this Young adds that the pattern of the need for hope within despair and trouble is a crucial interpretative insight. This pattern is so fundamental and widespread in the biblical text that the central event of the atonement must surely be seen in the light of it as well. This conviction arises not least from relating the pattern in a moving way to the experience of the possibilities for hope in the midst of the challenges of caring for Arthur. It also draws on the Bible's willingness to acknowledge that the present is very unsatisfactory. The cross must render the possibility of hope credible within the despair and trouble of that unsatisfactory present.[13]

Interpreting the Cross: A Double Reparation

To address this, as mentioned briefly earlier, Young proposes that two things can be seen taking place at the cross, a kind of "double reparation."[14] The first part is that Jesus, our representative and the perfect worshipper, makes a sacrifice of obedience and for sin. We are able to take advantage of his sacrifice through faith. Here, Young interprets the cross in strongly sacrificial terms. She discusses other approaches, including aspects of the justice model as well as Christus Victor. While each has some attractions, in the end she concludes that through them the church has lost touch with its Jewish roots. Sacrifice aligns us most closely with the early church making inevitable use of inherited tools of language and worship readily available to them to talk about the things of God. Particularly important for Young's way of talking about the cross are the sacrifices of the Passover lamb and the Day of Atonement.[15] As well as containing themes of liberation, both of these addressed not only individual moral sin but the community's wider corporate failure. They unmasked the violence and culpability of all of society, particularly when the fears or resentments of a group become focused on an innocent individual or minority. This unmasking was achieved by allowing that violence and culpability to be ritualized in the drama of sacrifice (a way of thinking about the scapegoat). Enacting that drama also became an opportunity for communal participation in thanksgiving for the aversion of judgment.[16] Celebration and thanksgiving took place through the shared eating of the sacrificed animal. For Young, drawing out the various parallels with Jesus, the drama of the cross, like that of sacrifice, exposed the sin and the complicity of the whole community in that sin,[17] giving the atonement a significance that is at least as much corporate as individualistic. At the communion meal, celebration and thanksgiving are shared by the community for what the sacrifice has achieved.

The other side of the double reparation is that God takes responsibility for the wide gone-wrongness of creation and makes some sort of reparation for it.[18] In proposing this, Young refers briefly to the idea that as part of the event of creation God withdrew to an extent. Space was made for creation, which is inevitably imperfect, since creation is not God. This reflected the nature of God's love in allowing independence to creation, but it also allowed the possibility of corruption, accident, and even the demonic within creation. That kenotic approach to creation is not expanded upon in any detail. However, it allows for the claim that from then on God has been willing to be fully present and responsible for such a creation. At the cross, God is present not only in Jesus as our representative but in himself, bearing out of love the consequences of how creation is.[19] The significance of this double reparation is that, through it, the cross demonstrates that God deals with sin, but more than that. Just as God is present in and with Jesus in the suffering and tragedy of the cross,[20] we can expect him to be present in all human suffering and tragedy.[21]

No mechanism is proposed by which this accountability-through-presence provides reparation for the gone-wrongness of creation. It may be that Young feels instinctively that any such proposal would be inadequate. Her suggestion is that the light and darkness approach of John's Gospel might be useful. At the cross the darkness of the world does not disappear as if by magic, nor is it explained away. Somehow it is transformed by the presence of God, rendering it bearable. However, an important conclusion that does emerge is that "atonement is effected by the very presence of God."[22] The Old Testament narrative of Job provides a kind of parallel here, since it was the presence of God that satisfied Job's desire to call God to account, rather than a ticking off of objective answers to his list of complaints. Jesus' perfect sacrifice for sin remains important, but in Young's proposal it is made complete by God's presence, whereby he takes responsibility for the gone-wrongness of creation, what might be called "atonement-as-presence."

The way that this double reparation connects with present lives is also interpreted in sacrificial terms. Jesus has offered the perfect, ultimate sacrifice once for all. However, the continuing worship of the church in response to that can also be spoken of as sacrifice. Christians, Young suggests, saw baptism, martyrdom, repentance, praise, thanksgiving, and thank offering all as worship and as ways of entering into Jesus' sacrifice and getting its benefits. They all stand in for the bringing of a physical sacrificial offering, which is hardwired in humanity's sense of what is required to approach God.[23] We therefore have access to the benefits of this double reparation by, on the one hand, recognizing the loving presence of God in the midst of trouble (since God's presence is also what makes the suffering arising out of any aspect of creation's gone-wrongness bearable, providing hope in despair) and, on the other hand, responding to God in worship, which, being sacrifice, makes real to us the sacrifice of Jesus.

Lest this all begin to appear too theoretical, it is worth grounding it in what Young says about Arthur. Arthur can only ever take part in the life of the church if others are involved. That in itself underlines the inherently corporate nature of worship, and indeed of salvation, that others are involved in our relationship with God. That corporate dimension is also deepened by the way in which God's presence is discovered through Arthur. As well as the assurance of God's presence providing daily hope and strength, Young detects it in what she calls the vocation of Arthur's life. This can be revelatory, in demonstrating the true vulnerability of all people, and it can be redemptive. Through him, good responses and behavior are evoked,[24] but also the sometimes negative responses to his presence demonstrate our need for some sort of atonement.[25] Lastly, relating back to the idea of the "diversity of hopes" that emerged above, Young is not looking for Arthur to be "fixed" in the sense of being brought into alignment with a "typical" body or mind either in this life or come the resurrection. Arthur is embodied as he is, and there must be continuity with that, as well as transformation, in the age to come, whatever that might look like.[26]

Encouragements and Open Questions

Young's account provides two particularly helpful and encouraging initial insights that can be put to work in beginning to look for an inherently inclusive account of the cross and the atonement. The first is that it encourages a willingness to grapple with life as it is. There is undoubtedly much in life that stems from sinfulness, the moral failure of individuals and groups, whether deliberate or not, and that leads to suffering and pain. In biblical terms the history of that is traced back to the fall in Genesis 3. However, mixed in with that there is also much in life that takes the form of variety, accident, and contingency that can be a source of distress, even despair, but that is far less easy to identify with moral sin in the same way. What is more, we deceive ourselves if we think we can fully distinguish the knotted strands of that combination and disentangle them. This is the complex "gone-wrongness" of the world, and it leads to the second insight, which is that both of those aspects of life, the moral and the contingent, must in some way be addressed by God at the cross. While the cross must address what can be identified as sin, it must surely address all aspects of life that cry out for hope within trouble and despair. Not least, these are powerful, pastorally effective insights, connecting everyday experience with the cross.

While this account opens up these two positive lines of thought, it does, however, leave other challenges and questions open that will have to be addressed to form a more complete picture of the sort of event that the atonement is. First, insisting on a primarily sacrificial understanding of the cross, as the earlier discussion has shown, asks too much of one theoretical model. For example, interpreting the worship of the church as sacrifice is not at all unreasonable but does not of itself suggest that the sacrifice model should take precedence over justice or victory, both of which make use of sound biblical resources. Worship is just as likely to include a cry for and commitment to justice, as well as a celebration of the victory of the atonement. Indeed, it seems the poorer for the lack of them. Similarly, a convincing account of the atonement should connect to the strengths of each of these ways in which the church has shared the meaning of the cross as well as recognizing the limits of correspondence of each.

Second, concerning the role of Jesus, in this account of him as the perfect believer and worshipper, he acts principally as our representative before the Father. However, all three of the prevailing ways of understanding the cross make as much, if not more, of Jesus' substitutionary role at the cross. Here, that role seems to have faded into the background. Even just sticking with sacrifice, while there is clearly more to it than a mere substitution of the animal for the sinful person, an account of sacrifice without a substitutionary dimension seems unnecessarily thin, presenting only part of what that model has to offer. At the cross, Jesus is not only the perfect worshipper but the perfect sacrifice as well.

Lastly, turning to the other side of the double reparation, the emphasis on God's presence is positive but seems to leave a crucial question unanswered. If it is primarily God's presence (his willingness to "turn up") that brings atonement, then such an atonement would seem to be achievable through a combination of the incarnation and the revelation of God's continuing presence, perhaps in the manner of that to Job. The cross would then be acting primarily as an offering of perfect worship together with a revelation of God's character and his willingness to accompany creation in its suffering. The sacrifice offered may address moral culpability, but this double reparation leaves unanswered the question of what change is wrought by the atonement for the rest of the gone-wrongness and contingency of the world. Young's proposal of atonement-as-presence seems to leave us with a subjective answer (we are confident of a sense of God's presence within human tragedy) to an objective question (how, following the cross, are things no longer as they were as regards the whole contingent nature of creation and life?).

THE POSSIBILITY OF GOD'S PARTICIPATION

To recap briefly, comparing the ideas and language at work in disability theology and in the ways the church has spoken of the cross has revealed that while some ideas and metaphors cross that boundary between them, they do so partially at best. That has suggested that the answer to bridging these two will instead lie in revisiting what sort of event the atonement is and what its relationship with disability might be. Paying attention to the testimony of real lives has kept that question grounded and has contributed both the idea that there is a diversity of hopes as to what transformation the cross might bring about and the insistence that our interaction with the cross must move away from a predominantly intellectual one. Frances Young's account has provided some first steps toward a response with her discussion of a wide, complex moral and contingent gone-wrongness, and thoughts on how all of that might be addressed in our main account of the cross.

In the end Young leans toward an interpretation of "atonement-as-presence," but that leaves open questions about what has objectively changed at the cross, beyond what can be said by interpreting it as Jesus' offering of a sacrifice. In the space it has opened up, however, a different interpretive course can be charted. The analysis can be pressed much further, suggesting that at the cross God is not only present to the whole predicament of creation but is in some way intimately, actively, and creatively participating in it to bring an objective transformation to all aspects of it. What might be called God's initiative of "atonement-as-participation."

Indeed, revisiting some of the themes in Young's account, but with a focus on ideas of participation, begins to shed some new light on the way ahead. At the cross Jesus makes a perfect sacrifice of obedience (worship) which is effective in dealing with our culpability for sin, intentional and otherwise, and in healing our moral relationship with God. Sticking with the sacrificial emphasis, participation can be seen operating with equal significance in two directions. Jesus in his humanity participates as our representative (our high priest, following Hebrews) in the need that humanity has for the atonement that sacrifice can bring. In response, we can participate in Jesus' sacrificial offering through understanding our worship as a form of sacrifice. What is more, that participation can be understood as a corporate affair as we, who already participate in the corporate person of Adam, can become included in the corporate person of Christ, the corporate body of Christ, and a corporate image of God. At the same time, God's presence and accountability at the cross can be taken as a suggestion that since creation (not only at the focal moment of the cross) he has in some way participated in the risk of creation's contingent nature. Exploring the cross in this way, not just as where God is present in the complexities of life but where he is participating in them to bring actual change, might well open up the way for the more fruitful conversation between disability theology and the atonement that seems so necessary.

II

PROPOSED INTERACTIONS

4

Atonement-as-Participation

An Inherently Inclusive Account

PARTICIPATION: PROTOCOL, KNOWLEDGE, AND DIVINE INITIATIVE

The discussion so far has demonstrated the need for a significant theological movement. It is from a position, almost an impasse, where the cross, disability, sin, inclusion, and healing sit awkwardly together to where the cross becomes the firmest foundation for a distinctively Christian theology of disability, inclusion, and healing. There are hopeful indications that such a movement might be possible. Mapping out the main themes and objectives being pursued in disability theology and bringing some order to the otherwise unwieldy field of atonement theology has laid the groundwork. But it has also demonstrated that as they stand these do not provide the resources that can draw the two fields more fruitfully together and bring about that theological movement. Instead, the way forward seems to lie in revisiting the very idea of what sort of event or divine action the atonement is. At the cross, God in Christ dealt effectively with sin. But to say that is not to say enough. Frances Young's approach has invited a willingness to see that the atonement at the cross must address the whole human predicament, indeed the whole contingent nature of creation. The suggestion here is that this might best be done by exploring what it means for the cross to be the focal point not just of God's presence but of his deep participation in his creation. When that is done, it holds the prospect of opening up a theological space in which the theologies of disability and the cross can interact fully and flourish together, and of discovering an account of the atonement at the cross that inherently includes people with disabilities right from the start.

It is hardly news to suggest that God's relationship with his creation and with humanity involves him participating with them. The Holy Spirit of God is intimately involved in every breath of life and in God's working both with his people and with the nations throughout the Old and New Testaments. The incarnation of Jesus, where the Word becomes flesh and lives among us (John 1:14), is perhaps the most dramatic and immediate example of God's participating, or joining in, with human lives. And the New Testament ends with John's apocalyptic vision that looks forward to the fulfillment of all things, when the dwelling place of God will be with humankind for eternity (Rev 21:3). What is happening in the present discussion, though, is that that idea and the meaning of God's participation are being pressed much further and with deliberate intent as regards what was going on in God's action at the cross. The first step in working toward that and developing the idea of atonement-as-participation involves working out what it means to talk of God's participating deeply in the contingent nature, or riskiness, of creation itself.

"Participation" is of course a word used with varying shades of meaning in all sorts of contexts. Therefore, using it well involves being clear what meaning "participation" is taking on here and what work it is being asked to do.

Participation as a Protocol, Not as a Model

To talk of atonement-as-participation and apply it in the ways so far suggested, it is important to be clear what sort of thing it is intended to be. Most importantly, it is not a new or separate model of the atonement in the way that sacrifice, justice, and victory are. It is not that those need to be replaced or another added to fill in some gaps. Instead, the idea of atonement-as-participation acts as what might be called a "theological protocol" for approaching discussions of the atonement as a whole. As such, it is something that should guide the application of any model used to explore what God brought about through Jesus at the cross.

What is meant by a "theological protocol" can be demonstrated by comparison with other concepts that act in a similar way. Examples would be the claim that the atonement is God's initiative, or that it relies on Jesus' humanity and divinity, or that through it God in some way addresses sin. Talk of the atonement is widely understood to be talk of this kind of action or event. Such protocols help to provide some agreed foundation of the type of action or event that the atonement is. The models, whether sacrifice, victory, or justice, are then deployed as ways of describing and explaining what God was doing through that sort of atonement. Theological protocols help to guide and discipline the way in which the metaphorical resources of each model are so deployed. They do similar work to, for example, the christological statements in the Chalcedonian definition. In that case, talk about Jesus Christ is understood to be talk about the sort person who has been described by those statements.[1]

Participation, Knowledge, and God

"Participation" is a broad term, and it appears across many theological and philosophical areas of debate. What will become important in the present discussion, however, is the part that the notion of participation plays both in the way we understand God himself to be acting, and in the way we can speak of ourselves as human beings having knowledge of God, and access to the benefits of the atonement. There is a strong link here with a wider shift taking place in philosophical thinking about knowledge in general. The shift is in favor of the argument that knowledge, particularly personal knowledge, arises more from involvement and participation than it does from analysis.[2]

For many years, a Cartesian idea of knowledge has had something of a monopoly. Following the thinking of René Descartes, knowledge has been assumed to arise through a process of separating or abstracting ourselves from that which we would like to observe and know. Thus, separated by the exercise of our consciousness, the object of our interest is analyzed, and conclusions about it are drawn. This conceptual maneuver is assumed to allow us to claim that our knowledge is objective. This has become a habit of thinking that has created a Cartesian anthropology, or way of understanding humanity, which separates our own being from the world and from other beings, separates mind from body, animate from inanimate, and so on. It can also be said to have led in turn to a Cartesian approach to theology, where there is a presumption that God is essentially separate from the world but perhaps intervenes from time to time.

In contrast, the shift taking place is toward what is termed a phenomenological approach to knowledge. The assertion of that approach is that to know the world properly we must participate in it and indeed become immersed in it. Such an approach proposes that all things relate to and affect each other in some way and that the Cartesian separation at best lacks self-critique as far as that interaction is concerned. The theological aspect or corollary of this way of knowing lies in a presumption of God's constant involvement in creation, birth, life, death, and resurrection. Talk here of participation therefore anticipates a knowledge of God which goes beyond analytical proposals about God and is derived from the experience of his intimate involvement in all things. It should be acknowledged that without care it is possible for such talk of God to veer off in a panentheistic direction, seeing God's existence as essentially within his creation and blurring the crucial lines of his otherness. That is certainly not necessary. The essential characteristic of the life of God as eternally dynamic and participative is as easily, and more convincingly, found in an orthodox Trinitarian, relational understanding of God as Father, Son, and Holy Spirit.

Participation as Divine Initiative

The idea of the cross of Jesus Christ as the focal point of God's deep participation in his creation seems to hold promise both as a guide or protocol for what sort of event it is and as a way of exploring more fully what it means to know the God who is revealed there. Those initial thoughts lead on to the larger question of how, in what manner, God himself can be said to be present, active, and participating in his initiative of the atonement at the cross. There is an objective aspect to this, which is to ask what light is shed on the change wrought by the cross when it is seen as the place of God's deep participation in the predicament of creation and how that should be shaped by the insights of disability theology. There is also a subjective aspect, which is to ask how approaching the cross as God's participation in this way opens up a way of seeing how that change is recognized by or within humanity, inclusive of its full range of ability and impairment, and how it becomes connected to particular lives.

GOD AND THE RISK OF CREATION

Our lives as creatures, as part of God's creation, are full of contingency. Things are as they are, but often we can see that they might have been otherwise. We are as likely to be surprised by joy and wonder as by distress and pain. This seems to be true of the way events unfold and of situations we encounter, such as the existence of a disability. In some ways it is also true of the decisions people make and the way they behave, whether with respect to disability or to anything else. One might choose one action or another, to behave this way or that way. The difference here is that in human decisions and behavior, freedom, agency, and accountability also come into play. This is creation as we encounter it in real life. To speak meaningfully of God's participation in creation must surely be to speak of his participation in this sort of creation. That means grappling with how to conceive of God's relationship with this sort of contingency and the riskiness of the way life is, and how that relationship works out when God addresses his creation and his creatures through the incarnation and, crucially, the atonement of Jesus.

Talk of creation in this way points to Frances Young's brief comment that God in some way withdrew to allow space for creation. That echoes similar comments made by others, but it needs considerably more flesh on its bones to contribute to an account of the atonement that relates the cross to both the contingent and the moral aspects of life, enabling it to be fully inclusive of all humanity with all its variety and disability.[3]

The idea that God withdrew to allow space for creation finds its roots in the Old Testament's emphasis that God, YHWH, is other than the world (over against a pagan pantheism which identifies many things in the world as manifestations of God). However, to infer that such otherness implies a separation of God from the world is not correct and indeed has long proven unhelpful. It has allowed creation, because it is considered to be separate and therefore not sacred, to be devalued and exploited. Instead, God's otherness has to be held in tension with his presence, or immanence within creation. Aspects of the doctrine of the Trinity are helpful in reflecting on how that tension is maintained. The Holy Spirit is involved in bringing creation to being but is also present within creation, maintaining its every moment and every breath of life. This requires that in the act of creation God both creates and enters the world.[4]

That assertion of God's otherness and his act of creation also has to sit alongside the equally important doctrine of *creatio ex nihilo*, creation out of nothing. For creation out of nothing to be taken seriously as a theological concept, and for creation to be other than God, that *nihil*, or nothing, must first be conceived of and allowed some sort of existence. This is where the suggestion arises that God in some way withdrew to allow that existence. While on the face of it this suggestion might itself seem to appear out of nowhere, the notion of God's self-limitation is firmly linked to the Jewish doctrine of the Shekinah of God:[5] that God could (and in his humility would) limit himself such that his presence could be with his people in the tabernacle, in the ark, in the temple, and in exile.[6] Taking up this idea, the infinite God would, in keeping with his character of humility, withdraw into himself to allow the space into which he would act creatively. This withdrawal of God allows the *nihil* out of which *creatio ex nihilo* can take place.[7] This has significant implications. It allows creation to be other than God and therefore allows creation not to be perfect as God is perfect. At the same time, it allows a deep and constant participation of God in the world without falling back into pantheism.[8] At his own initiative, God who is the creator takes on a role of servant, helper, and companion of his own creation.

An important implication of this line of thought is that God's self-withdrawal has created a nothingness that from then on threatens all of creation with a return to that nothingness, and against which God's participation maintains creation. That state of affairs, with creation from the beginning of its existence being at risk from the *nihil* from which it was created, provides meaningful theological space for contingency, accident, unexpected variety, and, in the present case, disability. In that sense the risk from the *nihil* is neither inherently good nor inherently bad. However, that original nothingness has also acquired a more menacing aspect that arises within life in the form of sin as moral choice.[9]

Another helpful way to conceive of creation out of nothing is to focus more directly on God's relationship with perishing and death. Rather than following the pattern of God's willingness to limit his Shekinah glory so as to be present to his people, the emphasis here is on God's willingness to be in relationship with, and accountable for, the perishability (the possibility of death) that is such a present part of life. Rather than God in some way withdrawing, or contracting, to make a space for creation, God chooses to be in relationship to perishability, or nonbeing. In so choosing, God provides the possibility of creation out of that nonbeing, or *nihil*.[10] Both these ways of describing *creatio ex nihilo* illustrate of course the strain that this concept puts on language. Neither is claiming to describe God's act of creation "as it is." They explore it by making metaphorical use of human concepts of space and relationship to say useful things about an act of creation that ultimately has mystery at its heart.

The second approach to creation out of nothing, God's willingness to be in relationship with perishability, also invites the question of whether perishability or death itself might be more complex than it appears at first sight. This possibility might also prove significant when going on to consider disability more directly. Our instinct is to regard both the nothingness that threatens life and the tendency of life to veer toward it as wholly negative. However, perishing itself is perhaps more ambivalent than that, capable of having both positive and negative aspects. On the one hand we can find within it the fitting boundary to what is real. That boundary is not necessarily the end of being as long as it has about it the possibility of becoming. In this case, perishing is a return to the possibility out of which being arose and might arise again. On its own, that suggestion seems rather vague and not particularly satisfying, but when the Christian understanding of the resurrection, of new life out of perishing, is brought to bear, it takes on great significance. The negative aspect of perishing, on the other hand, is that which removes any possibility of becoming. In that sense, perishing or death is "a negatively virulent emptiness without a place in being, a destructive undertow, a negative ontological whirlpool, a 'nihilating nothing' (*nihil nihilans*)."[11]

Again, it is moral evil, or sin, which has given death this other property of being an enemy, a hostile nonbeing.[12]

Although this dichotomy can sound abstract, it is reflected strongly in our own mixed reactions to death. Death, particularly that of someone close, is in so many ways utterly negative. It seems to rob both the one who has died and us of all sorts of possibilities the future could have held. The sense of loss and waste, especially when a death is untimely and unforeseen, can be almost overwhelming. At the same time, however, particularly when someone dies who in biblical language is "old and full of years," death has about it an aspect of being the proper boundary of life. In a broader sense also, the fact that life is limited by death gives meaning and significance to what is done during life, since what is done in life makes use of a limited resource. While these are only the briefest of comments on a complex and sensitive subject, they resonate with the idea that perishing can have both negative and positive elements that can, at least in principle, be separated out, and that God's addressing of those elements through the atonement should also be differentiated in some way.

Drawing these thoughts together provides a platform from which to say something about the manner of God's participation in creation with all of its contingency and risk. There are two essential elements to God's participation. Through *creatio ex nihilo* God is responsible for the involvement of nothingness and perishability in creation, and for the risk and contingency that result from that. At the same time God is willing, in accompanying his creation, for the consequences of that contingency, both moral and otherwise, to befall him. Just as our experience of both the contingent and moral nature of life is such that things befall us which might not have done, so by analogy God is willing to be subject to things befalling him. The emphasis on both positive and negative in this is again important. Not only suffering but joy might befall God, as it might befall us.[13] Not only sin but faithfulness might be encountered. In some limited sense God might be said to be willing for such things to be a "surprise" to him. They are a possibility, but not a necessity, of creation.

The suggestion of things befalling God has typically arisen in the past around the question of the impassibility of God, whether God can suffer. There is no intention here to equate disability with suffering. Rather the point is whether things can befall God and yet he remain eternal, unchanged by them. It is probably true that our responses here are influenced by the worldview of our times. In the past the idea of God as impassible seemed plausible and indeed could lead to illuminating discussion of the nature of divinity. In the present, with a prevailing view of the world as a network of relationships, it seems more consistent to speak of a relational God who would suffer in a way that is somehow analogous to the way in which suffering befalls us.[14] While that is both relational and pastorally useful, the question of how God remains unchanged by such suffering is still there. Conversely, if somehow God has remained untouched, or at least unchanged, how can he be said really to have participated?

Perhaps the most helpful formula for holding these challenges in creative tension is to say that while God does not desire suffering, he is willing for it to befall him, but is not overwhelmed by it. That is because although suffering is alien to him, God has chosen to make that alien thing intimately his own, giving it purpose and meaning. His willingness to do so reveals part of his eternal character. The idea that something is alien but that God chooses to make it intimately his own has roots in the meaning of God's love through the Old Testament and into the New. That love seems often to be expressed in terms of suffering, particularly the suffering of anguish over the behavior of the one loved (Israel), which befalls God and which he makes intimately his own, particularly as he forbears to punish fully and works to restore. It is seen again to the extent that the suffering servant in Isaiah, picked up by the New Testament in its reflections on Jesus, is also taken to reveal the character of God. We might say that as God accompanies creation, and human beings in particular, he suffers with them in empathy, he suffers because of their rejection of him and their spoiling of his creation, and he ultimately suffers for them in the death of Jesus on the cross.

Participation, Suffering, and Eternity

There is certainly an uncomfortable tension to be faced up to here. While acknowledging the pastoral strength of an analogy with human suffering, talk of God's suffering should not suggest that it is entirely the same as ours. Since God is eternal, it must be that God is not changed by suffering in the way that we are. This is not because God is in any way indifferent to it, indeed quite the opposite. As creator, sustainer, and redeemer he is more intimately and eternally involved in the joy and pain of his creation than we ever can be. There is nothing about it of which he is unaware. Therefore, while we rightly assert that in Jesus, who is fully human and fully God, God suffers, we have to hold that in tension with the fact that it is neither necessary nor correct to say that God suffers, in God's self, and is affected by that suffering, in a way that is just like human suffering.

A positive way to sustain this tension is through a stronger doctrine of incarnation. If Jesus of Nazareth is truly divine, then what we see revealed in Jesus is a glimpse of what is eternally true of God. We also assert that the flesh of Jesus of Nazareth truly represents, and somehow incorporates, all flesh. In that case, in knowing that it really is God who is fully, intimately involved and participating in the suffering of the man Jesus on the cross, we know that God is eternally and intimately involved in all such suffering. A fuller doctrine of the incarnation draws God's participation more, not less, deeply into the human experience of suffering.[15] It also suggests that atonement-as-participation expresses something that is an eternal feature of God's relationship with all of creation and humanity, and not merely an alternative descriptive theoretical model of what happened on the cross.

Disability, Contingency, and Risk

Having said all that, another important distinction is also pressing for attention here. Talk of the "risk" of creation is itself at risk of the ever-present trap of smuggling in a normate presumption that disability is essentially a negative thing. When the word "risk" is used, it generally carries a sense that all is well, but there is a possibility, a risk, of things going badly, which would result in suffering or cost. Hence the concept of the assessment of risk that underpins the insurance industry.[16] *Creatio ex nihilo*, as it has been described here, contains possibilities. There is the possibility for humanity which has freedom and agency to act well, in line with God's desire for flourishing, or to act otherwise, as explored in Genesis 3 and throughout Scripture. This can be called the moral contingency inherent in creation, but it is not a neutral thing, as it involves sin and all the complications of decision and habit. It seems reasonable, however, to speak of the risk inherent in God's allowing humanity freedom of will, since it is the risk that they will turn away from God's good will and choose a path that leads to suffering and cost. On the other hand, there is the possibility of variety throughout creation and in humanity, some aspects of which we call disability. This is a much broader sense of contingency, where to speak of risk seems to presume that any such variety outside of what is regarded as statistically typical is negative. The testimony of people with nontypical bodies and brains and of those close to them makes it abundantly clear that that presumption is profoundly misconceived. Life with a nontypical embodiment may well have its own complications, many but not all of which come about because of a society that is unwilling to adjust. It is also a source of joys and insights as particular to that life as to any other. A willingness to recognize this distinction between moral contingency and broader contingency in God's project of creation is essential to a fruitful discussion of disability and the cross.

Having considered what it means to talk of the contingency, or risk of creation, both moral and otherwise, and God's involvement or participation in the existence and consequences of that contingency, the next step is to shift the focus of attention to Jesus. When that happens, the question becomes how all of this is expressed in the flesh of the incarnation and reaches its deepest, most intimate point in the atonement of Jesus on the cross.

THE ATONEMENT AS GOD'S DEEPEST, ONCE-FOR-ALL PARTICIPATION

The Word Participates in Flesh and Death

God's participation in the contingency and risk of creation finds its fullest, most profound expression and affirmation in the incarnation and atonement of Jesus. God's character of humility and grace, his willingness to be in relationship with nothingness and perishability, and his willingness that the consequences of how creation is might befall him all come to a head as the drama passes through the crucial point of the person of Jesus and his death on the cross.

Expressed in terms of God's withdrawal to allow space for finite creation, that withdrawal is a first act of the grace or humility by which God self-defines his character. Consistent with the idea of the Shekinah of God, his willingness in humility to limit himself, this grace is demonstrated in his presence with his people, Israel, and fulfilled in the incarnation and in God's self-surrender on the cross. The importance of the incarnation here is that God not only takes death into himself, he also participates unreservedly in the realities of human life. Like all human life, that of Jesus stands under the burden and experience of the law, death, sin, and guilt all around him.[17] Then on the cross, and perhaps seen most vividly at the moment of Jesus' cry of abandonment,[18] God in Christ enters into the *nihil* that has threatened creation and fills it with his own presence and life. This paves the way for the eschatological new creation whereby the hold that the *nihil* has had over creation is destroyed.

Talk of withdrawal and humility in this way is not intended to go down the path of treating the self-humiliation of the incarnation and atonement as a christological kenosis (Jesus Christ emptying himself temporarily of aspects of his divinity in order to be born and live as a man). Rather, it is the fullest revelation of God's eternal character. In the language of having to do with perishing, God became incarnate in a body that was subject to the realities of perishing and ultimately subject to death on the cross. Through this God became intimately involved in perishing in the living, then dead, Jesus and in the struggle with nothingness that issued in the resurrection. Here, through being willing to be in relationship with perishing, God took the *nihil* into his eternal being and gave it a place. The positive and negative possibilities of that nothingness are each given a place. That which is negative, the annihilating power of death, which has arisen from sin and a turning away from God, is borne by God and dealt with without his being annihilated by it.[19] That which is positive, a proper and fitting boundary to life which has the possibility of becoming, becomes the resurrection.

The idea of befalling again helps to draw these thoughts together. The incarnation does not befall God, since it is his initiative, but the taking on of real human flesh and living real human life is a demonstration of God's willingness for the consequences of evil and contingency to befall him. On the cross moral evil, not a necessity of creation but seemingly an inevitable risk within it, befalls him at the hands of humanity. Here God takes death, which is alien to him, and makes it most intimately his own. Importantly, all of that is not somehow left behind at the resurrection. As indicated by the wounds of the cross in Jesus' resurrected body, the risen and ascended Jesus remains the crucified Jesus.[20] Therefore in God's revealing himself eternally as one who can overcome the *nihil* and nonbeing, his suffering what befalls him is, and remains, central.

An important, consistent understanding of creation, incarnation, and atonement is emerging. This is that the threat, risk, or contingency that accompanied *creatio ex nihilo* and in which God was intimately involved as creator, is entered into by God in Christ through the particularity of the incarnation and in the most intimate way at the atonement on the cross. That atonement represents a dealing with the *nihil*, or perishing, that has a finality and completeness and fittingness about it. On the cross, God's participation in the contingency and risk of creation reached its most profound point. The "hermeneutical key" that was intended to keep this whole discussion on track is again useful here: through the particularity of the suffering and death of Jesus, this universal ontological change, which is effective for all time, is brought about. Following that event, things are not as they were. To borrow the expression from Hebrews 7, 9, and 10, God's atonement-as-participation was "once for all."

The Manner of God's Participation

Revisiting the event of the cross and the atonement in this way and understanding it as the deepest, once-for-all participation of God in the contingency and risk of his creation and their consequences opens up a space in which the atonement addresses the complexities of real life. The contingency and risk in which God participates, and the threat of nothingness over creation that lies behind them, certainly involve the risk and consequences of poor moral choice. This is sin, which seems to crouch at the door of every aspect of life and for which there is human culpability and accountability. But that threat of nothingness over creation clearly also emerges in the more complex web of contingency in creation that is not moral sin but is often very difficult to unpick from it. That contingency gives rise to accident and variety and out of it arises much suffering and joy, which makes it of particular interest in the context of disability. This complexity needs to be explored more thoroughly and that takes place in the following discussion of alienation, disability, and the language of sin.

Before launching into that however, it is useful to take a moment to draw out and summarize the main elements of what can be said so far about the manner in which God appears to participate in the contingency and risk of creation and in the human predicament. God as creator is responsible for the part that nothingness, perishability, and contingency play in creation. As he accompanies creation, God is open to the risk of things befalling him, including joy, suffering, and evil. God is willing to take that which is alien to him and make it intimately his own. Through the incarnation, God in Jesus Christ is open to the consequences of nothingness, perishability, contingency, and indeed moral sin befalling him. At the atonement all of these find their most profound expression, once for all. Not only do these things fully befall God in Christ, all of this that is alien to God he takes and makes intimately his own. By his presence on the cross God also demonstrates that he is accountable for the way that creation is. The atonement seen in this way, though it is once for all, is a revelation of a participation that is eternally true of God.

This way of understanding God's participation arises from acknowledging that to treat all of the contingency and risk of creation in moral terms is too simplistic. It recognizes that while moral sin and accountability should never be played down, much of the contingent nature of life, with its joys and sorrows, is difficult to place in a binary sin/not-sin analysis. The willingness to see the risk of creation as both moral and contingent allows for a fuller, inclusive doctrine of atonement at the cross and opens the way to speak more confidently of sin, disability, and the cross together.

ALIENATION, DISABILITY, AND THE LANGUAGE OF SIN

One of the hard questions that set this whole venture in motion concerned the difficulty of including sin, disability, and the cross in the same conversation. It ran along the following lines: if the gospel has the cross at its center, where God was in Christ, reconciling the world to himself (2 Cor 5:19), and if the cross is all about dealing with sin, which is at its heart moral failure, then it begs the question of what place there is for saying that at the cross God addresses the issues, the challenges, and the suffering surrounding disability.

That way of talking about the cross seems to insist that, to be addressed there, disability and all about it also has to be, at its heart, a matter of moral sin.

This sense of a "sin model" of disability, that admittedly seems to be present quite often in the biblical text, has been an awkward, unresolved sticking point for developing a theology of disability, particularly when questions of healing or transformation have arisen. It seems to require that if the difficulties and suffering, of whatever sort, that disability can cause are to be dealt with by God through the cross and the atonement he wrought there, then disability has to be part of the fall in Genesis chapter 3, to which the cross is God's once-for-all response. There might be attempts to nuance this by saying that in some way disability is a result of the wider effects of the fall and is not really a moral issue in the same way as ongoing human moral failings, such as murder and dishonesty. But that seems unconvincing. As generally understood, the fall is essentially a moral matter, all of its various and persistent effects flowing in one way or another from the primal capitulation of Adam and Eve to temptation and their disobedience to God. Indeed, the experience of those living with disabilities and chronic illness, whether Christian or not, is often one of stigma. There is a sense of being judged by others on the basis that there is something "wrong" or "fallen" about their condition, which has echoes of the fall and sin about it, regardless of whether it is consciously conceived or expressed in specifically religious terms.

Atonement-as-participation, however, is beginning to make this picture look more hopeful. The insights from current disability theology have highlighted our tendency to make normate assumptions about what the human body and mind "ought" to be like and what we "ought" to expect God to do in situations that differ from what we might at any time judge to be the range of typical human morphology. That awareness has led to the exploration above of God's role as Creator (of humanity along with everything else) that takes seriously the variety of humanity that we actually experience in the world around us. As God participates intimately in all of the moral and contingent risk of *creatio ex nihilo* and of sustaining and accompanying his creation, the incarnation, and especially the atonement, are found to be best seen as God's deepest, once-for-all participation in, and addressing of, all of that risk and contingency and their consequences. This is a fuller concept of the atonement.

An important aspect of this fuller concept of the atonement is that it requires a willingness to move away from a view that what we identify as disability can only be understood as a result of the fall, of the primal moral failure of humanity. While moral sin remains moral sin, for which we are accountable and which is dealt with at the cross, a willingness is required to see disability, and indeed all the great variety of humanity, as part of the contingent nature, or riskiness, of creation. But this is what opens up the possibility of talking of sin, disability, and the cross together and asking what the cross, standing at the center of the gospel, has to say about the whole phenomenon and experience of disability. Much of our response to those with disabilities has been, frankly, sinful, but approaching the existence of disability in the first place within this idea of the contingent nature of God's creation opens the way for a far more constructive response, founded on the cornerstone of Jesus and the cross.

Completing that picture and filling in that discussion also involves asking very directly what it is that atonement-as-participation understands God to be addressing and dealing with on the cross, what target God has in his sights there, and what language best captures that.

Atonement and Explanation Relativity

A number of the ideas that have arisen so far can contribute to this question of what it is that the atonement addresses. An important factor in making good use of them is recognizing that what counts as a legitimate answer to the question (indeed, to any question) is influenced by the frame of reference of the person looking for that answer. The prevailing models of sacrifice, justice, and victory so far examined have tended to date to express the target of the atonement clearly in terms of sin. However, a disability perspective has indicated that there is much in the experience of life that is significant, negative, and causes suffering, and yet which seems to fall outside of a concept of sin which is presented just in terms of moral evil. Actual life presents a complex mixture of contingency and moral sin which is often difficult to disentangle, what Frances Young called a wide gone-wrongness in the world. The end of the last chapter expressed this as giving rise to the "diversity of hopes," whereby it is mistaken to presume what sort of transformation someone with what we would perceive as an impairment "ought" to look to God to achieve through the atonement.[21]

The way the prevailing atonement models have commonly been expressed and this challenge to them from a disability perspective are examples of what can be called "explanation relativity."[22] This is the idea that what counts as a valid explanation is heavily influenced by our frame of reference. It also recognizes that such an explanation often presupposes other explanations that lie behind it. Applying this idea of explanation relativity here is illuminating. If our frame of reference does not particularly encompass disability and begins with concerns about ethics, the fall, and moral sin, then the prevailing models, expressed mainly in sin terms, function very well as explanations of the atonement. They provide various ways of exploring how God deals effectively with moral sin and the impact of that on humanity. They also, crucially, presuppose that any other matters that might be brought into the picture (aspects of wider gone-wrongness in creation, say) are also in some way the results of moral sin. The result is that anything that in our own judgment is considered to be "wrong" in the world is all put under that sin umbrella.

If, alternatively, our frame of reference is more firmly rooted in a social model of disability, as much of disability theology is, then what counts as an explanation of the atonement is rather different. It is one that emphasizes the transformation of the social structures and attitudinal issues that generate much of the experience of disability. The seeming irrelevance, or at least inappropriateness, of speaking of moral sin in situations of profound impairment, particularly intellectual impairment, precludes much of such language from the explanation and certainly distances it from any link between disability, the fall, and moral sin. However, the account of the atonement being developed here, starting with God's participation in the contingency and risk of creation, provides the possibility of an explanation that bridges these two frames of reference and anticipates that in the atonement God addresses and deals effectively with all of this complex mixture of contingency and sin, allowing creative, constructive responses to the above hard question to be proposed.

Alienation as the Target of the Atonement

This idea of explanation relativity also sheds some light on the comparison of the prevailing models of sacrifice, justice, and victory. The frame of reference of each model results in a sort of "pairing up" of the model with the target or targets it assumes God to have in his sights through the atonement. Under the sacrifice model, the atonement provides a ritual cleansing from the pollution of sin or reestablishes a relationship broken by sin. Under the justice model the guilt, or the debt of guilt, arising through sin is removed or satisfied by the atonement, and a covenant is restored. Under the victory model, the powers that oppress humanity (sin, the law, death, and Satan) are vanquished in the atonement and the oppressed are set free. In each case, the language used for the target of the atonement is related to the model as a whole and is part of what that model contributes to our overall perception of what God achieves through the atonement. Each is a valuable part of the picture.

That pairing up prompts a similar, productive question to be asked about atonement-as-participation, even though it is proposed as a guiding "protocol," not as a separate theoretical model alongside those others. If the atonement is God's once-for-all participation in the risk of creation and the human condition, it seems worthwhile to look for language that expresses the nature of the target or objective of that participation.

Perhaps the best expression for the complex mix of moral and contingent risk that atonement-as-participation has in its sights is "alienation." Again, this is a word often used to talk of aspects of the human predicament, and it needs to be carefully fleshed out here. A place to start doing so is with a focus on alienation from God. On the cross, God in Christ participates most deeply in humanity that has lost meaningful communion with God.[23] There, alienation and participation form parts of the process of forgiveness. In human terms, the forgiver and the forgiven are alienated from each other by whatever it is that has taken place between them. Forgiveness could be described as a journey that demands movement from both sides. The forgiver does not stand apart and offer a pardon from a distance but must in some way enter into the world of the forgiven and make an effort to understand why that person did what they did in order to offer a forgiveness which includes the possibility of establishing a new relationship. At a human level, then, the forgiver to some extent participates in the life and world of the forgiven, which is a costly process and one that anticipates a response, or movement, from the forgiven. The divine parallel and pattern of that human process (indeed, the source of it) can be found on the cross, and in particular at the point of Jesus' anguished cry: "My God, my God, why have you forsaken me?" (Matt 27:46; Mark 15:34). At that point Jesus has entered into the world of those in need of forgiveness. He has suffered all the particular sins of those immediately around him (jealousy; love of power, both civic and religious; moral failure), and the full impact of that is that he participates in the experience of humanity, which has lost communion with God, the one whom Jesus calls Father. The deepest point of God's participation is in humanity's alienation from himself.[24]

However, alienation spoken of in this way is still something that primarily results from sin as conscious moral choice. It is the willful misbehavior of human beings that has led to their alienation from God and to the need for a forgiveness that deals with sin and reestablishes that relationship. What this says about sin is correct and must not be minimized or lost sight of, but more is needed. A wider perspective comes from contemplating destructive and alienating human behavior beyond the individual. Examples might be to ask how a group or population can become implicated in an event like the Holocaust or the Rwandan genocide, or how a society finds itself eradicating a class of human beings, children with Down syndrome, from its future population through prenatal testing with hardly a protest against the presumption that such a eugenic initiative is desirable. The whole complex nature of our human relationships is in view here, those with ourselves, with others, and with God, all of which have a brokenness about them that must surely be addressed by God through the atonement.

This deep sense of connectedness seems to lie at the heart of, for example, Saint Augustine's doctrine of original sin and the inheritance that it hands to humanity.[25] It seems true that the very material (our situation, social structures, culture, politics) out of which we construct those connected relationships, and even construct our very personhood, are in some pathological way distorted by a history of sin.[26] There is no need to press Augustine's suggestion that we each inherit biologically a culpability or guilt for the sin of Adam to argue that, by comparison, modern notions of the freedom of the will and of moral choice are superficial. In reality the will is bound and conditioned by a very broad and rather dark inheritance. We are at least from birth socialized into a world distorted by sin so that, while original sin is contingent rather than necessary to being human, it is hard to claim that any person, group, or society is ever "in neutral" before God.[27] There is choice through which we contribute to this inheritance. There is accountability for that choice, but that does not stand in place of our solidarity with the whole of the world as it is.[28]

This challenges what have become core elements of a modern individualistic frame of reference and an individualized interpretation of those relationships. Those are an inalienable individual freedom of will and a natural morality that says "I am responsible only for what I do." These core elements have come to be presumed to exist without the need for any reference to God. Yet such individualism is a denial of the reality around us. Humanity as a whole is culpable for much, including its responses as a society to the contingent nature of creation (for example, the existence of disability). But we struggle to recognize our solidarity in such because we cannot identify it with specific acts of the individual that we judge to be wrong. In fact, pursuing this just a little further, true human existence is ex-centric. Human existence takes place in relationship with the rest of creation, with others and with God. It is the disorientation of those relationships, through a host of influences and choices, generating a deep and complex alienation, that lies at the heart of what the doctrine of original sin was trying to articulate.[29] What this adds to the present discussion is that it helps to broaden the idea of alienation, which is the target of atonement-as-participation. Alienation encompasses moral sin, in terms of the product of the actions of individuals, but also a much deeper, pervasive disorientation of relationships that binds humanity and society as a whole.

This is a helpful broadening and complicating of what is in view, but the focus is still mainly on alienation arising one way or another from individual or corporate moral sinfulness. Bringing a disability perspective to bear adds a further and essential dimension. There is the fairly obvious point that society's (and indeed the church's) response to disability is often ambivalent at best. The inclusion of disability in equal rights legislation is an essential and welcome response to that, but it does not necessarily warm the hearts of those who do not consider themselves disabled and move them in friendship toward their brothers and sisters who have disabilities. That sense of an underlying separation for any group that finds itself "other" than the mainstream of the statistically "typical" population is a form of alienation that is a mixture of circumstances and responses.

Pursuing this further, a more complex aspect of alienation comes to light when I listen to my friends Martin and Diane. I find them both keenly aware of the varied facets of our relationships, not just with others but also with ourselves. Martin has lived with multiple sclerosis for many, many years. As his condition has progressed, he and his wife, Eve, have found they are able to form something of a truce with how his body is at each stage, only then, sooner or later, to feel it has betrayed them again with a further deterioration. While Martin might talk of "*this heavy body that I push around every day*," he also talks with passion of the way that as he travels around on his own by train, that same body opens up conversations and opportunities for others to glow with the satisfaction of offering real, valuable help to him. Diane, caring for her son Paul, who has severe autism, can be almost worn out with concern and a longing for an end to the terrors that Paul's autism can cause him. Yet at the same time she can marvel at the profound joy Paul finds in the intricacies of nature, a joy that seems beyond the grasp of most of us.

Martin's and Diane's situations can seem on the face of it unusual and rather particular, but in reality what they highlight is that in the course of ordinary lives our relationships even with our own bodies and minds, as well as with other people, incorporate contingency, difficulty, and a mixture of joys, griefs, and tensions. This is part of what has led to the insistence within disability theology scholarship that the human body and bodily experience, with all its variety, should be seen as a source, indeed sometimes as a starting point, for theological insight.[30] One of those insights is that we can feel as much alienated from our own selves, or bodies, as from others or from God.

Without the need to resolve all of the tensions that have come to the surface in this brief review, what has emerged here is that "alienation" is effective in gathering together the complex moral and contingent matrix in which creation and humanity find themselves and that atonement-as-participation is addressing. By doing so it helps to identify what type of event the atonement is. Other words might of course have been considered as candidates to do this work as alternatives to "alienation." For example, "exclusion" or "isolation" might be regarded as suitable obverses to "participation." However, they both seem to give questions around a theology of access priority over other theological aspects of disability. "Lack of community" might also serve, but perhaps does not lend itself so well to one's relationship with oneself and experiences that are personal or private to the individual. Frances Young's term "gone-wrongness" might also have been adopted. However, wider conversations have indicated that the "wrongness" element of it seems to bring in its wake a presumption that all experiences of contingency are bad or wrong, which is a presumption rightly resisted by wider disability theology.

The term "alienation" seems better able to capture the broad raft of circumstances addressed by God's participation. These can include the experiences of pain; of diverse bodily and cognitive form or function; of attitudes encountered in society; of a sense of being of a different class or category of person (social constructs of "us and them"); of physical exclusion or lack of access; of our response to our own body, to God, and to others, whether related to disability or not; and of the effects of intentional or unintentional, personal, and corporate moral sin. Alienation understood in this way is what God's action of atonement-as-participation had in its sights that terrible Friday afternoon at Golgotha.

Alienation and the Positive and Negative of Perishability

An uncomfortable relationship still waiting to be resolved here is that involving sin, disability, and the salvation secured through the cross. For that it is helpful to draw on the idea explored above, that perishability is ambivalent, having the possibility of both positive and negative aspects. The significance of this thinking for atonement-as-participation and disability theology lies in suggesting that the same distinction about perishing might be carried over into considerations of contingency, disability, and alienation. If it can be said that there is an aspect of the perishability of mortal life that is positive and has dignity as a boundary to life, yet also an aspect which is alienating, it might be said that there are aspects of the contingency of mortal life (in the present case, of disability) that are positive and have dignity as part of what shapes a particular life, yet also there are aspects which are alienating. The positive aspects are rightly emphasized in the disability theology literature in protest against normate assumptions. The alienating aspects are found in personal sin, in personal experiences of alienation and suffering, and in encounters with an unaccommodating world. The mixture of experiences in Martin's and Diane's accounts above resonates with that suggestion. Approaching disability in this way allows us to say that just as God in Christ took to himself and dealt with effectively what is negative and alienating in death that arises from sin, so God in Christ took to himself and dealt with effectively what is negative and alienating in contingency (and in disability). Conversely, there are aspects of contingency (and disability) that it is entirely legitimate to expect to be preserved through the resurrection.

The value of recognizing positives and negatives as part of alienation and atonement is illustrated very well by John Hull's theological writing and testimony on his experience of becoming blind during his adult life.[31] He says that as the various texts in the Bible are on the whole written from a sighted frame of reference, darkness and blindness can be understood inadvertently to be entirely negative and alienating, particularly given the great themes of light and dark, seeing and blindness that so often emerge in the text. However, Hull's experience of blindness has suggested that this is an oversimplified understanding. For example, in the Genesis 1 account of God as creator, darkness appears first as chaotic and threatening. When God creates light, however, darkness does not disappear. Instead, darkness is given a place, and God is discovered to be Lord over the darkness as well as the light.[32]

Having said that, there are aspects of darkness and of blindness that remain alienating and threaten a return to chaos. For example, rich and poor people who are blind live in the same "natural" world of blindness, which is quite different from the sighted world. But at the same time they often live in strikingly different socially constructed worlds of wealth and poverty. Indeed, many people who are blind or have other disabilities find themselves confined socially to that world of poverty.[33] There is much in the natural world of being blind that Hull would want to keep, it being full of possibilities of becoming. By contrast, the socially constructed world of poverty that seems to attach itself to blindness is most certainly alienating and must be addressed, critiqued, and transformed.

Participation, Alienation, and the Diversity of Hopes

In summary, then, adopting atonement-as-participation, God enters into, takes to himself, and deals effectively with all that is alienating. This includes sin, the moral evil that has broken relationships and alienated us from God and from one another. It includes the deeply ingrained sinfulness of social and political structures into which we are socialized from birth and which shape not only how we act but our very personhood and our perception of what is good and bad. It includes our own often varying and ambivalent reaction to disability. And it includes the experiences of pain, confusion, and exhaustion that seem to cut us off from life as it might be. As well as entering into all that is alienating, God also enters into all that is positive. This is everything in life that is not part of that "nihilating nothing." It includes every action and experience that is full of joy and grace and that retains "the possibility of becoming." God enters into all of this and preserves it through the resurrection.

This interpretation of what is happening at the cross provides a response to what sort of event the atonement is. It opens up the possibility of taking disability and the variety of humanity seriously and exploring how God addresses all of this through the cross without pushing every situation into a binary sin/not-sin analysis. Alienation as the target of that atonement, as that in which God intimately participates and which he deals with at the cross, provides a way of speaking of the breadth of what is addressed there by God that also encompasses sin, disability, healing, and salvation, again without pushing disability and sin together in unhelpfully simplistic or binary ways.

Part of the discipline of developing that proposal (enshrined in our "hermeneutical key" for keeping the discussion on track) has been the intention that, on the one hand, it should be universal, having the whole of humanity in view with all its variety, including what we identify as disability. On the other hand, it is equally important that any such proposal should be particular. It should make sense in the context of individual situations of disability, in the particularity of lives affected, often profoundly, by particular disabilities. Otherwise, there is a risk that the whole thing becomes too general and theoretical to be of practical use in the day-to-day experience of life and Christian ministry.

When that discipline was applied earlier in asking what an inclusive atonement would look like, it gave rise to the challenge of taking seriously a "diversity of hopes" as to what the atonement achieves in relation to particular situations of disability. It also recognized the level of speculation involved in looking forward to what the specifics of the resurrection body and mind might entail. Friends and acquaintances whose voices were listened to in that part of the discussion, together with wider testimony in the disability theology literature, showed up the folly of any presumption by those without such impairments that they can judge what "ought" to result from the atonement in terms of such transformation.

Dealing with alienation, however, atonement-as-participation opens up a way of addressing that diversity of hopes constructively by moving away from a binary sin/not-sin analysis that insists either that everything about disability is bad and to be eliminated, or good and to be preserved. Listening to Martin, confined to his wheelchair by multiple sclerosis and finding ways to live with each stage of deterioration, and listening to Diane, caring for her son Paul who lives with severe autism, that complex mixture is clearly evident. Matters such as identifiable personal moral failure, or discrimination, presumption, and cruelty in response to disability are readily identifiable as targets of the atonement in terms of sin, for which there is accountability and for which forgiveness is needed. But there are other aspects of living with disability where what is alienating in that life experience is more complex and personal and less easily rendered in the language of sin, but where the fact that God in Christ deals effectively with what is alienating and preserves what seems good opens a more constructive space for the interaction of the atonement, hope, and disability.

Pressing that further asks what the atonement might be said to achieve for someone with profound intellectual impairment. Again, atonement-as-participation removes the need to place all aspects of the life of a person with profound intellectual impairment into binary categories of sin or not-sin. It recognizes that there can be aspects of that person's life, both in relationships and in her or his reception by the world, that may be alienating, though the evidence of how that alienation is experienced may be subtle and partial. Nonetheless, it opens a space within which we can speak of our solidarity with that person in our corporate human need for the atonement wrought for us by the grace of God through the cross.

Atonement-as-participation, alienation, and a recognition of a diversity of hopes therefore allow two crucial assertions to exist side by side. One is that the presence of impairment and the lived experience of disability are fully validated as integral to humanity as a whole and as a meaningful part of individual lives, as disability theology rightly demands. The other is that, because of God's work of atonement at the cross, the presence and the experiences of impairment and disability are not the final word.

Participation and Sin

The hermeneutical key has proven itself useful in keeping the universal and the particular in view. But it has another side to it that ought to be tested at this point. The large claim within the key was that at the cross God dealt effectively (and objectively, not just ritualistically) with sin. That key has worked well up to this point in coming to grips with how the prevailing models of the atonement operate and in interpreting current disability theology. It has kept the discussion focused, not allowing the idea of the atonement to become diluted or vague. Here as well it raises the challenge of whether speaking of atonement-as-participation in the way it is being developed is succumbing to a temptation to slide away from the concept of the cross dealing with sin and human moral accountability, in favor of a somewhat value-neutral contingency and risk inherent within creation.

This is a good challenge, but the response to it is robust. Atonement-as-participation does not move away from God's objective of effective dealing with sin. It insists that sin is dealt with at the cross. However, it also insists that to say so is not enough. What is emerging is that there is more to speak of at the cross than just identifiable moral sins, in a world where so much of the suffering in life, so much that God would be expected to deal with effectively, seems to lie outside a description organized just around the fall and sin as identifiable moral choice. Atonement-as-participation, and alienation as a way of articulating what God addresses through it, suggests that the hermeneutical key, while clear and useful up to this point, is itself ultimately too narrow. What is required and is provided here is a broader sense of what it is that is that God addresses through the incarnation of Jesus Christ, and ultimately through the atonement at the cross.

BEING HUMAN: CONNECTING EACH LIFE WITH THE CROSS

Atonement-as-participation has so far focused on what God has done, his objective action through Jesus Christ, the cross, and his presence within that. But just as important is how human beings enter into and experience what God has done, its subjective outworking. The question is how we understand the transformation wrought through the past event of the cross and resurrection to become connected to a life in the present. To phrase the same thing in more Pauline terms, while we know that Christ has died and risen, we know that sin and death have lost their sting, and we know that the Holy Spirit has been poured out, how do we come to respond and to know that we and others are "in Christ"?

The review of the prevailing models of atonement demonstrated the importance of retaining a moral influence understanding as a means of addressing this subjective outworking of the atonement. This was not as a separate model in itself but something that balances and augments the more objective focus of the prevailing models grouped under ideas of sacrifice, justice, and victory. Part of a convincing affirmation of the objective achievement of the atonement, that an actual atonement has taken place, lies in the subjective experience of the transforming work of the Holy Spirit in this life, both personal and institutional. That transformation begins with an encounter with the atonement, which takes place through experience, witness, or at Baptism or the Eucharist, and gradually impacts all areas of life and relationships.

There are a number of elements to how this all works out, including how we come to perceive or apprehend the existence of the atonement event and the benefits it offers in the first place; who is allowed or expected, and on what basis, to have a share in those benefits; and how they might indicate that they are doing so. Classical formulations from Scripture include the encouragement to "repent and believe in the good news" (Mark 1:15), or the assertion that "everyone who calls on the name of the Lord shall be saved" (Rom 10:13). While any such apprehension or response is understood to be quickened by the Holy Spirit, it can easily be assumed to be principally a matter of individual intellectual and emotional understanding, as well as acceptance of and response to knowledge about the atonement.

The most obvious insight from a disability perspective is to challenge that way of interpreting those formulations not as incorrect but as inadequate. A participation in the benefits of the atonement which turns on a requirement to "repent and believe" potentially breaks down in the context of intellectual, or indeed emotional, impairment. Where "repent and believe" requires a sufficient intellectual understanding of the person and work of Christ to be able to articulate those things and an intellectual and emotional commitment to reflect those concepts in future living, we are already placing limitations on who has access to the atonement and on what basis. The conundrum seems greater for people with intellectual disabilities. It might be presumed that those whose impairment is more apparently physical can "know God" and participate in the atonement in an intellectually and emotionally "typical" way. If this describes our frame of reference, we are pushed to find an alternative understanding of what it means for those with intellectual disabilities (and possibly others with complex impairments, or indeed living with dementia) to respond to and participate in the atonement. If not a completely separate alternative, our position at least seems to demand a way of extending "our" main explanation of what it is to participate in the atonement to "their" special case by applying some sort of concession.

However, the contention here is that disability is not a special case as regards the atonement. Humanity, for whom the benefits of the atonement are secured by God in Christ, is humanity as we find it in all its variety, that variety being part of the contingent nature of creation. There is no other, ideal, or typical humanity. What is required is a main account of the atonement and our participation in it that addresses humanity as a whole. The argument above has proposed atonement-as-participation and alienation as a theological basis for such an account. That argument also provides a theological basis for exploring this more subjective, human side of the question.

Atonement-as-participation conceives the atonement as God's once-for-all deepest, most intimate involvement in the actuality of how things are. God's involvement is not theoretical or idealized but, through the incarnation, is in humanity as it is. This is reflected in God's openness to the risk of things befalling him, both good and bad, as discussed above. If the atonement arises through God's intimate participation in the predicament of humanity, with all its variety, then it is consistent, when considering the question of connecting the atonement with present lives, to insist that humanity, in all its variety, is fully able to participate in the atonement's benefits. Carrying through that insistence that all of humanity must be able to participate in what God in Christ has done through the cross requires some resources. Three strands of thinking are helpful here.

Ways of Knowing God

The first is to pick up the earlier brief examination of the connection between "participation" and the study of theories of knowledge. The movement noted there was that of going beyond an analytical, or Cartesian, way of knowing to a phenomenological, or affective, one that recognizes the need to be immersed in or participate in something to gain real knowledge of it. Christian, particularly Protestant, ideas of faith and response have often tended to emphasize words, concepts, reason, and understanding. However, in the face of cognitive disability or mental health challenges, that approach stumbles and proves to be inadequate, unless those with intellectual impairments are simply to be regarded as incapable of engaging with God.[34]

A different, more constructive basis for participation in faith and spiritual life is required. One way to approach that is to affirm that the life of Christian faith and response to God involves the great combined biblical commands to love God and love one another (Matt 22:34-40; Mark 12:28-31; Luke 10:25-28). Those commands do not stand in splendid isolation from one another to be applied separately or alternately. Rather, they are perichoretic. They interweave one another in the sense that each gives life and meaning to the other and is incomplete without its twin. Our relationship with God is bound up in our relationships with one another, such that we cannot fully grasp our relationship with each other without at the same time developing our relationship with God, who is the source of all life. Conversely, we cannot develop and participate in a meaningful relationship with God outside of a growing participation in relationships with each other.

The point that emerges from this is that while intellectual knowledge is useful, other more affective forms of knowledge, forms arising relationally, are as important in recognizing and responding to God's initiative, whether in the grand sense of the atonement or in a daily appreciation of the gift of life. Thus, through relationships with others, those with cognitive disabilities can encounter God and respond in a way that might be termed "conversion."[35] That might be extended to suggest that there are more affective forms of repentance, again reflected in the development of relationships rather than in propositional statements of confession. If responding to the atonement is captured in the phrase "repent and believe," then it should be possible to conceive of that response taking a less analytical and propositional form.

This is an important argument, with practical and ecclesiological as well as soteriological implications. On the one hand, it resists a presumption of demonstrable, articulated intellectual assent as the principal requirement for participating in God's saving act. On the other hand, it challenges our presumptions about which persons act as "gatekeepers" to the atonement in terms of assessing who is a disciple of Jesus Christ, who should be baptized, who should share in the Eucharist, and (particularly in a context of congregational governance) who should be a church member. The suggestion here is that it is those who are closest to people with cognitive impairment that are best placed to make, or at least to help guide, those judgments. Such judgments would be based, again, on affective, relational knowledge of the one in their care, rather than on an analytical assessment of competencies by others who stand outside of that relationship.[36]

God's Accommodation

A second strand of thought that is relevant to this human aspect of how we come to connect with atonement-as-participation arises from the doctrine of God's accommodation. It is not hard to find evidence of a presumption that because the concepts involved in a relationship with God can seem complex, such a relationship is not available to those with intellectual impairments.[37] It is also certainly true that the Bible on the whole has an intellectually able frame of reference that affects how it expresses things, just as it was noted earlier that in its use of light and dark the Bible has a sighted frame of reference. Scripture therefore often makes its points about response to God in terms of seeing, hearing, obeying, following, and seeking wisdom. Lack of awareness of that frame of reference can contribute to this often unexamined presumption that intellectual and language capacities and the learning and articulation of a set of beliefs constitute faith and worship. That presumption can sometimes manifest itself in anecdotes from times where those with intellectual impairments have been present in congregational worship. On occasion, some signs of "joining in" might be noticed by others, or worship might be shaped and conducted in a way that makes such an indication of joining in more likely to appear.

This sort of inclusion of "them" in what "we" are doing does not contain within it any real theological basis for participation. Such a basis can, however, be found in the doctrine of divine accommodation. The doctrine is found widely expressed in Christian and Jewish thought. The likes of John Calvin and Gregory of Nyssa write of God's accommodating to what we can comprehend through his use of language, through the incarnation, and indeed through all of his self-revelation.[38] The point is significant for this present discussion of all of humanity being able to participate in what God has done at the cross. If we believe that God accommodates to the capacity of human beings in general to comprehend him, there is little justification for assuming that his accommodation would not encompass people with intellectual disabilities, or that there might be a point beyond which God is unable or unwilling to accommodate. Accommodation is not just a tool used by God but a demonstration of the extent of his love. Accommodation is not the watering down of what is complex but the choosing of a mode of communication of that which is relevant to all.

The significance of God's accommodation for this discussion is twofold. On the one hand, it is consistent with the comments above on ways of knowing: affective ways of apprehending and responding to God's initiative are no more or less dependent on God's accommodation than intellectual or analytical ways. On the other hand, accommodation is part and parcel of God's participation in his creation, culminating in the atonement. Otherwise, his participation would be something that God does but that remains at best theoretical for us, something that lies beyond the possibility of our real practical engagement with it.

Corporate Participation in the Atonement

The third strand of thought that helps to resource the insistence that all of humanity must be able to apprehend and participate in what God in Christ has done through the cross is the recognition that our apprehension of God is as much a corporate affair as an individual one. The testimony of people reflecting on the experience of Christian life with children who have disabilities perhaps makes the point most eloquently.

For Faith, a mother of three children with disabilities, each of them embodies an insight into God. Her youngest, with autism and scoliosis, is for her a "walking miracle" of God's provision and healing. Her daughter who has Down syndrome brings to her God's welcome and freedom from fear each day. And her eldest, who has suffered significant physical trauma, is the presence of the returned Prodigal Son in the family. It is a corporate, family experience of God's saving work. In a not unrelated way, Frances Young's suggestion was that part of her son Arthur's "vocation" is to reveal to us the corporate nature of the person of Adam and the person of Christ and of what it means to be made in the image of God. Since Arthur's participation in the life of the church can only move beyond the merely theoretical if it involves others, he affirms that the image of God is not inherent to the isolated individual, and that the body of Christ is not a collection of such isolated individuals. It is fundamentally a corporate organism, inclusive of the variety of disability. We are only ever "in Adam" in solidarity with others, as we can only be fully "in Christ" in solidarity with others, not just as individuals.

Atonement-as-participation opens up the theological space to explore these reflections further. God's participation in the contingency and risk of creation and in the predicament of humanity within that, reaching its deepest point in the atonement, is a participation in all of the complex moral and contingent nature of life. Given the strongly systemic, corporate, interrelated picture of life that has emerged during the discussion of alienation here, it would seem inconsistent to suggest that the salvation achieved by God through that participation is atomized to the individual. It clearly has profound meaning and implications for the individual but seems to arise through something much more corporate. This is also something affirmed by the unguardedness of people with profound intellectual impairment. They make no pretense at independence, demonstrating that their (and by extension perhaps all) spiritual life certainly is personal but is better understood as a corporate, rather than individual, experience.[39]

We are all dependent on others for our encounters with God. Our knowledge of God (and in the current discussion our knowledge of the profound significance of the cross) is personal but not individualistic. This is consistent with the assertion that we recognize Jesus in the marginalized, that the body of Christ is always corporate, and that we encounter God especially in Christian friendships and relationships. This is not a bid for universalism but rather a question of how we understand the process through which any person comes to apprehend and respond to God's saving, reconciling, redeeming initiative of the atonement.

It is true that much is said elsewhere about Christian life being a corporate affair, even to the point that it could be said the church is not really or fully the body of Christ unless it has the most vulnerable at its core.[40] And the goal of the atonement is not simply to produce individually saved persons but the creation of a new (corporate) people, the people of the new covenant. However, the point being made here, one that flows both to and from atonement-as-participation, is that we are dependent on each other in our very apprehension of and response to Christ and the cross. If life is essentially interdependent, it would not be surprising that participating in the benefits of the atonement, wherein all of life is addressed by God, is similarly interdependent. Again, this can be related to the discussion above of different ways of knowing and suggests that we deceive ourselves in thinking that we can approach the atonement individually and (only) analytically. Atonement-as-participation affirms what lies behind the testimonies of Faith and Frances Young, that the activity of apprehending and responding to the atonement is for all of us a corporate one, in which each is dependent on the other and on being open to the other's ways of knowing.

CONCLUSION: AN INHERENTLY ACCESSIBLE, INCLUSIVE ATONEMENT

Thinking about the cross with disability in mind and taking seriously humanity as it actually is, with all its variety, requires a rethinking of what happened through Jesus Christ on that cross. The insights of disability theology demand that we revisit what sort of event the atonement is. It is absolutely right to say that at the cross sin was objectively and effectively dealt with. We are culpable for our moral failure, for our identifiable bad actions and inactions, our bad words and silences. At the cross these are dealt with by God, and through the cross forgiveness for them is offered. But to say that is not to say enough. Those things are alienating, they harm people and break relationships. But there is also much in life that is alienating, that harms people and breaks relationships, with God and with each other, that does not so readily fit into a binary sin/not-sin analysis. And yet we also look to God, at the cross, to address those things. After all, it is ultimately because of Jesus and the cross that the word of God in the end declares that "Death will be no more, mourning and crying and pain will be no more" (Rev 21:4).

In response, what is proposed here is that the atonement, through the cross of Jesus Christ, is God's deepest, once-for-all participation in the contingency and risk of creation. There, God takes all that is alienating, makes it his own, and overcomes it; he also takes all that is good and, through the resurrection, preserves it and brings it to fulfillment. The risk of creation that this speaks of is a complex mixture of the risk of moral failure, for which there is culpability, together with the contingent nature of life and our responses to that. This atonement-as-participation is not proposed as an alternative to existing models of the atonement nor as a supplemental model. Instead it is a response to that prior question about what sort of event the atonement is. The way it should be used is therefore as a "theological protocol" to guide the deployment of any such model. In fact, when the prevailing models of sacrifice, justice, and victory are revisited (below) in the light of atonement-as-participation, their great stores of metaphorical resources for talking about the cross prove to be at least as rich as they have been to date, if not more so.

The purpose has been to discover an account of the atonement that is inherently inclusive of people with disabilities, rather than one that seems only able to equate disability with sin or to include people with disabilities by concession, as some sort of theological special case. Atonement-as-participation approaches the cross from that inclusive frame of reference. It sees the cross as the central pivot of the great drama of redemption. God's participation at the cross is consistent with (indeed it is the fulfillment of) his original participation as creator in the risk of *creatio ex nihilo*. The whole phenomenon and experience of alienation from God and from each other is perceived as arising from a complex mixture of moral risk and culpability, as well as the contingent nature of life as humanity actually encounters it, with all of its variety, accident, and, in the present case, what we call disability. The atonement is God's deepest participation in that contingency and risk, and in all that causes our alienation, rendering the atonement inherently inclusive of humanity with all its variety of impairment.

An important part of that picture is that it recognizes that there are those aspects of the contingent nature of life (here, disability) that are alienating and those that are not, and that those without disabilities are not best placed to identify which is which. This opens up the theological space to talk of sin, disability, the cross, atonement, and healing together without imposing a binary choice between regarding disability as all bad and to be eliminated in the age to come, or all good and to be preserved. That broader sense of the atonement as God in Christ taking to himself and dealing with all that is alienating therefore recognizes and provides space for what has been called here the diversity of hopes. The clear acknowledgment of the complex nature of the contingency and risk of creation and of the diversity of the experience of alienation arising from it, avoids the tendency to assume that anticipating the kingdom of God involves anticipating a homogenization of bodies and minds. That also perhaps begins a movement toward paying better attention to the lived experience of actual bodies as a source of theological insight.

Exploring the emphasis on God's intimate participation in his creation and our human predicament has also led to a significant move away from a presumption that we apprehend and respond to the atonement only through intellectual faculties or that we do so only as individuals. In that way, any discussion of participating in the benefits of the atonement naturally encompasses situations of intellectual impairment, as well as benefiting from the light that such situations throw on the vulnerability and interdependence of all human beings.

Understood in this way, the atonement at the cross, where God was in Christ, reconciling the world to himself, is indeed accessible. In fact, it goes further than that. To speak of an accessible atonement might still perhaps suggest that the atonement was primarily, or originally, for the able-bodied. It could risk sounding like God conceived and enacted his response to the predicament of creation and humanity for those with "typical" bodies and minds and then later, finding that people with disabilities also wanted its benefits, modified it in some way to make it accessible and let them in. Atonement-as-participation, however, with alienation as its target, understands that the cross of Christ, that deepest revelation of the eternal character and purposes of God, has been inherently accessible and inclusive of all humanity from the very beginning.

5

The Cross as the Foundation for Disability Theology

AN INCLUSIVE FOUNDATION

If the cross of Christ is the foundation and criticism of all Christian theology,[1] the question here becomes whether atonement-as-participation enables the cross of Christ to take on that foundational and critical role in developing a distinctively Christian theology of disability. The other side of the same question is whether that distinctive Christian theology of disability can argue its case as a whole more confidently and convincingly when undergirded by the central theological foundation of the atonement at the cross.

To date the major themes of disability theology have interacted with the atonement in only a limited and partial way. The particularity of the incarnate, crucified, and resurrected body of Jesus has been found to reveal aspects of God's identification with humanity inclusive of impairment. But there has been little engagement with what that body signifies at the core of Christian theology, the universal claim that sin is dealt with and a cosmic reconciliation with God is brought about. The hesitation in engaging with that claim has not been surprising, given the history of a seemingly awkward relationship between disability, sin, healing, and the cross. However, just as atonement-as-participation has opened up an understanding of the cross that allows these to be disentangled then brought back together more constructively, it also seems to hold out an urgent invitation to explore the possibility that the cross might indeed be the best foundation or cornerstone from which to pursue the objectives of these major disability theology themes.

This is not merely a theoretical or organizational matter, one of locating the atonement in its proper place in the constellation of Christian doctrines in order to keep everything tidy. It is a matter of asking whether disability theology can draw from a deeper well than it has to date as it pursues its various objectives of understanding disability in the light of what we believe about God. It is a matter of asking whether its confidence and boldness can be nourished, deepened, and strengthened by its being rooted in the fundamental Christian soil of the cross, where God addressed the whole of the human condition, dealing with all that alienates and bringing what is good to fulfillment through the resurrection.

A way of responding to this invitation and of exploring this possibility is to reconsider the major themes of disability theology that were reviewed earlier. The main objectives being pursued within each theme can be identified, along with the theological ideas from which their arguments have mainly drawn to date. That should provide the opportunity to ask in each case whether atonement-as-participation does indeed allow the cross, and God's action of atonement there, to play that foundational and critical role in a distinctively Christian disability theology.

PARTICIPATION AND THEOLOGICAL ANTHROPOLOGY

Atonement as a Foundation for Anthropology

The first main theme of disability theology examined earlier was disability-perspective theological anthropology, exploring what it is to be human. The question now is whether atonement-as-participation allows the cross to act as the foundation from which that theme can best pursue its objectives.

The main objective within this theme is to establish convincingly that those with disabilities are of equal worth, in our own eyes as well as in God's, as those whom we regard for the time being as not having disabilities. Possibly the most significant part of that has been examining what it means to talk of all of varied humanity being made in the image of God. That entails seeking a basis for claiming with confidence that there is no sense of the image of God being defined primarily with the typical or ideal human being in mind, and then making theological allowances to extend that image, by concession, to encompass a "special case" of those with disabilities. Arguing that all people are made in the image of God does not include suggesting that the difference, or variety, represented by disability should be treated as irrelevant or simply not mentioned. The point is that our idea of humanity made in the image of God should incorporate and honor that difference as an inherent part of what that image is, rather than straining to accommodate it. Perhaps the late Nancy Eiesland, activist and theologian, captures this most succinctly when she declares, "Our bodies participate in the *imago Dei*, not in spite of our impairments and contingencies, but through them."[2]

The practical version of the same question comes down to how the church treats those with disabilities, whether it treats them as "them" or as "us." An example again is my friend Diane and her son Paul. When a leader in a church asks why it is only her child who cannot sit quietly in worship, or when the preacher speaks of the image of God in terms of a freely intercommunicating Trinity that makes little sense in Paul's world of autism, it raises the question of where he fits into that image and, as a result, what place the church has for him. The challenge and the goal is for the church not just to tolerate or accommodate Paul but to find a full and valid place for him as "us," claiming by its actions as well as its words that he also is indeed made in God's image.[3] This part of disability theology is looking for a sound and convincing theological basis for making that inclusive claim.

When this theme was reviewed earlier, three significant and creative lines of argument for an inclusive idea of the image of God were found to be at work. Briefly, these were (i) that there is evidence, particularly through Jesus, of God's solidarity with those with impairments; (ii) that our worth as human beings depends on God, not on us—it is extrinsic; and (iii) that biblical images of the age to come affirm those with impairments. These are considered in a little more detail below, but it also seems that behind each of these three lines of argument lies a single prior question about God's attitude and actions toward the whole of humanity.

For the claim that all are equally made in God's image to be convincing, it must be possible to assert with confidence that at the moment when God most profoundly reveals his love for his creation and addresses humanity and the whole human condition (at the atonement), God's concern and his action inherently encompass the full variety of humanity and humanity's whole predicament. The purpose in developing atonement-as-participation has been to do precisely that by responding to those concerns that have made disability sit awkwardly within our main account of the atonement and the cross to date. This account of the atonement does not insist that we say that disability is all good and to be preserved, nor that it is all to do with sin and to be eliminated. It does not assume that God's new creation, brought about through the cross and resurrection, must entail a homogenization of bodies and minds to a "typical" pattern in the age to come. And it affirms a much broader sense of how we apprehend and respond to God's initiative, such that no life is assumed to be unable to connect with it. As a result, those with disabilities are already, from the outset, fully "within the camp" of humanity that is addressed by God through the cross.

With that inherently inclusive starting point in mind, it is worthwhile looking again at those three lines of arguments around the image of God identified above to see whether that inherently inclusive account of the atonement does provide each of them with a stronger foundation on which to build.

The Image and God's Solidarity with Humanity

To summarize this approach, the incarnation of the living Word of God in Jesus of Nazareth reveals God's identification with humanity in general through the particularity of Jesus' body and experience, being subject to all the vagaries and risks of life. There is no suggestion that Jesus had any impairment that we would identify as a disability. However, through his passion and at the cross, Jesus was disabled to the point of death. That reveals not only a solidarity with the existence of impairment but with the experiences of exclusion, rejection, and degradation that so often accompany it. This solidarity continues through the cross and into the resurrection, as evidenced by the wounds of the cross carried in his resurrected body.[4] Added to those matters that focus on Jesus' own body is the evidence of his ministry in which he clearly sought out and identified with the marginalized, including the sick and disabled.

Responding to that line of argument, these aspects of Jesus' life, and of the cross and resurrection in particular, do indeed reveal important things about God's solidarity and identification with those who live with disabilities. They are undoubtedly insightful and pastorally useful in saying something about the image of God. But although they draw on aspects of the cross, they do no business with its principal, large claim, the crucial significance of what God does there. The whole drama of redemption passes through and finds its deepest meaning in this central point of the cross. There, a cosmic reconciliation takes place, dealing with all that alienates us from God. Atonement-as-participation asserts that that central point of the drama of reconciliation is in its very nature inclusive, encompassing all of varied humanity. This therefore provides a firm theological foundation from which to assert that whatever any particular aspect of the incarnation, cross, and resurrection does to reveal and restore the image of God in humanity, the whole is inclusive as a matter of course.

An important implication of this is that it frees up each of the points made about revelation, summarized above, from having to do all the work, or from being stretched unreasonably. For example, the progressive disabling of Jesus' body through the stages of his passion, right up to his moment of death on the cross, readily allows a claim of identification and solidarity with visible physical disability. Less apparent is such solidarity with a whole range of other less visible impairments. The same could be said about the physical wounds from the cross in Jesus' resurrected body. They say much about acquired physical impairment, less about congenital conditions or intellectual impairment. But if the true starting point and basis for inclusion is more fundamental, rooted in what God is doing through the atonement, then what Jesus' passion and his resurrected body reveal about solidarity with humanity inclusive of impairment can be celebrated as examples, or instances, of that deeper, underlying inclusion.

The Image of God as Extrinsic to Us

The second line of argument explored the idea that the worth of the human being, expressed in being made in God's image, must be extrinsic to the person. There is a convincing logic to this proposition, that if the worth of a human being found its origins in any intrinsic human attribute or function, then inevitably some people with disabilities would fail to qualify. This is addressed by saying that undifferentiated worth, and therefore undifferentiated inclusion in the image of God, is based instead on God's gifts. These have an inherent element, located in the gift of life itself, and an element located in God's gift of friendship, the telos of which, drawing on Roman Catholic terminology, is full communion with God.[5] Completing the picture, the gift of God's friendship is said to lead to freedom, and that freedom is secured through God's judgment, made public through the death and resurrection of Jesus.[6]

The idea of God's friendship toward humanity is powerful and again of great pastoral value. However, it would seem it could argue its case more convincingly, particularly for its twin inherent and teleological elements, by beginning with the atonement. In Christian theology the atonement is the only basis for the telos of full communion with God, or stating the same thing in other language, for inclusion in the new creation. As the writer to the Hebrews might put it, it is the blood of Christ that has washed away the pollution that spoiled our relationship with God. That blood has established that relationship and friendship in a new covenant. Atonement-as-participation understands our main account of this as fully, inherently inclusive of all humanity. As to the gift of life itself, atonement-as-participation emphasizes the intimacy of that gift. It is not given by a God who is in any way remote from the recipient. He participates intimately in all of the contingency, risk, and implications of that gift, the living out of which can prove to be a source of both joy and alienation for us. Ultimately, at the cross God takes full responsibility for the way this gift of life is.

Approached in this way the argument operates slightly differently but perhaps more robustly. Atonement-as-participation provides an inherently inclusive theological foundation for each of the two elements of God's friendship. When it is argued that the worth of the human being is extrinsic to us, based in God's friendship, the elements comprising that friendship are already known to be inherently inclusive. Therefore, the inclusiveness of the image of God and the worth of the human being becomes an outworking of our main account of the cross as God's inclusive drama of redemption. This seems a stronger ordering of the argument than proposing God's friendship as the initial main idea, with the cross acting as an illustration of it.

This discussion is not unlike the rather different flavor given to the *imago Dei* by the church fathers. The approach of much disability theology, for understandable reasons, is to seek to find the image of God reflected inherently, equally, and essentially passively in each individual, requiring no particular attributes, achievements, or response from the individual to establish it. However, the Fathers regarded the full image of God as something that is inherent only to Jesus Christ but something in which we might participate.[7] Following Irenaeus' concept of recapitulation, Jesus as the new Adam goes over all of the ground on which the first Adam, and humanity following him, has failed. Jesus, however, as the perfect, faithful human believer and worshipper, succeeds and gives all things past, present, and future new meaning.[8] The point of this here is that the foundation for participating in what Jesus has in this way secured, and therefore in the true image of God, is the atonement, which was Jesus' crucial step in the work of recapitulation. That atonement is equally foundational for the place of disability in the image of God as long as disability and its challenges are part of our main account of what God addresses at the atonement, which is how atonement-as-participation understands it.

The Image of God and Eschatology

The third line of argument for the inclusion of people with disabilities in the image of God arose from discussion of eschatological texts in Scripture. Assuming that those included in such eschatological pictures reflect more fully the image of God that humanity currently reflects in part, what those texts say about disability and inclusion ought to be helpful.

The parable of the great dinner in Luke 14:15-24 was given as an example. It is a parable about inclusion, which Jesus told in response to someone who declared what a blessing it would be to be included in the feast (or to eat bread) in the kingdom of God. The argument is that the parable demonstrates that those with disabilities are invited to participate in the kingdom of God just as they are.[9] Exegetical questions raise their heads over reading that argument from the text, in addition to the comments made earlier. One is whether that picture of a great feast painted rhetorically by Jesus through the parable presents a description of the age to come which, though clearly figurative, nonetheless makes this claim that people of diverse embodiment would remain as they are in that coming age. It is possible that their surprising inclusion in the parable was principally intended to make a sharp point about the assumptions that Jesus' listeners in positions of wealth and power in this age might make about who will be present and honored in the next, rather than a point about their physical (or mental) state there.[10]

That said, the thrust of the line of argument making use of this and other texts is that there is material in Scripture that supports a robust resistance to normate presumptions that the anthropology of the age to come will entail the homogenization of bodies to conform to a "typical" pattern. Far from being an academic hermeneutical point, the intention is that such inclusion of those with disabilities in the kingdom of God should act as a basis for transforming normate assumptions about their part in humanity, church, and society in the present: they have a fully valid place in each, just as they are.

However, in response it might be said that such an argument seems to press us into a binary choice between two opposing theological views. Just as one might follow that argument and resist the idea of homogenization, one might object to such a reading since that there may well be aspects of the lived experience of "the poor, the crippled, the blind, and the lame" (Luke 14:21) which they would rather were not preserved, just as they are, in the kingdom of God. While those aspects are likely to include the social elements of shame and poor responses to difference, they might well include a more complex interplay of social, physical, cognitive, and emotional elements of their lives that have led to an experience of alienation from God and others.

The suggestion here is that atonement-as-participation provides a more confident underlying theological basis from which to argue the eschatological case. The atonement, after all, is the event that inaugurates the age to come. Participation in the vibrant picture of the eschatological celebration dinner must be on the basis of whatever transformation has been secured through the cross and resurrection, and on the basis of freedom from whatever it is that God in Christ has thereby overcome. Any reflections beyond this on what such inclusion might entail (with the caution that such are inevitably speculative) must be consistent with it. Atonement-as-participation opens up the theological space for an atonement that is less polarized in its assumed outworking. It does not demand that everything about the life experience of disability be excluded wholesale in the new creation, as in some way related to sin. It also does not demand that it all be retained, stifling the protest that some aspects of that experience are indeed alienating. Instead it anticipates a new creation in which what is alienating has been dealt with and in which a diversity of hopes is fulfilled.

PARTICIPATION AND A THEOLOGY OF ACCESS

Atonement as a Foundation for Access

The overall objective of a theology of access is to address and then remove a whole range of barriers to the full inclusion and participation of those with disabilities in ecclesial life and worship in particular, as well as in society more generally. There are strong links here to the disability rights movement, lending this part of the field its significant advocacy element. Indeed, the arguments and the strength of testimony in this area can at times give the impression that disability theology equals a theology of access. What is hopefully being demonstrated here is that the field of disability theology comprises a number of important themes of which access is one, and that behind all of them are questions about God's relationship with creation and humanity that reach their critical point at the cross. This is not to downplay the scale of the challenges that a theology of access addresses. Without meaningful access to worship and ecclesial life, engagement in other areas of disability theology is unlikely even to begin.

The complexity of the challenge of access is also intensified by the fact that, like disability itself, exclusion from participation often involves more than one factor. A number of aspects of one's identity and circumstances that can lead to marginalization can be involved at once, including impairment, race, sexual orientation, employment/unemployment, gender, and educational background. In other words, inclusion in terms of enabling physical access to ecclesial life (and of that access being utilized, resulting in actual physical presence and engagement) may involve addressing interlocking issues that extend well beyond replacing the steps up to the church sanctuary with a ramp.

As with theological anthropology above, the earlier review of the field found a number of arguments that are generally put forward as bases for a theology of access and for supporting the case for inclusion. In summary these were (i) the fact that Jesus is God's gift to all of humanity, and therefore all should have access to worship him; (ii) the distinctive emphasis within Jesus' ministry on being present to those whom society seemed to regard as outsiders; (iii) an emphasis on the Holy Spirit, both as the person of the Trinity who has historically appeared rather marginalized and as the one who acts as our advocate and forms the church as a hospitable community; (iv) a call for the body of Christ to have the most vulnerable at its core; and (v) a spirituality that emphasizes friendship and recognizes a common human vulnerability.

Each of these lines of argument certainly contributes to building up a rich picture of access and participation. Each has its own emphasis and resonance, providing a particular insight relevant to situations that might be encountered in worship, Christian fellowship, or mission. However, behind each of them also seems to lie a more basic assertion, or possibly a presumption, about God's relationship with humanity. Any theological claim to physical, social, or ecclesial access and inclusion surely presumes an underlying claim to what might be called spiritual access to God: the claim that no one is excluded from the possibility of approaching God or from inclusion in the body of Christ. The various lines of argument above are examples of this presumption in action. But both aspects of the presumption are ultimately constituted by the atonement. Our access to approach God the Father in its fullest, most intimate form arises through the Son, whose death on the cross precipitated the tearing of the curtain in the temple, symbolically opening the way for all into the Holy of Holies, the place of God (Matt 22:50, Mark 15:38, and Luke 23:45). Our inclusion in the body of Christ arises from participating in the death and resurrection of Jesus, symbolically through baptism, and revisited and reinforced at every celebration of the Eucharist.[11]

If the atonement is indeed to be the foundation of that basic presumption of access to God, then it is essential to a theology of access that there is no question of disability (of whatever sort) being considered a special case, somehow outside of our main account of that atonement or included only by a special extension of that account. Adopting atonement-as-participation as a guiding protocol for the sort of event the atonement is addresses this directly. The emphasis on the atonement being God's deepest participation in the risk of creation recognizes the contingent nature of life. It recognizes the legitimate place of what we call disability in the variety of the human flesh that Jesus assumed in the incarnation and represented on the cross. Atonement-as-participation identifies all that is alienating (those aspects of life for which there is clear moral culpability as well as those that are harder so to categorize) as what is addressed by God through the atonement. That allows both sin and disability (the existence and the experience of it) each to have its own full place at the table in any discussion of atonement and the cross without an unnecessary or awkward conflation of the two. What is more, this approach to the atonement based on God's participation in the contingency and risk of creation and in the situation of humanity as it is, in all its variety, provides a basis for speaking of how we apprehend and respond to God which is inclusive, particularly of those with profound intellectual impairment.

This inherent inclusivity of God's self-defining action through the cross therefore provides the theological foundation for asserting inclusive access to God. The positive, constructive elements of a theology of access listed above are an outworking of that underlying assertion. They can be taken briefly in turn, looking at each from the perspective of this inherently inclusive atonement-as-participation. Taking the first one noted, at the cross, God in Christ does not withhold himself but participates fully in the risk of creation and the predicament of humanity, including suffering the effects of sin, echoed in Jesus' cry of forsakenness. This is God's wholly inclusive gift of himself to all humanity, indeed to all creation, opening the way to the Holy of Holies for all who will come. This affirms that the gift of Jesus from his birth was for all and that all have access to him in worship.

Turning to Jesus' ministry, whether in prayer, compassion, healing, or in calling those around him to account, that ministry is a foretaste of the kingdom of God. The wholly inclusive atonement, through which the way was made for that kingdom ultimately to be brought in full, affirms each of Jesus' acts in his ministry as an instance of that inclusiveness.

Emphases on the work of the Holy Spirit in forming the church and on the church as the body of Christ are both significant building blocks of a robust theology of access. The radical inclusiveness of Pentecost in Acts 2:1-12, when the Holy Spirit spoke through the disciples to everyone present, and the inclusiveness of the body of Christ in, for example, 1 Corinthians 12, are key resources. Each of these phenomena is inaugurated by the inherently inclusive atonement, followed by the resurrection and ascension of Jesus. They are again an outworking of the radical inclusiveness of the cross.

The development of a spirituality within the church based on friendship and a common vulnerability is also significant. Our friendship to one another is a reflection of God's friendship toward us, as individuals and as a community. The idea that those with disabilities reveal to us the common human situation of vulnerability and interdependence has also already been discussed. The point here is that God, the judge of all the world, is the one to whom we are all ultimately vulnerable. It is at the cross, where God participates in our predicament, that his response of friendship to that complete vulnerability is demonstrated and is fully inclusive. The inclusiveness of God's response to us is the foundation for a spirituality of inclusive access to participate in the life and worship of the church.

Having explored this underlying point about an inclusive spiritual access to God, through the atonement, being the foundation for building a theology of access, it is also useful to consider other particular discussions, or movements, that have been underway in the area of the theology of access and to consider whether atonement-as-participation also offers insight at those levels. Two examples are the consideration of rights and of presence.

Access and Rights

A legitimate question encountered in relation to a theology of access is whether its objective is essentially to provide a theological justification for the disability rights movement. It might be expected that a theology of access would start by seeking an articulation of the rights of individuals both to be present and to participate.[12] On the whole, disability theology literature tends not to make extensive use of the language of rights, although the liberation or advocacy aspects of the field are often close to it and might be read in that way.

However, an approach that begins with the idea of rights soon runs into difficulties. One difficulty is similar to that encountered when an argument for humans being made in the image of God turned on any reason or ability of the individual. Such an argument fails because by such a measure some, particularly those with intellectual impairment, will not meet those criteria. Here, similarly, a rights approach is usually based primarily on ideas of self-representation, what is often called a "minority group model."[13] Because those with profound intellectual impairment are unable to engage in self-representation and in the exercise, or indeed the comprehension, of rights, that approach struggles to be truly inclusive.

A second difficulty is that while the idea of self-representation and the exercise of rights is, for good reason, inspiring for many with disabilities, that assertion of rights seems to offer little that will transform the attitudes of the currently able and that might soften hearts and move them toward those with disabilities.[14] A danger of the language of rights and inclusion is that, while it makes its point against exclusion, it seems to perpetuate a sense of "us and them" and an assumption that someone has been excluded that never really moves beyond a sort of tolerance, or at best a restricted or distant hospitality.[15] What is needed is a change in attitude that results in those with or without disabilities seeing "them" as genuinely, inherently, "us." The securing of rights may follow, but it seems that what is required before that is a sense of shared need, of compassion and solidarity, one that also values the alterity of disability as a crucial part of humanity.

Atonement-as-participation contributes here by starting in a different place. It begins with solidarity, that we are all "us." What joins us as human beings before God is found in the common experience of alienation from God and each other, in all of its moral and contingent complexity. The need for that alienation to be addressed by God is both individual and corporate. The place where God addresses and deals with it once for all is the cross. To lay claim to the atonement achieved there by God in Christ is to lay claim to something that is as inherently inclusive as the alienation it deals with. It is to lay claim to something that requires me to admit that I need others to help me to apprehend it, that entails recognizing solidarity in alienation and recognizing that if I do not assert access to it for others, I cannot claim access to it for myself.

Access and Presence

Another movement which is under way within writing on the theology of access is toward expressing participation and access in terms of the significance of presence. Rather than starting with questions about activities, it is the presence itself of those with disabilities that lies at the heart of access to, and participation in, worship. As Block puts it succinctly in her work on hospitality: "The identity and mission of the church are explicitly tied to who is present and who is absent."[16] Indeed, it could be said that the significance of the incarnation and of Jesus' ministry begins not so much with what he does but with the fact that he is present among humanity, and present to the marginalized, inviting them to be present with him, not in a segregated way, but equally with others. If fullness of life for all people includes, among other things, the mediation of God's presence and grace by others, this cannot properly be achieved by means of segregation, where those with or without particular disabilities participate only with those in similar circumstances.[17] It requires full participation in human experience by all, where none is protected from the joys, sorrows, and expectations of the other. It is through fully valued membership of, and presence in, the Christian community that the mediation of God's presence and grace occurs. This is not to suggest that there is no merit at all in particular groups of people within the church meeting together to enjoy worship in ways that they find especially helpful. However, it does strongly anticipate that that would be the exception rather than the rule.

A challenge to carrying through such a proposal in practice lies in our expectations of each other. In particular, it lies in whether those without disabilities have any expectation of the divine being mediated through those with disabilities. The church may well be keen for people with disabilities to be present as it gives the church a feeling of inclusion. They might also welcome the reminder of our shared human vulnerability and interdependence. However, the challenge is for the church to go beyond that and to expect the gifts of the Holy Spirit to be given and received to and from every member of the body, of whatever embodiment.[18] That argument reaches beyond mere access into matters of people with disabilities exercising pastoral and other ministries within the church. However, starting from that point of view, it could well be that presence, properly understood and without excluding the activities that might flow from being present, may represent the essence of a theology of access.

As with other lines of argument, there is an underlying presumption that must come before this argument for understanding presence as the essence of access and participation. It is the presumption that those with disabilities should neither have to demonstrate their contribution to be valued and included by the church, nor have worship extended to them by concession, but a presumption that they will be present as a matter of course (or, conversely, that their absence would be unexpected and protested). This requires that our main account of God (in the present case of the atonement) naturally incorporates all of humanity in all of its variety. None is included as a special case. The purpose of atonement-as-participation is to present a main account of the atonement that shares this presumption. To the extent that it succeeds, it enables the atonement to act as a theological foundation from which to argue for this account of access in terms of presence.

A final observation is worth making on this point about access, presence, and atonement. When those writing from a disability frame of reference consider what inclusion in worship means, it is very often participation in the Eucharist that is taken as the critical test.[19] Since the Eucharist, so central to worship, is the revisiting and celebration of the cross and the atonement wrought there through the broken body and spilled blood of Jesus, this underlines how important it is that our idea of inclusion, access, and presence grows out of our understanding of what is so vividly celebrated there.

PARTICIPATION, HERMENEUTICS, AND HEALING

Atonement as a Foundation for Hermeneutics

Deliberately reading the Bible from a disability frame of reference, or disability-perspective hermeneutics, aims to set our reading of the Bible free from normate presumptions about disability and to move to a way of reading that encompasses and affirms the perspective of those with disabilities. The normate presumptions in question are both our own and those of the biblical authors, who like us were people embedded in their own times and cultures. Such presumptions are particularly those that portray, read, or interpret disability in a negative light. That might be as a sign of bad or weak character, or as something that results from sin, or that represents wider conflict or decline in the narrative, or as something that fulfils a merely functional or illustrative role in the workings of the text. The portrayal of disability in the Bible is certainly complex and varied, and normate presumptions manifest themselves in the Bible much as they do across so much of literature. So often it seems that disability is used as a device, either as part of sketching out a person's character or as a metaphorical reference to something else going on in the text.[20] The objective of disability-perspective hermeneutics is, as far as reading the Bible is concerned, to chart a different course.

Setting down hermeneutical guidelines for reading from a disability perspective is an important aspect of pursuing this objective. The earlier review identified guidelines intended to help the reader to see people who appear in the text and who have disabilities as dramatically significant characters, finding greater depth in them through careful attention. Another facet to hermeneutics is listening to those readers[21] of Scripture who themselves have diverse embodiments and whose perspective in reading is informed by their life experience. There ought to be a sound basis for saying that the text welcomes such readers, inviting them to ask with whom in the text they should identify and what the text seems to say about their own situation. The healing narratives in the Gospels are particularly relevant here. A disability perspective often places an emphasis on a social construction concept of disability and on healing in those narratives as primarily a matter of social reintegration.

All of these elements are important parts of building a thoughtful and inclusive hermeneutical strategy. But as with anthropology and access, it seems that behind each of these, and indeed behind the overall objective of Christian disability-perspective hermeneutics, a prior, more fundamental matter needs to be addressed. It concerns identifying what it is that changes our underlying assumptions about God's attitude toward humanity and disability and that shapes what we expect to find when we read God's word. Hermeneutics is concerned with how we read the whole account of the drama of God, including his revelation of himself, his relationship with creation and humanity, and the outworking of his intentions and promises. The focal point or pivot of that drama is the cross of Christ and the atonement wrought there. For all its variety and richness, the long drama of God finds its central, definitive meaning in the person and work of Jesus Christ. The greatest revelation of Jesus and his work is found as the whole drama passes through the locus of the cross and on to the resurrection. Therefore, how we perceive God to be addressing and treating humanity in all its variety at that focal point must be what shapes how we read the rest of the drama.

If, for example, we understand the atonement to be only about God's dealing with moral sin, then those aspects of the lived experience of disability that one might expect God to address through the cross either have to be linked to and expressed in terms of sin, or they have to be incorporated in the work of the cross as some sort of special case, or they have to be left as an unanswered mystery. Atonement-as-participation, on the other hand, understands the atonement as addressing not just identifiable moral sins but all that alienates us from God, from others, and even from ourselves as we believe we could be, and does so without an insistence on a binary sin/not-sin dichotomy. It also understands the atonement as a place where God meets the challenges of disability, including a diversity of hopes around healing or transformation, both in this life and in the resurrection body.

The point of this for disability-perspective hermeneutics is that it starts with the confident assertion that at the very focal point of the cosmic drama of God, all of humanity, in all of our diverse embodiments, are included as principal characters. This inherently inclusive atonement provides a foundation from which to argue in favor of strategies for reading Scripture that take a deliberately positive and inclusive view of disability. From this inclusive frame of reference, the points raised above (disability in the biblical text, the reader with a disability, and how we read the healing narratives) are worth looking at again in more detail.

Disability in the Biblical Text

There are helpful hermeneutical strategies available for reading the text in a way that encounters those characters within it who have disabilities as narratively significant figures. One strategy noted earlier is to adopt three succinct guiding principles that (i) people with disabilities are created in the image of God, (ii) people with disabilities are people first and are not defined by their disability, and (iii) disability is neither evil nor necessarily to be eliminated.[22] A slightly different approach applies ideas found in postcolonial studies to the reading of Scripture. The particular aim there is to avoid people with disabilities in the biblical text becoming "invisiblized," or hidden behind a supposed spiritual meaning or purpose of their disability.[23] One way of doing so is to read the characters in the text with disabilities as significant because they symbolize a whole nation's very real suffering under foreign rule. That still treats them as a narrative device, however. An emphasis that avoids that is to treat them not as symbolic but as actual individuals who have been disabled by the effects of foreign rule and the realities of living under colonial occupation (for example, the imposition of food rationing or punishments). In this way those with disabilities can become "visible" as significant individuals whose particular life experiences, and the causes of those experiences, are being addressed, in the case of the gospel, by Jesus.

What these hermeneutical strategies have in common is that they choose to avoid the pitfalls of normate presumptions that the characters encountered in the text (at least to the extent that they have impairments) act as mere cyphers, illustrations, or thin narrative devices used by the authors to push the plot along. However, despite these reading strategies, and even after applying them, two challenges of how the text presents people with disabilities remain unresolved. One is that characters in the biblical text who have disabilities are generally presented as atypical, and that atypicality contributes something specific to the narrative. We would not wish to smooth over or ignore that contribution but rather to explore and understand it with confidence. The other is that the extent of involvement of those characters in the narrative, and hence the depth we are genuinely able to discover in them, varies considerably.

Examining the first of these challenges for a moment, adopting a participative understanding of the atonement certainly does not remove disability from the text. Nor does it remove the fact that biblical authors do often appear both to use disability metaphorically and to exhibit the influence of presumptions about disability from within their own temporal and cultural frame. An example of such a situation is the account of the man who has been lame from birth and who appears in Acts 3 and 4. In considering the significance of that man's disability in the text, it is instructive to know that the interpretation of disability in those days was much influenced by physiognomic handbooks, which were in wide circulation and informed the medical theories current at the time.[24] These handbooks assumed that signs of character could be read in physical attributes (the meaning of physiognomy). Impairments to feet and ankles, as well as the need to be carried daily to a place to beg, were widely interpreted as signs of weak, or soft, moral character. When healed, the handbooks would expect to see a robust character being (re)established and again visible in the healed or restored physicality. It may well be that in writing his account in Acts, Luke was deliberately usurping the normal application of those theories, putting them to his own use. Rather than the man being restored to the dignified gait thought typical of a man of substance, Luke has him jumping and leaping (Acts 3:8), emphasizing the disruptive enthusiasm of the new body of God's people.[25] Recognizing such physiognomic assumptions of the time, although to modern ears they make uncomfortable use of disability, remains an important part of engaging with the text and discovering what it is trying to say.

The second challenge, the often very different extent of each character's involvement in the narrative, can be illustrated by contrasting two examples from one gospel writer. The first is the man with the withered hand in John 3:1-6. The only information given about the man is his condition. His hand is restored, but it appears very much that his disability is used as bait by those trying to trap Jesus, then in a countermove by Jesus as an illustration of the rightness of his doing good (in this case healing) on the Sabbath. The man himself is neither named[26] nor developed and does not appear again in the narrative. It is hard to see that the text does much other than make use of this character and his situation to serve the plot and say something about others. A contrasting example is the man born blind, about whom the ninth chapter of John's Gospel provides a wealth of background detail. Though he also is not named, it seems convincing to speak of him as a rounded, dramatically significant character in his own right who forms his own views and engages in lively, challenging conversation. Even then there is still a need for positive principles for reading that avoid interpreting this blind-then-seeing man principally as an illustration of Jesus' power to heal or as a metaphorical critique of the spiritual blindness of those around him, part of the picture John is building of Jesus as the light of the world.[27] Nonetheless, the relationships between these two men, their disabilities, and the part they play in the text seem very different.

What all this illustrates is that while the hermeneutical strategies indicated above do provide positive methods for reading Scripture, they do not in themselves provide a theological foundation or justification for adopting those positive methods in the first place. They can leave the impression that they are tools to be deployed in an uneasy wrestling match with the Bible as a whole and with the God represented therein, both of whom in fact have an underlying negative view of disability. What is proposed here instead is that the whole interpretation of the biblical drama should be shaped or underpinned by the conviction that its central action and revelation of God at the atonement includes all humanity, in all its diverse embodiments, as principal characters. That inherently inclusive atonement at the cross shapes our assumption about God's attitude toward humanity and disability and correspondingly should shape what we believe it is legitimate to read from the biblical text. It therefore provides a sound argument for developing and applying the various hermeneutical strategies indicated here which, across the gaps of time and culture, are looking for that inherently inclusive meaning. As well as that, it allows the approach and the apparent presumptions of the human biblical authors to be examined and critiqued with confidence in the context of the presumptions and conventions of their time and culture. What they are saying through the use of those conventions can be acknowledged and explored without the fear that they might lead to the conclusion that the Bible as a whole, as the word of God, disparages disability.

The Person with a Disability as a Reader

Considering how readers who themselves have experience of disability encounter the text mostly comes down to asking how their world interacts with the world presented by the Bible and how their insights as readers are received. As in other areas of disability theology, paying attention to those with disabilities is paramount. An example would be to ask someone who is blind, or partially sighted, what they find in the Bible's extensive use of light, dark, seeing, and blindness, and indeed the fact that the Bible presents predominantly a sighted person's (or more broadly, an able-bodied person's) view of the world.[28]

We might listen to John Hull, mentioned briefly earlier, commenting on the account of Bartimaeus in Mark 10:46-52. Jesus asks Bartimaeus what he wants Jesus to do for him. It might appear that the answer is obvious to anyone: he must surely want his sight to be restored. But that answer is only obvious, either in the biblical world or in our own, to "us" who are sighted.[29] Other responses are possible in Bartimaeus' world. Hull describes being blind as having been given a "strange, dark and mysterious gift from God."[30] It is not a gift he would have asked for nor suggest others should desire, yet along with much trouble it has brought him insights and experiences, including experiences of God, he would not otherwise have had. For him, Jesus' question is more complex than it appears. That perspective affects our reading of the text, both in highlighting its able-bodied frame of reference (not to denigrate the text but to be honest about it) and in suggesting that there are more subtle questions about disability that without that insight we would not think to ask.

Equally, we might listen to Holly Joan Toensing's examination of the "demoniac" in Mark 5 in the light of mental illness and tragedy in her own family. It is crucial to go beyond rather one-dimensional interpretations that see this man only as a symbol of Jesus' intention to extend the kingdom of God to the Gentiles or as a human corollary to his calming of the storm at the end of chapter 4. Depth, significance, and connections are there to be discovered in the world of the man who lives among the tombs, close to the dead, and in how Jesus responds to him. These include the sheer scale of the condition he is dealing with (a whole herd of pigs could not sustain it and resist self-destruction); the community's ongoing struggle to understand and help him; his own feeling of being overwhelmed by his condition; and his unusual commission from Jesus to share his particular story widely, when Jesus had told others not to do so.[31]

What emerges from this very brief consideration of the person living with disability as a reader of the biblical text is the need for a firm ground from which to assert two things. A principle for reading is needed that both (i) affirms that a disability-perspective reading is not peripheral to a "main" reading of the text or to discovering the text's meaning, and (ii) takes seriously the levels of complexity that emerge when the world of the biblical text (often portrayed in only a few sentences) is illuminated by insights from those living with disabilities in the present. Setting atonement-as-participation as the foundation for hermeneutics affirms those with disabilities (both reader and biblical character) as principal players in the drama to which Scripture bears witness and therefore affirms their perspective as essential to a "main" reading. Indeed, our "main" reading of the text is impoverished without it. By providing theological space for a diversity of hopes and a discussion of what is or is not alienating, it also does not insist on a simplistic binary sin/not-sin interpretation of the life experience of those with disabilities either in the text or reading it. Just as importantly, it also affirms the crucial importance of the insights of disability-perspective readers in arriving at the theological protocol of atonement-as-participation in the first place.

Reading the Healing Narratives

The healing narratives in the gospels probably present the greatest challenge in developing a convincing disability-perspective hermeneutic. In fact, they might well be the most challenging part of disability theology as a whole. Given the sheer number and diversity of occasions on which the Gospels speak of people being healed through an encounter with Jesus, those narratives are clearly of great significance, but interpreting them from a disability perspective presents a number of problems. While one might argue that Jesus did not heal absolutely everyone he came across who might be a candidate for such healing, it certainly seems that he healed by far the majority. In the reports of those encounters, there seems to be little effort made to distinguish between disease and disability, making it difficult to determine whether Jesus himself differentiated his response between the two.[32] It is also possible to gain the impression, if only through implication, that it is those who are of "sound mind and body" that are capable of being proper followers of Jesus and having true access to the benefits of his atonement, since being healed by Jesus often seems to lead to the healed person following him as a result.[33]

Those are awkward points, but perhaps more troubling still is the connection between the healing narratives and the coming kingdom of God to be inaugurated through the cross and resurrection. That connection comes from the suggestion that Jesus' action of healing in some way prefigures the coming of the kingdom, whereby the power of God the Holy Spirit, at work through the atonement, is the same as the power at work in the healings. Certainly the cross and resurrection are the usual basis for praying for and expecting healing through the power of the Holy Spirit. But the problem is that if the atonement is all about dealing with sin, then it is hard to dissociate the disabilities and illnesses that Jesus heals in the gospels (and by extension any other disabilities and illnesses) from sin. This has been the source of much of the awkwardness around interpreting the healing narratives in the context of either disability or chronic, disabling conditions.

The hermeneutical strategies adopted to date and indicated above have mainly focused on dissociating sin from either disability or disease, and differentiating disability and disease from each other, challenging readings that fail to do so as arising out of normate presumptions. There is little objection to the idea of healing from disease, from which anyone could suffer, being seen as a foretaste of God's saving power. It is the idea that disability must be treated in the same way that is rightly resisted. The move within those strategies has been to direct the discussion away from a focus on the physical healing toward an emphasis on the holistic reintegration of the person both ritually and socially. There is emphasis on exclusion and inclusion, on avoiding loose application of metaphors found in the text and on Jesus' own willingness to cross social boundaries and show concern for those considered "unclean."[34] Another approach is to provide balance by indicating situations of nonhealing. There are not many such examples in Scripture, but a clear one is the apostle Paul's ailment that he describes as a thorn in his flesh.[35] God's response to Paul's prayers for healing was not to heal directly but to give Paul reassurance that God's grace was sufficient for him (2 Cor 12:7-10).

These reading strategies are undoubtedly helpful in broadening our view of the text and in questioning normate interpretations. However, they do not really resolve the underlying dilemma. They either provide broader appreciation but leave the question of the link between healing, sin, and the atonement unresolved, or they give the impression that a reading with an emphasis on inclusion and reintegration is an alternative, which should replace a reading that links the physical healing with the cosmic reconciliation to be wrought by God in Christ and that correspondingly seems to link illness or disability with sin.[36] That seems to beg the question of whether, and on what basis, one of these ways of reading should take precedence over the other, or whether there is any way of holding together the concerns that lie behind each of them.

A single, consistent answer to this is unlikely to be found within the confines of the healing passages themselves. Examples even from one Gospel writer display considerable variation in how the healing accounts proceed and in how Jesus himself seems to perceive the purpose of healing in this life. Sometimes there is a clear emphasis on a link between faith, salvation, and healing: Jesus tells the leper in Luke 17:11-19 that his faith has healed him, and the word for "healed" (σέσωκέν) also carries the meaning "saved." Sometimes there is an emphasis on reintegration: another leper is instructed in Luke 5:12-15 to show himself to the priest and make an offering as a public testimony to his healing. Sometimes there is no mention of reintegration but another emphasis, such as the prioritizing of compassion over religious regulations, as in the case of the man healed of dropsy in Luke 14:1-6. On only one occasion does Luke record Jesus asking a sick or disabled person what he himself would like to happen. This he asks of the blind man begging near Jericho in Luke 18:35-43, an account close to that of Bartimaeus in Mark mentioned above.

Revisiting all of this through atonement-as-participation, however, provides a different frame of reference from which to approach the healing narratives. It begins with the underlying relationship between God and disability by emphasizing a number of important points. Disability is part of the contingency and risk of creation. God's act of creation involves a complex mixture of both the risk of moral sin, for which we are accountable and also an openness to variety, accident, and contingency, some of which surprise us with joy, some not. It is often not possible to pick apart that complex mix or our varied and often inconsistent responses to it. God participates in all of that contingency and risk as he accompanies his creation and is willing for things to befall him. The incarnation of Jesus and ultimately the atonement at the cross is where God's participation is deepest and once for all. There, all that alienates us from God and each other, both moral sin and the effects of the contingent nature of creation, is dealt with by God. All of humanity, in all its variety, is therefore inherently included there.

That central, fully inclusive atonement should shape how the healing narratives are read, as it shapes how we read the rest of Scripture. Most importantly, it allows for a differentiated consideration of sin, disease, and disability. The healing of disease, which can afflict anyone, is a clear part of Jesus' ministry, just as it has been part of the ministry of the church, as well as of the medical and care professions. As part of Jesus' ministry that healing certainly presages a much deeper, complete healing of the world and reconciliation with God, from whom we are alienated, brought about through the cross. Part of that deeper healing and reconciliation is the calling to account, and offering of forgiveness, for sin. But atonement-as-participation does not conflate that with disability. The transformation of disability (for example blindness or lameness in biblical language) by Jesus does prefigure the atonement that deals with all that alienates us from God and each other, but it does not insist that disability has its roots in moral sin and the fall of Adam and Eve or that all aspects of it that those without disabilities think "ought" to be changed must be changed.

Because the basis for understanding God's response to disability is thereby rooted in the central event of the cross and the atonement, rather than just within the healing narratives themselves, this also allows us to recognize where Jesus nonetheless makes creative use of the presumptions of the time about disability, sin, and who we consider to be "outsiders," to make powerful points about the inclusiveness of the coming kingdom. But it is now possible to do so without the fear that what he is doing is entrenching a negative view of disability.

An example serves to illustrate this and to demonstrate how atonement-as-participation enables the cross to act as the foundation for a fully inclusive disability hermeneutic. The account in Luke 8:43-48 of a woman cured of bleeding which had afflicted and disabled her for twelve years incorporates many of the points relevant to the challenge of a disability-perspective reading. The woman, in the press of the crowd around Jesus, touches just the fringe of his clothes and is healed. Jesus insists that she declare herself, then he in turn declares that her faith has healed, or saved, her (σέσωκέν again). The account includes a variety of interesting exegetical matters, such as how Jesus was aware that she touched his clothes and what he meant by saying that power had gone out of him. There is also the relationship between the flow of blood, ritual uncleanness, and the sense of exclusion that resulted from it, which is arises out of the Torah (Lev 15:19-30). Because of this uncleanness, the reintegration that is emphasized in existing disability-perspective readings is very significant here and is part of a proper reading of the text.

However, there is physical healing as well, which is equally important, along with clear atonement allusions in the senses of oppression, liberation, salvation, and faith that the account provides. Although we do not have all the details, such as whether this was a hereditary condition or something acquired, the physical healing and its link to faith and salvation are as important as the social and ritual reintegration that takes place.

In approaching that physical healing, atonement-as-participation as a way of understanding the cross allows for confidence that the power of God to bring about cosmic reconciliation through the cross and resurrection is the same power that is the source of this woman's healing. It affirms that her healing prefigures the fullness of the kingdom of God in which mourning, crying, and pain will be no more. At the same time, it allows a full acknowledgment of Jesus' clear intent in reintegrating her, publicly, into society, freed from ritual uncleanness, also as a sign that in the coming of the kingdom of God outsiders become insiders through Jesus. However, it does not insist that all of this conflates her condition with sin. It does not insist that she has been carrying around in her body a badge of the moral failure of the fall that others do not have to carry. Through this very disabling condition she has been alienated from those around her and felt alienated from God. Indeed, since the bleeding was regarded as making her ritually unclean, that alienation even bore something of an official stamp. The cross will certainly open the way for her to be forgiven for sin, as it does for all of us, but that does not say enough. It is also the whole of that broader alienation that the cross addresses, since the cross is where the whole human predicament is dealt with by God.

That this lady should suffer from that particular condition is part of the contingent nature, or riskiness, of life that all people encounter to varying degrees. This is not to treat the existence or experience of such a disability lightly nor to pretend to explain it away. At the cross, God is also present as the one responsible for the fact that this is the way that creation is. At the same time, though, it is because life is fragile in this way that the decisions we make and how we behave hold real importance. In part, Jesus' healing and reintegration of this woman was also a critique of the often negative response of those around him to people in her and similar situations. The result is that atonement-as-participation allows the atonement to act as the foundation for interpreting Jesus' act of healing in its full sense, without a need to steer clear of discussion of sin and without a need to treat the disability or illness as mainly symbolic. All of these things which alienate us from God and from each other are addressed at the place of the cross.

PARTICIPATION AND DISABILITY-PERSPECTIVE SOTERIOLOGY

Soteriology in the Context of Disability

The themes of disability theology also include soteriology, the idea of salvation, and how that is affected by a disability perspective. There are clear links between this and the discussion of healing above, not least through the New Testament's use of the word group that provides σέσωκέν which, as indicated, can be translated as both "saved" and "healed" and that therefore carries with it a mixture of the two ideas. However, there is also something to be said about a disability-perspective soteriology that goes beyond that healing discussion. In that sense, "salvation" is functioning as a collective term for the whole of the benefits secured by God in Christ through the atonement. Salvation used in that way is not something confined only to Christ's passion and resurrection. It can be taken to encompasses the whole sweep of Scripture, something with its beginnings in the early chapters of Genesis, played out through God's relationship with Israel and with the world through Israel, ultimately secured through Christ, witnessed to by the church, and fulfilled eschatologically. Here, however, the question is more specifically how salvation, as secured by Christ's atonement, can be spoken of in the context of disability.

The overall objective of a disability-perspective soteriology could be summarized as arriving at a soteriological account that avoids normate assumptions and that particularly addresses how disability is included in the process of salvation. A range of approaches was discovered in the earlier review. Of these, the first two were closely linked. They placed the emphasis of what salvation means on the revelation of God's identification with humanity, with all its impairments, and on the bringing about of a subjective transformation in personal and societal attitudes and behaviors. That changed behavior would affirm the worth of the person with a disability. The basis for such change moves away from the work of God in Christ through the cross and atonement toward a more direct work of the Holy Spirit in the person and in society more widely, what might be called a pneumatologically enabled response.

The third way of dealing with the question was Frances Young's approach, retaining a focus on the cross but with the emphasis on God's presence there: Jesus is present as our representative to offer a sacrifice for sin, and God is present to take responsibility for life as it is, the "gone-wrongness" of the world, including the experiences of disability. This deep sense of God's presence at the cross becomes the basis for assurance of his presence with us in life, though it says much less about what sort of actual change or eternal life is secured through the cross. The last approach is very different. It certainly keeps a focus on the cross as the means of salvation. It does so by linking disability directly with sin and the fall. It therefore insists that an account of salvation must include the elimination of all that we consider to be disability, since such a change must follow from the defeat of sin.

These various accounts of salvation seem to be heading in quite different directions from each other. However, they are doing so because each has behind it a particular concern, arising for good reasons, about what is being said of the atonement. The pneumatological account, moving the focus away from the atonement, is concerned among other things to dissociate sin and disability, to reaffirm the value of the human being and indeed the value of all that is positive in the life experience of disability. The "elimination of disability" account is concerned to avoid slipping away from a thoroughly objective atonement that deals with all the effects of the fall. However, both of those approaches in their different ways seem to betray an underlying assumption that talk of an objective atonement can only be talk of moral sin. One approach finds that unacceptable in the context of disability and so moves away from it. The other approach embraces it but correspondingly insists that all the phenomena and experiences we judge not to be good must stem from the fall, which is a matter of sin. Both approaches also give the impression that they already know what God "ought" to address, or need not address, through the atonement. On the one hand, little need be addressed but attitudes and behaviors. On the other, all that is considered, from time to time and in our own estimation, to be limiting or objectionable about disability must be put right by God.

Young's emphasis on presence acknowledges that things are more complex. It asserts that talk of salvation can only be meaningful if it is possible to speak of hope within despair, and that is what leads to the emphasis on God's presence demonstrated at the cross. This is a broader sense of salvation, but it leaves open and unanswered what objective change that salvation brings about beyond Jesus' representative sacrifice for sin. In what way, for all humanity, are things not as they were after Good Friday and Easter Sunday?

The picture that emerges is of a disparity of soteriologies, pushed in very different directions by the concerns that drive them. The question is whether the proposed account of atonement-as-participation provides a better foundation from which to address those concerns without arriving at such seemingly fragmented and irreconcilable notions of salvation.

Atonement-as-Participation as a Foundation

A crucial outcome of revisiting the cross in the light of the insights of disability theology and arriving at an understanding of atonement-as-participation has been a willingness to move away from an assumption that to speak of an objective atonement can only be to speak of dealing with moral sin. That assumption is the large part of what is pushing the above accounts of salvation apart. Instead, the atonement is God's deepest, once-for-all participation in the whole complex mix of the risk of moral failure and the contingent nature of life that are part and parcel of creation. Within that understanding, God at the atonement addresses all of the effects of that mix that alienate us from him and from each other. This allows the recognition that there are elements of the lived experience of disability that are alienating and elements that certainly are not. It also allows us to speak of sin and disability together without conflating the two.

As a result, different aspects of the salvation account can be held together constructively and helpfully. The concern to see the subjective impact of salvation emerge as a transformation of sinful attitudes and behaviors across society can be held together with the concern that God will also address and deal with, objectively, the personally alienating aspects of the lived experience of disability. This could involve change or healing in this life, or something manifest in the life to come. As regards the "elimination of disability" view, the concerns driving it, that the negative effects of disability on a particular life should not be left unresolved by God through the atonement, and that God should deal with sin, are held together without the need to identify all of disability and its implications with sin and the fall of humankind.

In taking this approach, there is recognition that the interaction of moral sin and contingent life (here disability) is complex and often difficult to analyze into its component parts. This suggests (following the earlier discussion of ways of knowing God) that in many cases it will only be those intimately involved in a particular life who might have a full sense of what is alienating and what is not. It allows for the diversity of hopes to be acknowledged in our soteriological account. It moves away from the presumption that those without disabilities know, or can predefine, what aspects of a life lived with disability "ought" to be addressed by God through the atonement.

As regards Frances Young's discussion of the cross, although the concept of atonement-as-participation began with some of her insights, it has moved away from her conclusion that the atonement should be understood primarily as God's presence at the cross (and correspondingly in life). Interpreting it instead as God's initiative of participating intimately in the moral and contingent risk of creation allows the objective achievement of the cross to encompass not only Jesus' sacrifice for sin and God's presence within that but also the broader question of what has changed, objectively, for all of varied humanity, come Easter Sunday.

Atonement-as-participation does therefore provide a place from which to build an account of salvation that is inherently inclusive of disability. It allows for an understanding of salvation that retains a full account of the cross and the atonement and that allows the concerns behind the various soteriological proposals to be given due weight without the need to drive them apart.

The Soteriological Vocation of Disability

One other aspect of disability-perspective soteriology should be revisited here. It is the role that disability itself plays in the drama of redemption, or salvation. For all the caution that might be felt about demanding a functional value from disability, the idea of a "vocation" of those with disabilities often raises its head.[37] The suggestion is that people with disabilities reveal the true vulnerability and interdependence of all humanity, as well as that people with disabilities evoke at best an ambivalent reaction from society, demonstrating its need for an atonement of some sort, the conviction of that need being an aspect of God's judgment. In this way, those with disabilities participate not only as recipients of the benefits of the atonement but as people through whom an aspect of the judgment leading to atonement is mediated. On that argument, people with disabilities have a particular role within the drama of salvation.

As they stand, these are attractive suggestions. However, they are vulnerable to questions about whether they are looking for a functional value to "justify" disability—whether the existence of disability has somehow become a necessity in the soteriological scheme—and what this atonement, elements of which are thus mediated, achieves for those people with disabilities through whom that mediation has come. These questions all have a sense of "us and them" about them, since they ask how God uses "them" for the soteriological benefit of "us." Atonement-as-participation helps to strengthen the discussion here in two ways. On the one hand, it provides an account that is consistent with the notion that salvation, though profoundly significant for the individual, remains a corporate affair in that we are all dependent on one another for our apprehension of, and response to, God's initiative of atonement. That allows the revelatory vocation of disability not to be necessary but to be appreciated and celebrated. On the other hand, the recognition that there are aspects of disability that are alienating and aspects that are not is again significant. It provides the theological space for disability to play a positive role in God's soteriological purpose without the need to insist that it has that role by virtue of being inherently a negative or positive phenomenon. In doing so, as discussed already, it recognizes a diversity of hopes, which allows for a much more open discussion of what aspects of disability might be eliminated, changed, or retained through the dynamics of the salvation secured for us by the grace of Jesus Christ.

A BRIEF RECAPITULATION

Much ground has been covered here. Reconsidering the themes that are active across the field of disability theology and their objectives has shown how atonement-as-participation allows the cross to play a foundational and critical role for each. Before moving the focus to the continuity of this way of approaching the atonement with the way it has long been expressed through the prevailing models, it is worthwhile taking a moment to reflect briefly on what the exploration has discovered so far.

Three particular features of atonement-as-participation have been essential in opening the way for the cross to become the cornerstone of Christian disability theology and the place from which it can most effectively argue its case. These are (i) that the atonement is God's deepest, once-for-all participation in all of the risk of creation, which involves both the risk of moral failure/culpability and the contingent nature of life, and recognizing that these are often deeply intertwined; (ii) that what is addressed at the atonement and transformed by the power of the cross and resurrection is whatever alienates us from God and others, acknowledging that, particularly in relation to disability, there can be a diversity of hopes in that regard; and (iii) that apprehending and responding to the atonement is not a narrowly conceived individualistic or intellectual process. These features generate an account of the atonement that is inherently inclusive, rather than one that has to be extended to disability as a special case. Applying these to the objectives of each of the themes of disability theology considered has allowed the following assertions to be made.

The cross and the atonement wrought there can be foundational to disability-perspective theological anthropology (what it means to be human) because the atonement is the point at which humanity and the human condition are most deeply participated in and addressed by God. The manner and depth of that participation means that any discussion of what it means to be human, of God's identification with humanity, and of what it means to be made in the image of God can begin from a place of confidence that God's definitive addressing of humanity at the cross is fully inclusive of humanity as it is, with all of its variety and impairments. All are "within the camp."

As regards a theology of access, since any theological argument for physical, social, or ecclesial access and inclusion should be predicated on spiritual access to God, an inherently inclusive atonement becomes its best foundation. It is through the cross that we have full access to God and inclusion in the body of Christ.

As regards hermeneutics, the focal point of the biblical drama, through which the whole of that drama passes, and which should shape a Christian reading of the rest of Scripture, is the cross and the atonement. The fact that there is a sound basis for that atonement being inherently inclusive and addressing the challenges of disability provides a theological foundation for reading all of Scripture from that frame of reference and for applying with confidence the positive hermeneutical strategies that are proposed in the literature. What is more, atonement-as-participation recognizes that the alienation God addresses at the cross is a complex mixture of moral sin and the contingent nature of creation. That allows the healing narratives to be read as a sign of God's great work of reconciliation and as something rooted in the power of the cross, without any need to conflate disability and sin.

As regards disability-perspective soteriology, atonement-as-participation provides a theological foundation for moving away from an assumption that to speak of an objective atonement is confined to speaking only of addressing moral sin. The other side of the same coin is that it does not demand that everything that gives rise to alienation, and that is dealt with at the cross, must be expressed in terms of moral sin. This sets the soteriological account free to be one that encompasses both a resolutely objective reconciliation with God and the demand for subjective evidence of personal and societal change experienced in this life.

6

Continuity of the Traditional Models

The atonement at the cross, as God's once-for-all, deepest participation in the contingency and risk of creation and in our human alienation, provides the soundest foundation for a Christian theology of disability. It is a way of understanding the atonement that is inherently accessible and inclusive of all humanity, with all its variety and impairments. Of course, in the day-to-day world of actual people asking questions about God and endeavoring to live out the life of Christian faith, there is another side to this: whether understanding the cross as atonement-as-participation has continuity with the way in which the gospel of Jesus Christ has long been shared, week by week, in the life of the church. It is all very well to propose such an idea, but its usefulness also hangs on whether a clear line can be drawn that connects it with those powerful models of the cross as Jesus' sacrifice, justice, and victory. These are the ways of speaking of the cross that give form to preaching and to the ministry of the gospel. They are the images drawn upon when the church wants to say what is happening at sacramental moments, such as baptism and the sharing of the Lord's Supper, moments when the Holy Spirit once again draws aside the veil and enables all of those present to come close to God. If the connection with these images or models cannot be made, if there is no such continuity here, little has been gained.

The idea of the cross as God's atonement-as-participation is intended to guide the way in which any model is used to describe what is happening at cross. In that way it acts as a "theological protocol." Therefore, the heart of this question about continuity is how well each of those models functions in bringing biblical and metaphorical resources to bear to describe and explain God's action at the cross as atonement-as-participation. That entails casting each model alongside atonement-as-participation and asking how well its resources can communicate the central ideas that have led to seeing the cross in this way. This includes whether the model helps us to explore and express the things that alienate us from God, others, and ourselves and the benefits of that alienation being addressed at the cross. It includes how well it encompasses the complex mix of moral failure, the contingent nature of life, and a diversity of hopes. It includes how well the model can speak of the cross as God's deepest, once-for-all participation in all of this and in the human predicament of suffering, joy, and sin and God's taking responsibility for how creation is. It also includes whether the model helps us in speaking of Jesus' death as demonstrating God's willingness for things to befall him and to take what is alien to himself, making it intimately his own without being diminished by it. In other words, it is a matter of putting each of these prevailing models quite seriously to the test.

Just as important in asking each model to do this descriptive and explanatory work is identifying the boundaries, where the limits of a model's correspondence to what God is doing on the cross lie. As already discovered, recognizing when the limit of the analogy between the subject, here the atonement, and the metaphors provided by the model has been reached introduces discipline into the use of the model. It also prompts fresh questions about the subject and about what sort of model might pick up the work of analogy beyond those boundaries. In exploring the continuity of these prevailing models when speaking of atonement-as-participation, recognizing their limits remains as significant as finding where their correspondence is strong.

SACRIFICE-AS-PARTICIPATION

Beginning this task with the sacrifice model takes us back into the Torah and the worship life of Israel. Because of its focus on the restoration of relationships damaged by sin, the offering of a sacrifice readily provides metaphorical resources for speaking of the alienation of parties to those relationships. Under the Levitical system of sacrifice, this is mainly expressed as sin, being moral failure that alienates us from God. In addressing that, sacrifice also allows talk of cleansing from the pollution of sin, moral weakness, and ritual error. This goes beyond a focus just on personal sins, however. There is an acknowledgment of the complex nature of sin and of our frequent inability to discern its contours from our standpoint in its midst.[1] That comes through in the emphasis on unintentional sin within the instructions for the various sacrifices (as distinct from intentional, "high-handed" sin identified in Num 15:30-31, which requires exclusion from the community). It extends to the culpability of the whole community for unintentional sin where it is difficult to discern the origin or source of a particular failure or weakness.[2] That communal involvement is particularly clear in the instructions for the Day of Atonement (Lev 16), which allow the language of sacrifice to explore a sense of alienation that goes beyond the individual and God to the community and God. As a ritual act of the whole community, it even extends into interpersonal relationships and the restoring of a community damaged by sinful attitudes or behavior. A great strength of the sacrifice model here is that its specific purpose was to declare that the alienation of sin is dealt with, that pollution is cleansed, and that all parties have a fresh start.

When all of this is applied as a model of atonement, this fresh start is constituted by the forgiveness of sin achieved at the cross. When the model is applied in that way, an extension is clearly being made to Levitical sacrifice in that the perfect sacrifice of Jesus is treated as making forgiveness, cleansing, and renewal of relationship available in relation to any sin. This is a significant development, bridging the distinction between intentional and unintentional sin that existed in the Levitical code.

However, the sacrifice model comes up against a limit of its correspondence when we turn to the wider contingencies of life. It has less to say about alienating experiences that seem to lie outside of an analysis based just on moral sin. The sacrifice model would certainly speak to society's often poor response to disability but not so much to the sheer difficulty of some of the experiences of living with disability attested to across disability literature and testimony. Correspondingly, the sacrifice model does not particularly provide metaphorical resources for engaging with the diversity of hopes as to what is addressed, transformed, or healed by God through the atonement beyond dealing with personal and corporate moral sin.

One response to that observation might be to turn to the Passover sacrifice for assistance.[3] The Passover sacrifice was connected to an experience of being set free from an involuntary, imposed, oppressive situation (slavery in Egypt) where an analogy could be drawn with some aspects of living with disability. It was not a Levitical sacrifice for sin but more an obedience that led to shielding from sin's effects. As part of the Exodus narrative of liberation, the Passover sacrifice was a protection from judgment rather than the action that in itself brought about freedom from oppression. But having said that, the fact that the Passover lamb is intimately bound up in God's action of setting free does helpfully broaden the scope of the sacrifice model. By moving in that direction, the language of the Passover sacrifice and its related liberation is also beginning to drift into that of the victory model, discussed in more detail below. These are good examples of recognizing limits of correspondence, that although sacrifice performs very strongly in terms of a complex sense of alienation resulting from personal and communal sin, there are aspects of the wider experience of alienation from God and each other where sacrifice is more limited and other models must pick up the work.

The ability of the sacrifice model to speak of God's participation in the contingency and risk of creation stems from the fact that God's provision of the sacrificial system was part of his gift of the Torah. Through the Torah God provided a comprehensive way of life for the people of Israel, set free from slavery in Egypt and called to be a light to the nations. The Torah was celebrated by Israel as a demonstration of God's intimate participation in the life and dangers of their community. Psalm 119, to take a single example, is an extended celebration of the Torah, its wisdom, and the sense of God's intimacy that it creates. God's initiative in providing the sacrificial system was part of that intimate involvement, allowing for offerings of thanksgiving and fellowship, as well as those directly addressing the risk and consequence of moral failure. This included God's willingness to treat the sacrifices offered as effective in dealing with sin and to act toward the individual and the community on that basis. It recognized that the alienation caused by sin could not be fully and effectively dealt with by human beings but required God's participation.

The whole sacrificial fabric of Israel's life therefore functions impressively as a model of God's participation, at least in the complex moral risk of creation. If that is so, then Jesus' death can be described as the once-for-all, completed, fully effective sacrifice in strongly participatory language. In human terms, Jesus was executed through the combined efforts and failures of those who opposed him. But in theological terms, God can be said to apply the full weight of the sacrificial system to that death, such that it becomes the deepest, once-for-all expression of God's participation in the alienation of humanity from God and from others that Jesus' death represents. The various metaphorical resources that sacrifice offers all contribute here. For example, death befalls the sacrificial victim as a result of the sin of the individual or the community. Hands are laid on the victim, and the alienation of sin is identified with (if not actually transferred to) that victim. The victim, together with the sin which is alien to it, is handed over to God. Correspondingly, what is alienating for us (and which is certainly alien to Jesus) is identified with him when sinful humanity lays hands on him, and in death he is handed over to God.

The correspondence here is interesting in many ways. The laying of hands on the sacrificial victim (Jesus) is treated as effective, even if it is unwitting. The death by execution that befalls Jesus becomes his initiative in handing all this to God, for example in Luke 23:46, which has him commend his spirit to his Father. The resurrected Jesus, who has taken what is alien and made it his own without being diminished by it, nonetheless bears the marks of a death which has now taken on the full meaning of sacrifice. As well as being marks of identification, perhaps these are also now a reminder of the eternal nature of God's intimate participation in the risk of his creation. What is more, God's initiative in providing the system and the fact that God is in Christ providing the ultimate sacrifice, while in no way reducing our own culpability, allow us to speak with confidence of God's being present at the cross as the one responsible for the way that creation is. The sacrifice model therefore functions consistently and effectively in describing Jesus' death in terms of atonement-as-participation as far as the complex alienation of sin is concerned.

Wider Thoughts on Sacrifice

Comparing the main atonement models and the themes of disability theology earlier highlighted that certain metaphors emerging from each of those models bring into sharp focus some of the awkwardness that has existed between the two fields to date. It is important not to lose sight of these or try to paper over them but instead to examine them in the light of atonement-as-participation in the same way that limits of correspondence are examined. Doing so raises new insights as well as providing confidence as to the actual extent of the analogy between each model and God's action at the cross.

In the case of sacrifice, two such metaphors came to light. The first was that if Jesus is the perfect, blemish-free sacrifice (as required of the Levitical victim), the claim that he particularly identifies with the life experience of people with impairments, a strong theme in disability theology, might seem to be weakened. This issue does not simply go away when the atonement is understood in terms of God's participation in the risk of creation. However, it is certainly helped by explicitly acknowledging both the rich correspondence of the sacrifice model in terms of moral sin and its limits of correspondence in describing a broader sense of alienation. This avoids conflating the ritual symbolism of Levitical perfection in dealing with sin with the insight of Jesus' embodiment of impairment at the cross. Pressing this point of Jesus' perfection further, the emphasis on God's full participation in varied and vulnerable humanity through the incarnation should, when the incarnate Christ becomes the crucified Christ, change our perception of what bodily perfection in a sacrifice is intended to signify. It had far more to do with what was going on in the heart and mind of the one offering the sacrifice, his or her open confession and unreserved desire for reconciliation with God, than with the visible particularities of the animal. This way of thinking runs parallel to the way in which the cross as victory changes our perception of victory from one secured through strength (typically "a mighty hand and an outstretched arm" per Deut 4:34, for example) to one secured through vulnerability.

The second potentially awkward idea was that Jesus is most closely identified with the consequences of sin at the moment, as he approaches death on the cross, when he can be said to have become, or been made, most clearly disabled. This seemed to bring disability and sin into uncomfortably close proximity. Again, however, this remains awkward only if this one model is pressed into doing all of the work of explaining everything about the atonement, and if the atonement is restricted to being expressed in terms of dealing only with moral sin. Where limits of each model are acknowledged, and where the cross is understood to deal with all aspects of alienation, moral and otherwise, the disabling of Jesus through his passion can be seen as an example of his identification with people with impairments without being forced to equate impairment itself with sin.

JUSTICE-AS-PARTICIPATION

Moving from sacrifice to justice as a model for speaking of the cross opens up again the great wealth of metaphorical resources coming from a range of understandings of justice and law. Earlier these were separated into four ways of thinking of justice (albeit that these are not sealed categories and they inevitably overlap): (i) justice as keeping the Old Testament covenant; (ii) justice as providing satisfaction to restore God's honor and dealing with the debt of guilt arising from offending it (Anselm and a medieval, feudal concept of justice); (iii) justice more in terms of forensic guilt, innocence, penalty, and the law court, more closely associated with the Reformation; and (iv) justice as day-to-day transactions subject to the right application of law or custom. If justice is going to function well as a model for describing and explaining atonement-as-participation, then each of these ways of thinking about justice should be expected to have something to contribute toward the core ideas of alienation, God's participation in the contingency of life, and Jesus' death as God's willingness for things to befall him.

Beginning with alienation, as we did when looking at sacrifice, where the justice emphasis is on covenant, the metaphors for alienation arise from the breaking of the covenant through moral and ethical failure. The correspondence is extensive, since in the Old Testament the covenant was the basis for relationship with God. Moreover, it was the basis for the creation and ordering of community and for self-identity as part of that covenant community. Clearly there is overlap here with the sacrifice model, since sacrifice was involved in recommitment to the covenant except, as mentioned, for high-handed intentional sin. Describing the atonement of Christ in covenant terms (the creation of a new covenant) might therefore at first sight seem to run into the same limits of correspondence as sacrifice in having less to say about experiences of alienation arising from aspects of the contingency of life that fall outside of direct questions of sin. However, the call to return to the covenant, running like a connecting thread throughout the fabric of the Old Testament, emphasizes that the ritual of sacrifice is only ever a sign of something deeper. The underlying call is always for full justice throughout the community, not mere ritual observance. In two well-known examples, Amos 5:21-24 and Micah 6:6-8, God through his prophets rejects sacrificial ritual that is not accompanied by justice, righteousness, kindness, and humility. If there is to be continuity between old and new covenants, then the people of the new covenant must likewise be characterized in this life by those attitudes and behaviors. In the present case that includes a call to be fundamentally kind, just, hospitable, and inclusive of those with disabilities.

Shifting the emphasis from covenant to the law court, whether in feudal or later times, provides metaphors for alienation in terms of guilt, condemnation, and unworthiness before God and others, arising from wrongdoing, or that which brings dishonor to the God we claim to worship. In any meaningful justice system there is of course the need for the one who is guilty to be rehabilitated, as well as the need to make restitution or to face a just penalty, and all of these aspects of the model can shed light on parts of the atonement Jesus is securing at the cross. However, other metaphorical dynamics here also say something about alienation. The cry to God as judge against persecution by others is a cry that is rightly heard and responded to in the court context. This could be the cry against deliberate unfair action against the individual. It could be the cry against the negative attitudes and reactions of others to, in the present case, disability. Experience of exclusion might not result from deliberate fault but from a general ingrained systemic insensitivity or ignorance across society of the needs of those with disabilities (normate presumptions). This takes the justice model at least some of the way into the contingent nature of life which goes beyond a simple "individual moral sins" description of alienation. Here the justice model is building a slightly broader correspondence than is achieved through the sacrifice model alone.

When the focus shifts once more, this time toward a transactional sense of justice such as ransom or redemption, the metaphorical correspondence operates slightly differently and broadens the picture further. The question of alienation becomes one of asking from what alienated state one is to be ransomed or redeemed. We might say this is from being a slave to sin (or to life's negative experiences) or from being under the power or sway of such things. Being in that state distances us from God, others, and even from our own selves, as we envisage how we might otherwise be. As mentioned earlier, trying to fill in too much detail here, such as to whom the ransom or redemption payment is made, risks demanding an unfair level of correspondence. However, that very lack of detailed correspondence also allows this element of the justice model to express any part of life (not just moral failure) in which alienation is experienced. We can say we have ended up "owned" by a master other than God through our own action, or that of others, or through a complex tangle of circumstances, and to speak of being ransomed or redeemed from that position is rich in meaning and pastoral possibility.

Taken as a whole, therefore, the justice model provides metaphorical resources for speaking of alienation that overlap helpfully with what sacrifice provides but that also extend the reach of description and explanation of the atonement into alienation arising from the wider contingency of life. This breadth of the justice model also provides more in the way of resources for speaking about the diversity of hopes acknowledged earlier. A person with a disability (for example, someone who has Down syndrome or uses a wheelchair) might or might not hope that God would change an aspect of his or her situation through the power of the cross, and that will depend much on the experience of living his or her particular life. That diversity of hopes can be better explored using the language of being redeemed or ransomed from oppression than that of restoring the covenant or satisfying God's honor.

Making use of the full breadth of the justice model in this way also makes a particularly useful contribution toward speaking of the atonement in terms of God's participation. It helps to address a possible weakness that this model can fall into if its focus is confined to law-court imagery alone. As noted earlier, Anselm's contemporary Peter Abelard avoided any such objective models because he believed they imposed an alien necessity upon God. They seemed to make God subject to a higher legal authority or principle, following which God "had to" apply a penalty for sin, for example. However, since the Old Testament (and indeed the New Testament) covenant is God's initiative, a covenant emphasis enriches the correspondence of the justice model significantly by addressing this directly. Justice is not a standalone idea, somehow independent of God or above God. It originates with God. God's placing of himself within the covenant relationship demonstrates both his humility and his participation in the risk of the covenant being broken. In

New Testament terms, in the Gospel accounts Jesus through the incarnation lives as a Jewish man participating in the inheritance of Israel's struggle to keep the covenant. The consequences of that covenant having been broken in various ways over time pervade his life, ministry, and death. These include living in a land long occupied by a succession of foreign rulers. They include divisive attitudes toward those considered unclean or sinful, as well as idolatry and the misuse of religious and political power. As declared through the Last Supper and its ongoing celebration by the church at the Eucharist, God in Jesus takes upon himself the responsibility, as the source of justice, of reestablishing that broken covenant and extending it to all.

As before, a law court emphasis also extends the correspondence of the justice model to areas other than covenant. Although the image and language of the court as a place of accountability is used at times in the Old Testament, forensic metaphors are perhaps more often applied to God's participation in our predicament through talk of Jesus himself. God in Christ suffers injustice as our substitute. Jesus also takes the role of our advocate or representative before the judgment of the Father. Where the law court emphasis contributes particularly strongly to an exploration of atonement-as-participation is its ability, after the manner of Job, to accommodate the idea of calling God to account for the experiences of alienation arising not just from identifiable sin but from all the contingent nature of life. This is applying the point made above that the cry for fair treatment is rightly heard in the court context. God's participation in the risk of creation involves being present on the cross where all that is alienating about life is addressed and where Jesus, again as our representative, utters that cry of alienation and forsakenness against God on humanity's behalf.

A transactional emphasis again adds to the whole a more compact range of metaphor but nonetheless an important one. In wanting to speak of God's intimate participation, the notion of "transaction" might seem to present God as a remote participant, one who hands over a payment and receives what is due to him as a result. However, the participatory sense returns with force when the nature of the "payment" is pursued. If redemption or ransom involve God in some way paying the price of human freedom, then perhaps the garden of Gethsemane is a place to put this part of the justice model to work. There, Jesus chooses not to withhold himself from paying (through himself becoming) what he seems aware will be the greatest possible price. However, Gethsemane also emphasizes (as do Old Testament passages about God redeeming or ransoming Israel or Judah) that the transaction is essentially a one-sided initiative, not a negotiation. God in Christ pays the price, but no one has a right to demand that payment. There is a connection here with the discussion about the nature of the risk of creation. The threat, or risk to creation, even though it may be personified in Satan, is not ultimately from a person, a counterpart to whom God could somehow ever be in debt, but from an annihilating nothingness.

When speaking of Jesus' death as revealing God's willingness for things to befall him, bringing a covenant emphasis from the justice model to bear is illuminating. It enables Jesus' death to be described in terms of the breaking of the covenant. God bound himself to the covenant, and any idea of breaking it is something alien to God, yet he bears its consequences. The death which befalls Jesus is real death, through which, in the tomb, we can say he is cut off completely from the covenant people. This was the Old Testament consequence for sin with a high hand (Num 15:30-31), where a sacrifice was not available as a remedy, which is also a good example of one model of the atonement taking over the work from another. At Golgotha Jesus also symbolically dies outside the city, or "camp," of the people.[4] Not only does God take the consequence of the broken covenant to himself in Jesus' death, he uses that very thing as the foundation on which he establishes the new covenant. Through the Last Supper Jesus makes it clear that he will take the alien things of his body being broken and blood spilled, the very emblems of the broken old covenant, and make them the ground, the eternal foundation, on which the new covenant is built. The covenant emphasis therefore proves particularly powerful for exploring this aspect of atonement-as-participation.

If the emphasis is more forensic, the thing which is alien to God and yet which he makes intimately his own through Jesus' death is the guilty verdict passed on the one who is innocent. Jesus then suffers what the people, humanly speaking, regard as the suitable consequence of that verdict, which is his death. With this emphasis Jesus' death is spoken of as a judicial punishment or penalty rather than representing exclusion from the covenant people. Jesus suffers fully what is alien to him, the guilty verdict and the penalty of death. He takes them to himself and deals with them without being diminished by them and demonstrates all of that through his resurrection.

In a transactional sense, Jesus' death would instead be described as a price paid. It is alien to God, as he is never and never could be in slavery or in debt to another. Nor is he or could he be under the sway or control of persons or circumstances except through his own initiative of participation in the risk of creation. It is a price which would destroy us and yet which he pays in our place to secure our freedom.

Wider Thoughts on Justice

Using the justice model as a means of describing and exploring atonement-as-participation has made it clear that the full range of understandings of justice and law and their metaphorical resources are needed if enough is to be said. Any one concept of justice on its own is inadequate. This is particularly the case as regards the question of God's responsibility for how life is and for moving to a frame of reference which includes both identifiable moral sin and other alienating aspects of the contingency of life.

Taking that broader view, there is a particular challenge that the justice model has suffered from, perhaps especially in a disability context. It has to do with the idea of guilt. There is no question that there is human culpability for sin. The problem has been what that idea of guilt before God in relation to sin is understood to mean and how it is apprehended, particularly in relation to people with intellectual impairment. The more forensic, courtroom forms of the justice model require the identification of moral wrongdoing and an appreciation of both guilt and the rightness of a just penalty for those forms of the model to function meaningfully as an explanation of the cross. This remains a potentially sensitive aspect of the justice model. But the discussion here indicates again that the way to address this is by recognizing the crucial importance of limits of correspondence, even within different aspects of the same model. Working with ideas of a covenant, broken by attitudes or behaviors but restored through God's friendship, or of a sense of being graciously redeemed from oppression, or of a life ransomed into freedom, is likely to bear much more fruit here than more analytical metaphors of forensic guilt, penalty, and substitution. As well as highlighting the importance of limits of correspondence, this cautions against a tendency to crown any one model of the atonement, or part of a model such as a law-court version of justice, as taking precedence over other models or being in some way the overarching model to which others are somehow subservient. It also cautions against falling into the mistake of treating the metaphors of any particular model, however strong their apparent correspondence to what is happening at the cross, as if they are describing the actual mechanism by which God's initiative of atonement proceeds.

VICTORY-AS-PARTICIPATION

The victory model, with its very different metaphorical resources of conflict or struggle and God in Christ as the one who defeats the enemies who seek to oppress humanity, proves to be particularly effective in opening up a rich and wide-ranging description of the alienation which is the target of atonement-as-participation. This is perhaps partly because deploying this model for talking about the cross naturally begins with the experiences of alienation in terms of oppression by these forces, rather than with a definition of moral sin. The model therefore readily identifies the complexity and interweaving of the forces that we find alienating. These certainly include the typically identified "tyrants" of sin, the law, death, and Satan. However, it seems justified also to extend them to the alienating effects of, for example, ingrained societal and medical-model attitudes to disability, or to the complicated experience of "being different," things which cannot necessarily be mapped directly onto one of those four standard loci. Whatever those powers and sources of alienation are, and however they interact with each other, their defeat through the atonement offers victory and freedom. This model is therefore especially effective in moving beyond a discussion that insists on moral sin as its sole focal point and in opening the discussion to encompass the diversity of hopes. The fact that it readily recognizes the complexity of life's experience places a restraining hand on those currently without disabilities when it comes to presuming that they know in advance what God "ought" to transform in the life of another who is living with disability.

In describing God's participation in the contingency and risk of creation, the victory model would have access to God's Old Testament record of defending Israel from her enemies, setting her free from Egypt, opposing her own injustices and bringing her back from exile in describing his participation in the risks facing his people. This close participation in the life of Israel can be seen as a particular (albeit extended) instance of God's deeper participation in all of creation's struggle, beginning with his judgment in Genesis 3:14-15 on the serpent who has acted to alienate humanity from God. In fact, Christus Victor, at least as Aulén presents it, has tended in practice to have much more of a New Testament focus on God in Christ. Following that focus, Jesus participates fully in the predicament of humanity when he becomes vulnerable to the attack of these forces befalling him through the incarnation. As he approaches the cross, he is literally taken prisoner and loses his freedom. The cry of forsakenness (alienation from God) from the cross places Jesus at the deepest point of our own sense of alienation and of the human struggle against the forces which threaten to destroy us and the relationships, human and divine, which shape our personhood.

If the model is allowed to extend back and draw also on those Old Testament references to God's involvement in our struggle or battle, an important aspect of applying it to atonement-as-participation becomes particularly apparent. It is that the atonement through the cross, as well as being the point of God's deepest participation in the human struggle against oppressive forces, redefines the source of victory, as already mentioned, from the might of God's outstretched arm in battle to Jesus' willing vulnerability to the risks of the forces that threaten creation befalling him.

When it comes to using the victory model to speak of God taking to himself what is alien to him, Jesus' death would be described as God's taking and making most intimately his own the greatest oppression and captivity that humanity could experience, being death itself. That oppression and captivity must be wholly alien to a completely sovereign God. Death also has a particular role in the victory model in this regard, since having the power to threaten and ultimately inflict death is the ultimate weapon of any tyrant against those under his or her sway.[5] In Jesus' own time and place, the fact that the power to inflict death as punishment sat with the occupying Roman forces is what gave the death and resurrection of Jesus its profound political impact. This event was an utter repudiation of the Roman Empire and its power, an empire which the early church regarded as the very embodiment of sin and death. There is no negotiation or covenant made with this ultimate oppression. Death is overthrown.

Wider Thoughts on Victory

The victory model, as well as overlapping with the other models, very clearly shows itself here to be stepping in and picking up the work where the other models meet their own limits of correspondence. In doing so it paints atonement-as-participation onto a broader canvas. However, it also became clear in the earlier discussion that some metaphors within the victory model, such as notions of triumph, victory, and overcoming, can seem awkward in a disability context if not handled with care. Too sweeping an application of those can run the risk, in a general sense, of the victory model becoming exemplarist: Jesus' unmasking, challenging, and undoing of evil can come to be presented as behaviors we should emulate, rather than as Jesus' once-for-all victory over death. In a disability context, this might seem to require those with disabilities to set and achieve goals in a way that is not appropriate to them, or it might encourage others to valorize those with disabilities or to ascribe to them a function of demonstrating the overcoming of adversity. This can also be a function of something else noted earlier, that the victory model can appear to be describing something mythical, an epic conflict among divine beings in a distant spiritual realm, whose qualities we are called to emulate.

The benefit of atonement-as-participation here is that it arrives at the atonement as the fulfillment of the long, thoroughly grounded drama of God's constant participation in the risk of creation, the cross being his once-for-all deepest participation in humanity's predicament of alienation. Part of applying any model in a way that sheds light on a subject lies in appreciating how that subject also affects the meaning of the elements of the model itself. In this case, applying the victory model to atonement-as-participation demands that those metaphors of triumph, victory, and overcoming must be redefined as arising precisely from God's participation, through Jesus, in our weakness, vulnerability, and dependence. Understood in that way, an exemplarist interpretation is far less likely.[6]

Another aspect to face up to here is the use of a victory model of the atonement in some healing ministries, which has been a source of awkwardness and irritation among people with disabilities and those who care for them. To summarize the theological approach often encountered in such ministries, the victory of the atonement is the basis for the victory over all sickness, which has its origins in sin and the fall, and within which disability is not generally differentiated. That victory is fully expected to be experienced in the healing of such sickness, through the prayer of faith, in this present life. A disability theology critique sees much this approach and how it is conducted as oppressive. It appears to impose its own view of what God "ought" to heal and to presume that God's own aim is to bring about conformity to a typical physical or mental pattern. It also appears to carry the accusation that any failure of disability to be so healed is a failure of faith, since faith in the atonement would deliver such a change.

However, atonement-as-participation, which recognizes a diversity of hopes and can speak with sensitivity of both death and disability as having positive and negative faces, opens up a space for responding to that critique. When the victory model is applied as a model of atonement-as-participation, that oppressive sense can be avoided. The statement made above, that "death is overthrown," seems on the face of it uncontroversial. Indeed, it seems sensible to extend that victory over death (via Rev 21:4) to incorporate all that would cause mourning, crying, and pain. However, does it follow that the victory declared should also be extended to incorporate everything that we label disability? Is disability, in all its aspects, also overthrown? The acknowledgement of a diversity of hopes that emerges from atonement-as-participation allows us to ask what is or is not alienating about the various experiences of disability. It allows space for a much greater differentiation to be brought into the discussion of the victory of the cross and of what the tyrants are that God in Christ is understood to have vanquished there. It also requires that we refrain from dictating to those with disabilities the terms of what constitutes victory or healing, and instead allow them and those who are their carers and know them most intimately to speak for themselves.

MORAL INFLUENCE, CONNECTION, AND PARTICIPATION

When the various approaches to models and theories of atonement were grappled with earlier in order to bring some greater discipline to them, the idea of a moral influence account of the cross was also considered. It was proposed that, while moral influence is not a separate theoretical model of atonement, its challenge of accounting for the subjective connection between ongoing present lives and the benefits of the atonement must surely be brought to bear whichever prevailing model is deployed. It should therefore be considered here also when testing the continuity of those three prevailing models as they apply to atonement-as-participation.

That earlier exploration found that taking disability into account, particularly when profound intellectual impairment is included, serves to sharpen these questions of connection. At the same time, however, insights already emerging within disability theology are helping considerably in forming a response. These are the ideas of different ways of knowing God, of God's accommodation, and of our participation in the atonement being as much a corporate affair as an individual one. Those ideas in turn discover a firmer footing and greater relevance when they are understood and expressed in terms of God's participation in the contingency and risk of creation and the realities of being human.

Asking how the prevailing models fare as models of atonement-as-participation also emphasizes the usefulness of those insights in developing an open, confident discussion about disability and the cross. An example of each makes the point. The comments on affective ways of knowing God help to address, within the justice model, the fact that requiring acknowledgment and articulation of guilt attached to an intellectual admission of wrongdoing seems awkward and inappropriate in the context of intellectual impairment. Acknowledging affective ways of knowing God helps in discerning this limit of correspondence but also in exploring what it might mean for a particular person to sense the need for atonement. It points to the possibility that the resources of the sacrifice model, with its practical emphasis on actions (often in community) that reestablish relationships, might have more to offer there.

The principle of God's accommodation in communicating his grace finds a similar strong connection with the sacrifice model, speaking of an enacted and experienced atonement rather than an intellectual one. When it comes to the insight of the corporate dimension of participation in the atonement, the victory and sacrifice models lend their resources to expressing how we celebrate together our freedom from what has oppressed us.

What is most firmly underlined here, however, is that when these powerful models of sacrifice, justice, and victory are deployed to describe and explain a thoroughly objective atonement-as-participation, it remains crucially important to call for the subjective dimension of the atonement to be accounted for and for insights like these to be pressed into service to do so.

A (VERY POSITIVE) CONCLUSION ON CONTINUITY

This has been a detailed look once again at these three prevailing models of the atonement, but in doing so something significant has emerged. Atonement-as-participation had already been found to provide a way of thinking about the cross that is inherently inclusive of people with disabilities. What has emerged here is that these models, with their long heritage in sharing and exploring the gospel, have shown themselves to provide as rich, if not richer, resources of ideas and metaphors for describing and explaining the cross as atonement-as-participation. As a result, the answer to the question of whether atonement-as-participation is consistent with, and grows out of, the gospel as already shared in churches week by week is emphatically "yes." The best resources of language for exploring God's initiative through Jesus at the cross as atonement-as-participation turn out to be these already prevailing models, or groups of ideas, that have informed the sharing of the gospel through the long history of the church.

That in itself is a great encouragement, but more can be said. What has also been pressing for attention is the importance of recognizing limits of correspondence between each of the models and the atonement when this "theological protocol" of atonement-as-participation is being followed. This is not simply to make the bland statement that each model has some strengths and some weaknesses. It is to assert that the intentional, disciplined identification and examination of those limits of correspondence is as important in giving an account of the atonement that embraces all of humanity, inclusive of its range of ability and variety, as is identifying the aspects of the models where correspondence is strong. A willingness to allow one model to take over the work where another reaches such a limit is essential.

The point can be illustrated in broad terms as follows. The sacrifice model is effective in a discussion of how atonement addresses sin and the complexity and subtlety of sin that goes beyond individual identifiable acts, as well as the breadth of relationships that sin affects. However, it provides less in the way of metaphorical resources relating to the alienating experience of things that fall outside of explanations focused on particular moral sins and as a result less material for a discussion of the diversity of hopes. The justice model has great breadth when different concepts of law and justice are embraced. That breadth encompasses a wider cry for fairness and for calling God to account for the way that life is than did the sacrifice model. What is more, the element of the justice model that has been called here a transactional emphasis is particularly suited to extending the correspondence of the model to the contingency of life that stretches beyond a moral failure explanation. Similarly, the victory model, while again providing resources for discussions of sin, also steps in and provides metaphorical resources for a broader range of life experiences which alienate us from God and from others.

This leads on to a further implication. Although the three prevailing models of sacrifice, justice, and victory, along with the subjective contribution that we might still call moral influence, connect fully with atonement-as-participation, this is not to claim that these therefore represent a "closed canon" of models of the atonement. The insistence on recognizing limits of correspondence would in any case be at odds with such a claim. These models certainly have much to say in terms of the alienation of moral sin in all its complexity and subtlety. They also function well, taken as a whole, in speaking into experiences of alienation arising from the contingencies of life that fall outside a sin explanation. But the balance of ideas found in these models also suggests that it would be worthwhile considering the place of other metaphorical resources, which have similarly sound biblical roots but which perhaps have not hitherto been to the fore because they seem to speak less immediately of moral sin and the fall. This could include expressing God's initiative and action through the cross and resurrection more boldly in terms of, for example, (i) exile and return, (ii) brokenness and restoration (or healing), or (iii) that which was lost and now is found. This present discussion and its discoveries seem to open the door for an exploration of these other metaphors and the descriptive and explanatory power that they in turn can add to the picture painted here of atonement-as-participation.

Conclusion

A KIND OF CONVERSION

Any change in how we perceive our relationship with God and how we understand him or his actions is a kind of conversion. That conversion, whether quick or slow, often comes from finding ourselves in an unexpected place, negotiating a different frame of reference in which our existing theological explanations of the world, of ourselves, and of God do not quite work. For me it was many years as a local pastor involved with a nearby campus for young people with disabling neurological conditions that demanded a revisiting of the gospel and a new encounter with Jesus and with the cross that stands at the center of that gospel. Those young peoples' lives and experiences and the world's various responses to them threw into relief all the moral and contingent complexity and frailty of human life. Such experiences demanded an answer to what place there was for these young people, and more widely for disability, in this gospel that talked of salvation, healing, sin, cross, and resurrection. What makes all of this a kind of conversion is also that it does not involve stepping into another frame of reference, doing some work, then stepping back, having found something interesting to append to our list of doctrinal ideas. Instead, it involves permanent change. Our own personal frame of reference can never go back to what it was. In that way, it is a work of the Holy Spirit, not just of theology.

This might sound like mere philosophical reflection, but it contains one of the most important points to be made in this whole investigation into disability theology and the cross of Christ. The person and work of Jesus, especially the atonement secured by God through Jesus on the cross, are central to the Christian gospel. To ask about disability theology and the cross is absolutely not to ask whether there is a particular way of understanding this atonement that seems useful just within a defined disability frame of reference. It is not to ask how our existing ideas of atonement, formulated in the context of people whose bodies and brains happen to fall within the statistical majority, might be extended by some theological maneuver or concession when called upon to say something about the special case of disability. To put it bluntly, there is no intention to retrofit the atonement with a ramp, ready to be deployed when requested.

We have little in the way of a convincing response to those young people unless, instead, our main account of the gospel inherently includes them from the start without any special maneuver or accommodation. That means permanently changing our frame of reference to one where our main account of the atonement at the cross inherently includes all of humanity, together with all its variety, including what we call disability. Rather than finding a way to make our account of the cross and the atonement accessible or inclusive, it is a matter of discovering that the cross of Jesus Christ and God's saving work there are fundamentally, inherently so. Moving to that different frame of reference, undergoing that kind of conversion, involves a willingness to move away from a view that what we choose to identify as disability can only be understood as a result of the fall of humankind and therefore a result of sin.

That willingness is what took the conversation right back to the point of examining what can be said about the nature of creation, God's *creatio ex nihilo*. Recognizing that creation is not perfect as God is perfect entails recognizing that creation contains both moral risk, the risk of sin for which there is human culpability, and a wider contingency that allows creation to include the unexpected, accident, variety, and, in the present case, what we call disability. That allows us to recognize that not only sin in the sense of moral failure, but also this much wider contingency, can be a source of distress and suffering and have the effect of alienating us from God and from others. Contingency can of course also be a source of joy and fulfillment. God's willingness to participate in all of that risk and contingency, as he loves and accompanies his creation, finds its most profound expression in Jesus. In the flesh of the incarnation, God participates in and represents all flesh, not an idealized version but flesh as it is. Jesus' life and ministry unfold in a world of sin and of contingency. And at the cross God, in Jesus, participates most profoundly, once for all, in our alienation from him and from each other. Sin and its alienating effects are dealt with, but so also is all else that alienates us and breaks those relationships. All that alienates, God deals with, giving it a place within himself without being diminished by it. All that is good, he preserves and fulfills through the resurrection.

This is atonement-as-participation. What has been discovered about it along the way is perhaps best summarized in the following few statements. Disrupted and reformed in this way, our main account of the cross and the atonement become inherently inclusive of all people, without any need to extend it to disability as a special case. Atonement-as-participation allows the cross of Christ, as the cornerstone of Christian faith, to take its place as the firmest foundation from which the themes and objectives of current disability theology can best argue their case. In each area of disability theology there is creative and innovative work underway, all of which is better underpinned by an inherently inclusive understanding of the cross. Atonement-as-participation provides the best foundation for a theology of healing, since it opens up a space in which disability, illness, sin, and healing can be addressed without conflating disability and illness with sin. Lastly, this is not a break with the way the gospel, centered on the cross, is and has been shared week by week in the life of the church. Instead it is the discovery that the gospel, rather than proving awkward in the context of disability, is inherently inclusive. And the ways the cross has been described and explained, using the models of sacrifice, justice, and victory, and all the treasures of biblical metaphorical resource they open up, continue to be as effective as ever as models of God's atonement-as-participation.

A WEALTH OF IMPLICATIONS

When atonement-as-participation becomes the way of understanding God's initiative at the cross, it must necessarily have far-reaching implications for the life of the church. Rather than trying to find a convincing argument for including those with disabilities within the life of this gospel-shaped fellowship, we discover that they are already at the center of it, waiting for the rest of us to join in. Hopefully, what has been communicated here is that the church's response to disability does not best begin by turning immediately and only to overcoming problems of physical access (important though that is) but by asking what place people with disabilities have in the very roots and foundations of the gospel. What we think about the cross, and about the sort of reconciliation, freedom, and forgiveness that was secured for us there by Jesus, must surely shape every aspect of the church, its Christian faith, and its life. Those assumptions about the cross are inevitably shared whenever we worship together and celebrate the Eucharist, whenever we read or preach from the Scriptures, get involved in healing prayer, prepare for baptism, or pursue lifelong discipleship. And that life of the church extends into the world as the church joins in with the mission of God. The church is called to be a foretaste of the kingdom of God in the world and to model the life of that kingdom, shaped by Jesus, the cross, the resurrection, and the hope of new creation. Again, the way the church appears to the world, and the way of living that it models, will inevitably be shaped by its understanding of Jesus and the cross. If the church is confident that that is fundamentally, inherently inclusive, it will show.

It is tempting to try to prescribe how this should look for every church. But to do so would be to fall into the trap of suggesting that all situations are much the same. Every life lived with disability is unique, and the lives and situations that find themselves labeled "disabled" vary extremely. Many have little in common with each other apart from the fact that they do not fall within a typical statistical range. In the same way, every church of whatever size will have within its fellowship, and within the wider community it serves, its own unique mixture of people, some of whom will have disabilities. That uniqueness and particularity cautions against sweeping prescription. Yet there are some opening comments that are worth making about the implications for important dimensions of church life of having as a default a well-founded confidence that the cross and the gospel are inherently inclusive.

The church's celebration of Communion, the Eucharist, is a good place to begin. It is a dramatic, vivid, ongoing celebration of the cross of Christ and what it says about the cross and about Jesus shapes the life of the church. The challenge is this: that perhaps we have not really shared Communion unless its starting point has been the inclusion of all before the cross that Communion points to. From the comments earlier on the theology of access, the cross provides access to God, to the Holy of Holies, to salvation, and to the new creation and is the ground for all other assertions of access and inclusion. If the cross is inherently inclusive, then to have genuinely celebrated it at the Eucharist, that celebration must have been undertaken in a way that begins with accessibility for those who are no longer a "special case" but who are at the center of the fellowship, those with disabilities. How that looks will vary with each church situation, its fellowship and community. But even if in some churches there are for now few physically present who have disabilities, the inclusion of the variety of ability in the fabric of the celebration, its words and actions, will say something profound and convincing about what is celebrated there: that at the cross God participated in and dealt with not only moral sins but everything that alienates us from him and from each other.

The implications for how we share Communion logically extend into the rest of worship, when the church gathers as the body of Christ. Many churches already provide very good worship opportunities for people with a range of disabilities in their own context. Doing so has allowed for a freedom to worship in ways not necessarily possible in other church services. However, the same challenge applies as to Communion: that we have perhaps not really worshipped unless that worship has explicitly and confidently presumed that it is for all who wish to respond to God. If we are worshipping God, who is most clearly revealed in Jesus, who for the salvation of the world went to the cross and rose on the third day, then the inherently inclusive nature of the person of Jesus and the cross will be reflected in the shape of our worship. This has all sorts of ramifications for organizing church gatherings that are not worked out in detail here. Not least of these will come from the presumption that the leadership of worship, indeed of the church, should also reflect the whole variety of impairment and nonimpairment. This is not to suggest an end to particular worship events for people with particular disabilities. Rather, the presumption of the inclusiveness of Christ of the cross means that, like any service, these particular ones are also events for the whole church that happen to be led by those with disabilities. At those times those with disabilities are leading the rest and sharing the gifts of the Holy Spirit with the wider church that needs to learn how to receive both in those events and at other times. Again, even if there are, for now, not very many with disabilities in a particular church, weaving that presumption of inclusion into the fabric of the words and actions of worship is a sound place to begin to change.

Within worship more generally there is also the matter of prayer for healing and the conduct of healing ministries. Much has already been said about the relationship between sickness, disability, sin, the cross, and healing. Much has also been said about how that relates to the biblical healing narratives, particularly in the Gospels. Prayer for healing rests its case before God on the power of the cross and the resurrection. The same Holy Spirit at work in Jesus' taking all that is alienating to himself, overcoming death, and preserving all that is good through the resurrection is invited to be at work in our own lives. But such ministry has foundered on the unhelpful conflation of disability and sin and on the lack of differentiation between disability and sickness or between the variety of humanity and what truly alienates us from God and prevents our flourishing. Its failure to differentiate effectively has led it to assume there is a failure of faith when those looking for healing have not experienced what such healing was expected to entail. Starting instead from a place that recognizes both moral sin and a wider contingency in the world, all of which is addressed by God at the cross, allows a confidence within a healing prayer ministry that ultimately God will deal with all that is alienating. Importantly, in doing so it frees us from the burden of dictating in advance what that ought to look like and of assuming failure where those expectations are not met all at once.

From there, perhaps the next place to visit is reading and preaching all of Scripture, not just the healing narratives. For Christians the cross gives the deepest meaning to the whole of the Bible. Confidence that the cross is inherently inclusive leads to a reading of the Bible that assumes an inherent inclusivity in how human beings stand before God, even if the culture in which the text was originally embedded needs to be examined carefully in that light. More practically, though, applying the same challenge as above: we have perhaps not really read Scripture until we have listened to the voices of readers who are not like us, in the present case those who have disabilities. The inclusiveness of the cross as our interpretative compass demands that what the Word of God speaks into a life lived with disability is as much part of its meaning as what it speaks into any life. At its simplest, preaching by those with disabilities is as crucial as any other. So is seeking out the insights of our brothers and sisters with disabilities in coming to grips with the Bible in the first place.

Lastly in these brief comments, for each Christian and the part he or she plays in the body of Christ, there is the question of discipleship. This is how as individuals and groups we go about growing, intentionally and through being open to the work of the Holy Spirit, into the people we are called by God to be. Such discipleship encompasses everything that has been said here, since it is our encounter with Jesus and the cross that, one way or another, has started us on that path. The way we see the cross, where Jesus is most vividly revealed, will shape how we grow and how Jesus and the cross are in turn reflected into the world through our own lives. The challenge here is perhaps this: to ask how we can truly grow as Christians, created in God's image and recreated by his inherently inclusive initiative at the cross if we do not also seek out as friends those who are included there and who are different from us. Our choice of friends, recognizing all its complexities and that we have closer and wider friendship groups, will reveal to what extent the inclusiveness of the cross has seeped into the fabric of our lives. In that way, people with and without disabilities truly befriending one another becomes a celebration of the gospel. It becomes a celebration of the whole of humanity for whom the Word was made flesh; for whom Jesus said to his Father, "not my will, but yours be done"; for whom he remained faithful to the last on the cross; for whom his death tore the curtain in the temple, opening the way to the Holy of Holies; for whom he lay cold in the tomb, rose on the third day, ascended, poured out the Holy Spirit on all flesh; and for whom he will return. And all of this is rendered inclusive and accessible by Jesus' inherently inclusive, accessible atonement at the cross.

Notes

PREFACE

1 Language, and the choosing of terms, can be fraught with danger. This book will adopt the terms "disability" and "people with disabilities." "Disability" is used to denote both the phenomenon of impairment of whatever sort and the lived experience of the person who has that impairment. "People with disabilities" reflects a preference to acknowledge the full personhood of any individual before discussion of an impairment. These terms also seem to be in keeping with present mainstream usage across the literature and in practice.

INTRODUCTION

1 From the opening reflection on Luther's statement that *crux probat omnia* in Jürgen Moltmann, *The Crucified God: The Cross of Christ as the Foundation and Criticism of Christian Theology*, trans. R. A. Wilson and John Bowden (London: SCM Press, 1974), 1.

2 For example, a recently published compendium comprising over one hundred articles and essays on the atonement contains none that addresses matters of disability. See Adam J. Johnson, ed., *T&T Clark Companion to Atonement* (London: Bloomsbury T&T Clark, 2017).

3 In his book focused on the crucifixion, Tom Wright makes the point that, although a full account includes resurrection, ascension, ultimate resurrection of all, and renewal of creation, "we must still insist that it is proper, necessary and vital to ask: By six o'clock on the first Good Friday evening, what had changed and how had that happened?" See N. T. Wright, *The Day the Revolution Began: Rethinking the Meaning of Jesus' Crucifixion* (London: SPCK, 2016), 169–70.

4 This phrase comes from an essay by Vernon White that explores in some depth the tension of this universal claim of atonement based on the particular event of the cross of Christ. White sets out his discussion of the central claim about the atonement for his

own purposes. His objective is to find an explanation for the claim that the event of the cross is effective across all time and space that to him seems both theologically and philosophically satisfying. Ultimately, White locates that in the experience of incarnation, temptation, suffering, and death equipping God with a moral authority to overcome those things. See Vernon White, *Atonement and Incarnation: An Essay in Universalism and Particularity* (Cambridge: Cambridge University Press, 1991), 10.

5 An example of writing at that end of the spectrum would be John Hick and Paul F. Knitter, eds., *The Myth of Christian Uniqueness* (London: SCM Press, 1988).

6 Nancy Eiesland argues strongly for this. See, for an example, Nancy L. Eiesland, *The Disabled God: Toward a Liberatory Theology of Disability* (Nashville: Abingdon, 1994), 90.

7 An extensive clinical taxonomy can be found in the work of the World Health Organization (WHO). These documents are intended to bring order to the diagnosis and classification of clinical situations across varied geographies and populations. They are extremely detailed and are kept constantly under review. See WHO, *International Classification of Diseases (ICD) version 10* (Geneva: WHO, 2010); WHO, *International Classification of Functioning, Disability and Health (ICF)* (Geneva: WHO, 2001); and WHO, *How to Use the ICF: A Practical Manual Exposure Draft for Comment, October 2013* (Geneva: WHO, 2013).

8 On the whole, the WHO's ICD/ICF approach has not been adopted or supported by people with disabilities and those organizations supporting them. Despite improvements, they are still regarded as presenting an overwhelmingly negative, medicalized picture of disability. See Jerome Bickenbach, "The International Classification of Functioning, Disability and Health and Its Relationship to Disability Studies," in *Routledge Handbook of Disability Studies*, ed. N. Watson et al. (Abingdon: Routledge, 2012), 51–66.

9 Where those testimonies are shared, the names of those involved have been changed.

1 DISABILITY THEOLOGY AND THE CROSS

1 Kenneth Surin makes the point that what he calls the first-order discourse is the one that allows the lived experience of the person with (in the present case) a disability to be articulated and explored and the questions, whether theological or practical, that it raises to be listened to without presuming that we have answers, or that God can be justified in the face of them. The second-order discourse is what is attempted in this book, being a theological response to that first-order discourse. See Kenneth Surin, *Theology and the Problem of Evil* (Oxford: Blackwell, 1986), 149–54.

2 There are several detailed reviews of the historical development of disability theology. For example, Eiesland, *The Disabled God*; William C. Gaventa, *Disability and Spirituality: Recovering Wholeness* (Waco, Tex.: Baylor University Press, 2018), ch. 1. There is also an insightful review of the much longer history of Christian theological engagement with disability in *Disability in the Christian Tradition: A Reader*, ed. Brian Brock and John Swinton (Grand Rapids: Eerdmans, 2012).

3 A classic sociological text on this view is Michael Oliver, *The Politics of Disablement*, Critical Texts in Social Work and the Welfare State (Basingstoke: MacMillan, 1990).

John Swinton adds a further dimension to this argument with the idea that attitudes to disability have also developed negatively with changing concepts of time and evolution as well as industrial productivity. See John Swinton, *Becoming Friends of Time: Disability, Timefullness and Gentle Discipleship* (London: SCM Press, 2017), 39–44.

4 Oliver, *Politics of Disablement*, xi.

5 The balance being struck is with what would be called a realist view of disability. That view would argue that the social model is valid but too limited. Any situation of disability has both "brute facts," which exist independently of how we react to them, and "institutional facts," which depend on language and social attitudes. To take the example of a person with Down syndrome, a brute fact is the existence of a particular chromosome. An institutional fact is the statement that that person has Down syndrome. This latter fact depends on language and a particular institutional understanding of the expectations of a human life and of the purpose or function of elements of the human body, but it does not affect the existence of the chromosome. See Simo Vehmas and Pekka Mäkelä, "The Ontology of Disability and Impairment: A Discussion of the Natural and Social Features," in *Arguing about Disability: Philosophical Perspectives*, ed. Simo Vehmas et al. (Abingdon: Routledge, 2009), 42–56 (47–49).

6 There are other voices on this matter of "models" of disability. For example, Deborah Beth Creamer suggests that both medical and social models have the weakness that each tries to be an explanation for the whole picture and thus fails to grasp the complexity of disability. Creamer suggests a "limits model" which starts with the variety of human limitations in ability as a norm and identifies any abilities we do have as gifts, which she considers to be a more inherently inclusive approach. See Deborah Beth Creamer, *Disability and Christian Theology: Embodied Limits and Constructive Possibilities* (Oxford: Oxford University Press, 2009), 93–96.

7 Eiesland's suggestion of God in such a wheelchair is not proposed as a sort of theological thought experiment but arises through the recounting of a powerful personal epiphany. See Eiesland, *The Disabled God*, 89.

8 A slightly different approach to the "disabled God" concept is that of Amanda Shao Tan. Tan's suggestion is that God's identification with the limitations of all humanity comes through the incarnation, not just through retaining the marks of the crucifixion. God limited himself, one might say disabled himself, by becoming a human person. Not only that, he became lowly and ultimately ostracized, despised, degraded, humiliated, and, on the cross, physically incapacitated. See Amanda Shao Tan, "The Disabled Christ," *Transformation* 15, no. 4 (1998): 8–14 (11).

9 Eiesland makes the point herself that she has focused mainly on physical disabilities in her reflections on disability in God. See Eiesland, *The Disabled God*, 94.

10 This argument is explored and developed most eloquently in Hans S. Reinders, *Receiving the Gift of Friendship: Profound Disability, Theological Anthropology and Ethics* (Grand Rapids: Eerdmans, 2008).

11 Reynolds characterizes this as "the cult of normalcy." See Thomas E. Reynolds, *Vulnerable Communion: A Theology of Disability and Hospitality* (Grand Rapids: Brazos, 2008), 98.

12 Reynolds, *Vulnerable Communion*, 187.

13 Jean Vanier, *Essential Writings*, ed. Carolyn Whitney-Brown (Maryknoll, N.Y.: Orbis Books, 2008), 103.

14 Jean Vanier, *Becoming Human* (London: Darton, Longman and Todd, 1999), 89.

15 Vanier, *Essential Writings*, 55.

16 Frances Young, *Face to Face: A Narrative Essay in the Theology of Suffering* (Edinburgh: T&T Clark, 1990), 143.

17 Reinders, *Receiving the Gift of Friendship*, 216.

18 David A. Pailin, *A Gentle Touch: From a Theology of Handicap to a Theology of Human Being* (London: SPCK, 1992), 102–5. Also Wayne Morris, "Transforming Able-Bodied

Normativity: The Wounded Christ and Human Vulnerability," *Irish Theological Quarterly* 78, no. 3 (2013): 231–43 (242), http://itq.sagepub.com/content/78/3/231.full.pdf+html.

19 This aspect of the revelatory vocation of disability is raised by Stanley Hauerwas in relation to people with intellectual disabilities in particular. See Stanley Hauerwas, *Suffering Presence: Theological Reflections on Medicine, the Mentally Handicapped, and the Church* (Edinburgh: T&T Clark, 1988), 175–78.

The parable of the sheep and the goats (Matt 25:31-46) is also explored in Amos Yong, *The Bible, Disability, and the Church: A New Vision of the People of God* (Grand Rapids: Eerdmans, 2011), 136–42.

20 The idea of this vocation of disability is also explored in some depth by Frances Young, writing about life with her son, Arthur, who was born with profound physical and intellectual disabilities. See Young, *Arthur's Call: A Journey of Faith in the Face of Severe Learning Disability* (London: SPCK, 2014), 150–58.

21 Yong, *Bible, Disability, and the Church*, 130–33.

22 As Reynolds sums up this objection: "There is no assimilation into normalcy in the new life to come." Reynolds, *Vulnerable Communion*, 208.

23 The development and personal experience of prenatal testing and the culture surrounding it is examined in detail in Brian Brock, *Wondrously Wounded: Theology, Disability and the Body of Christ* (Waco, Tex.: Baylor University Press, 2019), 59-96.

24 It is not uncommon to link this discussion to an underlying tendency toward a eugenic attitude in society generally. See Agneta Sutton, *Christian Bioethics: A Guide for the Perplexed* (London: T&T Clark, 2008), 89.

25 For example, Hauerwas, *Suffering Presence*, 68.

26 The experience of church in the context of autism is also reflected on in John Gillibrand, *Disabled Church—Disabled Society: The Implications of Autism for Philosophy, Theology and Politics* (London: Jessica Kingsley, 2010).

27 A useful gathering together of the elements that have made up a theology of access to date is provided by Jennie Weiss Block. Her own particular emphasis is on Jesus as the "copious host" who offers the outsider the right to become the insider. See Jennie Weiss Block, *Copious Hosting: A Theology of Access for People with Disabilities* (New York: Continuum, 2002).

28 Reinders, *Receiving the Gift of Friendship*, 283–84.

29 Block, *Copious Hosting*, 138.

30 Amos Yong, *Theology and Down Syndrome* (Waco, Tex.: Baylor University Press, 2007), 201.

31 There are a variety of views as to what Paul meant by the "weaker members" of the body. Brock, for example, resists the view that it is a reference to internal organs, suggesting Paul is usurping the typical contemporary practice of using the body as an analogy of empire, with a controlling inner organ. See Brian Brock, "Theologizing Inclusion: 1 Corinthians 12 and the Politics of the Body of Christ," *Journal of Religion, Disability and Health* 15 (2011): 351–76 (361–62), http://dx.doi.org/10.1080/15228967.2011.620389.

32 Hauerwas, *Suffering Presence*, 178.

33 Eiesland, for example, describes it as often being "a ritual of exclusion and degradation." See Eiesland, *The Disabled God*, 113.

34 Block communicates this by narrating an imaginary celebration of the Eucharist and asking why various people with disabilities seem not to be present. See Block, *Copious Hosting*, 115.

35 Gillibrand adds one of the closest connections to the atonement in this regard. He suggests that on the cross all the apparent ability, gifting, and purpose of Jesus' life and ministry end in a death which seems pointless and that at that moment "meaning and meaninglessness are fused." This allows Gillibrand to see in his son's disability (autism) both a meaninglessness and at the same time profound meaning in a connection between salvation and vulnerability, which adds impetus to his concern for access, in particular in his son's case to the connection provided through participation in the Eucharist. See Gillibrand, *Disabled Church—Disabled Society*, 104.

36 Yong, *Bible, Disability, and the Church*, 6.

37 Yong, *Bible, Disability, and the Church*, 13.

38 An excellent example of essays of this type is the collection in Candida R. Moss and Jeremy Schipper, eds., *Disability Studies and Biblical Literature* (New York: Palgrave Macmillan, 2011).

39 John Hull, *In the Beginning There Was Darkness* (London: SCM Press, 2001), 165.

40 Roy McCloughry and Wayne Morris, *Making a World of Difference: Christian Reflections on Disability* (London: SPCK, 2002), 64.

41 I. Howard Marshall, *The Gospel of Luke: A Commentary on the Greek Text*, The New International Greek Testament Commentary (Exeter: Paternoster, 1978), 314, 694. The translation of σέσωκέν as "saved" in Luke 7:50 appears quite consistently across Bible translations, for example, in the New International Version, New King James Bible, New Living Translation, and New Revised Standard Version. Its translation as "healed" or "made well" in Luke 18:42 appears in all of these apart from the New Revised Standard Version, which sticks with "saved" in that instance.

42 Yong, *Bible, Disability, and the Church*, 53.

43 Pailin, *Gentle Touch*, 128, 135.

44 Yong, *Theology and Down Syndrome*, 176–80.

45 Yong develops an overarching approach to his proposed disability-perspective systematic theology, which he calls "emergentist." This approach draws on the philosophical idea of emergence: that, for example, the range of human experience, properties, and abilities depends on the physical components and processes of our brains but cannot be reduced to those components and processes. Rather, we are more than the sum of our parts, though each of the parts is essential. For a summary of the philosophical development of the concept of emergence, see Timothy O'Connor and Hong You Wong, "Emergent Properties," in *The Stanford Encyclopedia of Philosophy*, ed. Edward N. Zalta, Spring 2012, http://plato.stanford.edu/archives/spr2012/entries/properties-emergent/.

46 Gillibrand, *Disabled Church—Disabled Society*, 146–47.

47 Frances Young, *Can These Dry Bones Live?* (London: SCM Press, 1982), 54.

48 Young, *Arthur's Call*, 119.

49 Frances Young, *God's Presence: A Contemporary Recapitulation of Early Christianity* (Cambridge: Cambridge University Press, 2013), 246.

50 Gould particularly argues against the formulation of a disability-perspective soteriology presented by Amos Yong. See James Barton Gould, "The Hope of Heavenly Healing of Disability Part 1: Theological Issues," in *Journal of Disability and Religion* 20 (2016): 317–34 (318), http://dx.doi.org/10.1080/23312521.2016.1239153.

51 Gould, "The Hope of Heavenly Healing of Disability Part 1," 324.

52 James Barton Gould, "The Hope of Heavenly Healing of Disability Part 2: Philosophical Issues," in *Journal of Disability and Religion* 21 (2017): 98–116 (104), http://dx.doi.org/10.1080/23312521.2016.1270177.
53 Gould, "Hope of Heavenly Healing of Disability Part 1," 331.
54 Gould, "Hope of Heavenly Healing of Disability Part 1," 325.

2 MAKING SENSE OF THE ATONEMENT

1 See, for example, the christological definition and its background in R. V. Sellers, *The Council of Chalcedon* (London: SPCK, 1953), 209–28.
2 John McIntyre, in his review of ideas of atonement, offers two possible reasons for this. It might be because for a long time there was no significant heresy surrounding the atonement to be refuted, as there was in Christology, and hence no pressure to undertake the work of developing a creedal statement as a defense of orthodoxy. Alternatively (or perhaps additionally) he suggests that the lack of soteriological theory could stem from the practice of the Eucharist. The drama of the atonement is acted out, with accompanying liturgical statements, each time the Eucharist is celebrated. Moreover, it is celebrated as something received from Jesus himself. Thus, soteriology becomes something we do, not just something we describe. McIntyre's observation that "the *plebs Dei* felt themselves to be under no constraint to investigate the matter in theological detail" is perhaps worth heeding should there be a temptation to make too much of our soteriological theory or to crown one model of the atonement over others. See John McIntyre, *The Shape of Soteriology* (Edinburgh: T&T Clark, 1992), 10–16.
3 Gustaf Aulén, *Christus Victor: An Historical Study of the Three Main Types of the Idea of the Atonement*, trans. A. G. Herbert (London: SPCK, 1931), 20–23.
4 Aulén, *Christus Victor*, 149.
5 Peter Schmiechen examines this possibility for ten ways of describing the atonement. He also suggests that each theological understanding of the atonement can lead to a different form of church. See Peter Schmiechen, *Saving Power: Theories of Atonement and Forms of the Church* (Grand Rapids: Eerdmans, 2005).
6 This analysis of the effects of Enlightenment trends in thinking, the corresponding argument in favor of an actual atonement, and recognition of the power of metaphorical language is eloquently set out in Colin E. Gunton, *The Actuality of Atonement: A Study of Metaphor, Rationality and the Christian Tradition* (London: T&T Clark, 1988).
7 Gunton particularly locates this move in theologians such as Schleiermacher. Gunton, *Actuality of Atonement*, 16.
8 A good example of this approach is found in F. W. Dillistone. He looks for parallels to the cross in ancient thought, drama, literature, Christian thinking, and wider human philosophy. Dillistone does not deny an objective atonement but suggests that it only takes on meaning for us when we can draw parallels with our own lives. F. W. Dillistone, *The Christian Understanding of Atonement* (Welwyn: James Nisbet, 1968).
9 Writing in 1988, Gunton here is perhaps referring indirectly to John Stott's book *The Cross of Christ*, published two years earlier and influential at a popular level. Stott presents penal substitution as the one governing model, based on the wrath of the sovereign God against human sin coupled with the loving self-substitution of God on the cross to take the penalty for the related human guilt. Stott emphasizes God's self-substitution as a way of addressing criticism that this approach drives a wedge between God the Father and God the Son. In Stott's scheme, any other image, model, or language around the

atonement is subordinated to the forensic model of penal substitution. See John Stott, *The Cross of Christ* (Leicester: InterVarsity, 1986), 168.

10 Adam Johnson has reviewed recent movements in debates around the atonement. One is away from what he sees as rather caricatured treatment of Abelard and Anselm and their ideas of moral influence or satisfaction. Another is away from the sort of assumption that appears to be held by Aulén, at least as it comes across from Christus Victor, that there ought to be one main, or best, model or theory. There is also a movement toward expressing sacrifice less in terms of the taking on of a penalty and more in terms of cleansing from sin. He notes an increasing openness to ideas of theosis arising from Eastern Orthodox studies, as well as to insights from work on covenant and on feminist, womanist, and nonviolent critiques. No direct link with theological thinking on disability is made, however. See Adam J. Johnson, "Atonement: The Shape and State of the Doctrine," in *T&T Clark Companion to Atonement*, ed. Adam J. Johnson (London: Bloomsbury T&T Clark, 2017), 1–17.

11 Colin Gunton argues that any metaphorical language used in relation to the atonement should be taken from the New Testament, where it is already being used theologically. See Gunton, *Actuality of Atonement*, 37, 48.

12 Gunton, *Actuality of Atonement*, 34.

13 G. B. Caird, *The Language and Imagery of the Bible* (London: Duckworth, 1980), 144.

14 Janet Martin Soskice, *Metaphor and Religious Language* (Oxford: Oxford University Press, 1985), 94 (emphasis original).

15 The discussion here draws particularly on work by Janet Martin Soskice, Paul Ricoeur, and Sallie McFague, all of whom rely at various points on principles set out by Max Black in the 1960s.

16 Soskice, *Metaphor*, 15 (emphasis original).

17 Sallie McFague, *Speaking in Parables: A Study in Metaphor and Theology* (London: SCM Press, 2002), xvii.

18 Paul Ricoeur, *The Rule of Metaphor: The Creation of Meaning in Language*, trans. Robert Czerny et al. (Abingdon: Routledge Classics, 2003), 292.

19 McIntyre calls these the positive and negative analogies. The positive analogy recognizes the correspondence between metaphor and subject, and the negative analogy recognizes the extent to which the two do not correspond. See McIntyre, *Shape of Soteriology*, 75–78.

20 Gunton, *Actuality of Atonement*, 51.

21 Max Black, *Models and Metaphors: Studies in Language and Philosophy* (Ithaca, N.Y.: Cornell University Press, 1962), 33.

22 Ian G. Barbour, *Myths, Models and Paradigms* (New York: Harper & Row, 1974), 27.

23 Ricoeur, *Rule of Metaphor*, 284–85.

24 Barbour, *Myths, Models and Paradigms*, 32.

25 To take three examples, Aulén complained that abstract objective and subjective theories had obscured the true drama, found in the "classic" idea of Christus Victor. Frances Young concludes that theories based on satisfaction, penalty, moral influence, and victory all fail the gospel drama in some way, and Wright, more recently, expresses a desire to move away from theories that fail to listen closely enough to the gospel as historical narrative. See Aulén, *Christus Victor*, 17-31; Young, *Can These Dry Bones Live*, 22–39; and Wright, *Day the Revolution Began*, 196–98.

26 For example, having objected to models or theories in general, Wright's own presentation of the atonement is couched in the language of victory and sacrifice for the forgiveness of sins.

27 Other proposals exist for ways of working with terms like model, theory, and metaphor. For example, as Oliver Crisp has set it out, a model is a simplified description of something that is complex, and a model contains simple ideas, called motifs or metaphors, as elements. Motifs and metaphors are also elements of a doctrine, which is a comprehensive account of a part of Christian teaching. A doctrine of atonement is expected to contain a mechanism by which the atonement takes place. There are also theories. While a model is a simplified presentation of facts, a theory is an overall explanation of them. There is much of interest in this account, but the resulting matrix of terms and relationships seems too complex to work with. The analysis is not particularly aligned with the wider scholarship on the functioning of metaphorical language, nor does it explore the significance of limits of correspondence. See Oliver D. Crisp, "Methodological Issues in Approaching the Atonement," in *T&T Clark Companion to Atonement*, ed. Adam J. Johnson (London: Bloomsbury T&T Clark, 2017), 315–33.

Similar comments apply to a proposal from Peter Schmiechen. He suggests ten theories of the atonement. Each theory is built on an image, such as the lamb or vine, which has symbolic value. To this he adds theological value, which says something of God; contextual value (its connection with people); and evangelical value (its ability to convey the gospel). These are certainly helpful ideas, but again there is no mention of the way metaphor operates or of limits of correspondence, making it difficult to see the boundaries of the claims being made. See Schmiechen, *Saving Power*, 5.

28 The enduring nature of these three models is demonstrated in reviews of atonement thinking by, for example, Colin Gunton and Paul Fiddes. Gunton accepts that victory is useful because it presents the atonement as drama, rather than as a transaction. Justice is also useful but can go astray when it becomes too individualistic or when we lose sight of the fact that biblical justice concerns the covenant with God, rather than the Western idea of a transaction or contract. For Gunton, however, the notion of sacrifice brings us closest to the heart of the matter, since it so directly addresses covenant, relationship, and grace. Fiddes also finds that these three have become the broadly dominant models for speaking objectively about the cross but points out the need to integrate these with a stronger account of the subjective element. See Gunton, *Actuality of Atonement*, 133; and Paul Fiddes, *Past Event and Present Salvation: The Christian Idea of Atonement* (London: Darton, Longman & Todd, 1989), 26.

29 McIntyre, in contrast, takes eleven different terms that are used in Scripture and treats them all as representing individual models of the atonement. His analysis does not distinguish the fact that some of these function as a whole model and others are more convincing as an individual metaphorical element of a model. McIntyre, *Shape of Soteriology*, 26.

30 Ben Pugh, in his review of atonement models, adds the idea of recapitulation, or the reversal of the sin of Adam, favored by Irenaeus. In recapitulation Jesus goes over all the ground on which Adam, and we who are "in Adam," have failed and remain faithful. Pugh suggests that this is a form of Christus Victor. The recapitulation idea seems less prevalent in more recent debate. Wiles also includes it in his review but concludes that it only remains relevant as long as the sin of Adam is conceived as a particular historical event with universal ramifications, reversed by the parallel particular historical event of

the cross. In more recent times, when Adam is regarded more as an incisive description of the human predicament, dealing with the pervasiveness of sin, the need to link two particular historical events falls away (a view with which Vernon White agrees). See Ben Pugh, *Atonement Theories: A Way through the Maze* (Cambridge: James Clarke, 2015), 25; Maurice Wiles, *The Remaking of Christian Doctrine* (London: SCM Press, 1974), 62–68; and White, *Atonement and Incarnation*, 26.

31 McIntyre, *Shape of Soteriology*, 69–73.

32 Soskice, *Metaphor*, 158.

33 Stott, *Cross of Christ*, 138.

34 Frances M. Young, *Construing the Cross: Type, Sign, Symbol, Word, Action* (London: SPCK, 2016), 31–32.

35 Gunton suggests that a change in role takes place at the resurrection, after which Jesus as priest is able to baptize with the Holy Spirit. This makes sense as regards the particular point about baptism with the Spirit, but it seems to miss the point pressed by Heb 7:27 that at the moment of sacrifice on the cross Jesus is already both sacrifice and high priest. See Gunton, *Actuality of Atonement*, 135.

36 Wright, *Day the Revolution Began*, 296.

37 Gunton, *Actuality of Atonement*, 112.

38 Caird, *Language and Imagery*, 156–59.

39 Gunton, *Actuality of Atonement*, 85–92.

40 This is a point explored in some depth by Michael Gorman, who argues that the concept of the atonement as the creation of a new covenant community, drawing on Old Testament covenant ideas, has been sadly neglected. Michael J. Gorman, "Effecting the New Covenant: A (Not So) New, New Testament Model for the Atonement," *Ex Auditu* 26 (2010): 26–59 (28).

41 Anselm, *Cur Deus Homo* 11, in *Basic Writings*, 2nd ed., trans. S. N. Deane (La Salle, Ill.: Open Court, 1974), 202.

42 Frances Young, for example, claims that Anselm's model did not appeal to Scripture but was developed as a philosophical reflection on the notion of legal justice and how it operated at the time. The idea has subsequently been related back to Scripture as it has been developed by others, and it could be said to have become scripturally based over time. There is scope to discuss further the comparative historical development of each of the models described. However, the discussion of them here is focused much more on how they are applied currently as interpretations of the atonement and how well they may or may not fare when examined from a disability perspective. See Young, *Can These Dry Bones Live*, 22.

43 A concise summary of the penal substitution idea, particularly as developed in the nineteenth century by Charles Hodge, and the biblical, legal, and ethical problems it presents is provided in Joel B. Green and Mark D. Baker, *Recovering the Scandal of the Cross: Atonement in New Testament and Contemporary Contexts* (Carlisle: Paternoster, 2000), 140–50.

44 While acknowledging its positive motives, Wright is deeply critical of the penal substitution mechanism that has resulted from it. He says this has become the idea that someone has to do something to make us good enough for God. The arrangement is that Jesus does the work of taking the punishment for our sin so that we are saved and go to heaven. Wright calls this a "works contract," which has smuggled in a subtle version of salvation by works. Wright, *Day the Revolution Began*, 299.

45 H. D. McDonald, *The New Testament Concept of the Atonement: The Gospel of the Calvary Event* (Cambridge: Lutterworth, 1994), 88–89.

46 The discussion here considers approaches taken to the atonement in the Western Christian tradition, which in terms of justice mostly focus on individual, or communal, guilt and innocence. Eastern cultures, which are based rather on notions of shame and honor, will inevitably interpret the atonement from that frame of reference. Such an Eastern viewpoint is not explored here, but a useful introduction to its impact on the interpretation of the atonement is provided in Timothy C. Tennent, *Theology in the Context of World Christianity* (Grand Rapids: Zondervan, 2007), 77–101.

47 Fiddes examines these "tyrants," concluding that each is in a way a corruption of something good. That even applies to death, which otherwise is a natural boundary to life. Fiddes, *Past Event and Present Salvation*, 114–25.

48 See McIntyre, *Shape of Soteriology*, 29; or Fiddes, *Past Event and Present Salvation*, 126.

49 This is a point particularly stressed by Gunton, who also suggests that the victory seen in this way is incomplete unless it carries over from the event of the cross into the ongoing life of the Christian and the church. Gunton, *Actuality of Atonement*, 62–77.

50 Paul Fiddes pursues this line of argument in some detail in response to the three prevailing models of sacrifice, justice, and victory being, on their own, too objective. Fiddes, *Past Event and Present Salvation*, 26.

51 Gunton, *Actuality of Atonement*, 161.

52 McIntyre, *Shape of Soteriology*, 49.

53 Alister McGrath, "The Moral Theory of the Atonement: An Historical and Theological Critique," *Scottish Journal of Theology* 38, no. 2 (1985): 205–20 (209), doi:10.1017/S0036930600041351.

54 Richard E. Weingard, *The Logic of Divine Love: A Critical Analysis of the Soteriology of Peter Abailard* (Oxford: Oxford University Press, 1970), 82.

55 Weingard, *Logic of Divine Love*, 150.

56 Fiddes, *Past Event and Present Salvation*, 140.

57 Updating New Testament language to express this restoration, Fiddes suggests that Paul's claim that "I have been crucified with Christ" (Gal 2:19) becomes "my ego is shattered by the crucifixion of Christ." This is what sets the self free from a state of endless self-justification to one of trusting in God. See Fiddes, *Past Event and Present Salvation*, 147.

3 SEEKING CONNECTIONS

1 The precise meaning of the laying of a hand, or hands, on the head of the sacrificial animal is not without some controversy. Milgrom suggests an identification of ownership, such that the spiritual benefits of the sacrifice are attributed to the correct worshipper. Rowley prefers an understanding of identification where the death of the animal represented a "spiritual death" of the offeror. Whichever is preferred, identification of victim with offeror remains the point. See Jacob Milgrom, *Leviticus 1–16: A New Translation and Commentary*, Anchor Bible 3 (New York: Doubleday, 1991), 150-53; and Howard H. Rowley, *The Meaning of Sacrifice in the Old Testament* (Manchester: John Rylands Library, 1950), 88.

2 The sacrificial language adopted by Paul for the atonement is explored by Bell, who links it to Paul's Christology in general as well as to the Levitical sacrificial system. Bell argues that Paul takes the idea of sacrificial identification and, in Rom 3:25 and 8:3 as well as

in 2 Cor 5:19-21, enlarges on it. The identification now operates in both directions: Jesus identifies with sinful humanity, such that humanity can identify with his sacrifice and resurrection. What was symbolic in the Old Testament system has now become "the most concrete reality." See Richard H. Bell, "Sacrifice and Christology in Paul," *Journal of Theological Studies* 53, no. 1 (2002): 1–27, www.jstor.org/stable/23969330.

3 John Dunhill has argued for a renewed understanding of sacrifice in Christian thinking by emphasizing its ordinariness in cultures where it is practiced. He has also argued for a closer connection between an understanding of sacrifice and more recent work on body theology. See John Dunhill, "Communicative Bodies and Economies of Grace: The Role of Sacrifice in the Christian Understanding of the Body," *Journal of Religion* 83, no. 1 (2003): 79–93.

4 Aulén, *Christus Victor*, 20–21.

5 Thomas Reynolds explores vulnerability as a basis for a theological understanding of disability and humanity as a whole. Reynolds, *Vulnerable Communion*, 208.

6 John Wimber and Kevin Springer, *Power Healing* (London: Hodder & Stoughton, 1986), 35.

7 John Wimber and Kevin Springer, *Power Evangelism: Signs and Wonders Today* (London: Hodder & Stoughton, 1985), 22.

8 Yong, *Theology and Down Syndrome*, 243.

9 The ideas from Professor Young reflected here have developed over the course of a number of publications. In many cases her writing explores the theology of the early church fathers and the relevance of their arguments for our contemporary theological thinking, as well as the theology of books of the New Testament. Those broader investigations are not particularly examined here but rather her ideas on the atonement, and on how we think theologically about disability, that emerge alongside that other work.

10 Young, *Face to Face*, 58.

11 Young, *Arthur's Call*, 119.

12 Young acknowledges that modern theologians expand the notion of sin from an individual to a corporate problem, a whole system that affects all people. However, she still considers this too restricted to the effects of intentional moral choice.

13 Young, *Can These Dry Bones Live?* 54–56.

14 Young, *Arthur's Call*, 117–18.

15 Young, *Construing the Cross*, 1–43.

16 Young, *Construing the Cross*, 22–30. Here Young is employing, but also critiquing, the mimetic concept of sacrifice and atonement developed by Rene Girard and others.

17 Young, *Arthur's Call*, 102.

18 Young identifies something of this connection in her review of the development of the creeds. She attributes to Athanasius "a sense that since God is the source of all, he must ultimately bear responsibility for the presence of evil in his creation" and does so at the cross. See Frances Young, *The Making of the Creeds* (London: SCM Press, 1991), 91.

19 Young, *Can These Cry Bones Live?* 58.

20 The significance of this point in Young's analysis is particularly highlighted in one of her contributions to a debate on the understanding of the incarnation. There she argues that it is important not to rush from cross to resurrection as if, appearing like some deus ex machina, the resurrection makes the tragedy of the cross turn out alright in the end because it proves that Jesus was God after all. Instead, for Young it matters that we recognize fully the presence of God in and with the suffering of Jesus on the cross. See Frances

M. Young, "Incarnation and Atonement: God Suffered and Died," in *Incarnation and Myth: The Debate Continued*, ed. Michael Goulder (London: SCM Press, 1979), 101–3.

21 Mary Schaefer Fast arrives at a similar point but from a study of Luther's theology of the cross. She suggests that one can deal with one's lot in life (or vocation, following Luther's notion, which Fast suggests might include that of disability) if one has a strong enough theology of the cross, where God is revealed in solidarity with all humankind. See Mary Schaefer Fast, "A Theology of Disability: Living as a Theologian of the Cross," *Journal of Religion, Disability and Health* 15 (2011): 414–30, http://dx.doi.org/10.1080/15228967.2011.620392.

22 Young, *Can These Dry Bones Live?* 62.

23 Frances M. Young, *Sacrifice and the Death of Christ*, repr. (London: Xpress Reprints, 1994), 82.

24 Young, *Arthur's Call*, 107–12.

25 Young, *Face to Face*, 143.

26 Young, *God's Presence*, 105–7.

4 ATONEMENT-AS-PARTICIPATION

1 For example, the sort of person who is "truly God and truly Man," or "begotten of the Father before the ages," or "like us in all respects, apart from sin." For the full Chalcedonian definition and background, see Sellers, *Council of Chalcedon*, 209–28.

2 Theories of knowledge and epistemology form an extensive field of inquiry and scholarship which is only hinted at in this brief summary. An excellent review of the shift in ideas of knowledge referred to here is provided by Anthony Balcomb. He particularly finds the roots of a phenomenological approach in Heidegger's concept of knowledge arising through "being-in" the world and also the study of "primal cultures." See Anthony Balcomb, "The Metaphysics of Participation: Exploring an Idea Whose Time Has Returned," *Journal of Theology for Southern Africa* 145 (2013): 18–34 (18).

3 The line of argument followed here takes various inputs from the work of Jürgen Moltmann, Eberhard Jüngel, and Paul Fiddes. They each develop aspects of what it might mean to speak of God's creation out of nothing and of the implications of that for contingency, risk, and suffering.

4 Jürgen Moltmann, *God in Creation: An Ecological Doctrine of Creation*, trans. Margaret Kohl (London: SCM Press, 1985), 9–15.

5 The Shekinah of God is itself an idea closely linked to that of *zimzum* (or *tsimtsum*) from Jewish kabbalistic thought. The idea of *zimzum* was introduced into Jewish mystical thinking in the sixteenth century by Isaac Luria, whose influence is explored in an account by Gershom Scholem. Luria began with questions such as "If God is 'all in all,' how can there be things that are not God?" and from there developed the idea of God's withdrawal, using earlier ideas of God's Shekinah. One aspect of *zimzum* is that God's withdrawal and the accompanying setting of boundaries carries with it an anticipation of the need for judgment (the correction and ordering of things). Scholem sees in this the original latent possibility of evil. Scholem regards Luria's concept of *zimzum* as a unique (and possibly the only) attempt at substantial articulation of creation out of nothing, which demonstrates the complexity and elusiveness of that seemingly simple formulation. See Gershom G. Scholem, *Major Trends in Jewish Mysticism* (London: Thames and Hudson, 1955), 260–64.

6 Jürgen Moltmann, "God's Kenosis in the Creation and Consummation of the World," in *The Work of Love: Creation and Kenosis*, ed. John Polkinghorne (London: SPCK, 2001), 137–51 (143).
7 Moltmann, *God in Creation*, 86.
8 A pantheistic interpretation would see each aspect of creation as a manifestation of God, rather than maintaining that God is other than creation yet participates intimately in it.
9 For Moltmann, whose theology was in many ways shaped by his experiences in World War II, this menacing aspect that moral sin adds to the nothingness threatening creation is brought into sharpest relief by the history of the Nazis and their concentration camps, such as Auschwitz.
10 Eberhard Jüngel pursues this line of thought. Part of his concern is to get away from arbitrary philosophical ideas of God as highest essence, or absolute causality, with attributes of infinitude and omnipotence. Instead, he suggests that there is a point where God, who is inherently creative, chooses to go out into nothingness and to have to do with the perishability that is our actual experience of life and death. See Eberhard Jüngel, *God as the Mystery of the World: On the Foundation of the Theology of the Crucified One in the Dispute between Theism and Atheism* (Edinburgh: T&T Clark, 1983), 184–85.
11 Jüngel, *God as the Mystery of the World*, 216.
12 Paul S. Fiddes, *The Creative Suffering of God*, new ed. (Oxford: Oxford University Press, 1992), 210–12.
13 Fiddes, *Creative Suffering of God*, 107–9.
14 Fiddes, *Creative Suffering of God*, 38–40. The impassibility of God has of course been the subject of much debate and can be a matter of some subtlety. Fiddes suggests that the worldview of the church fathers was influenced by Greek philosophical ideas that the changeability of the world pointed to an unchangeability of the perfect world of God. He compares this to the Enlightenment worldview of, say, the eighteenth century under which a rational theology cast the world as a machine and God as its remote designer. Under either way of thinking, impassibility could be maintained in a way that it cannot in the present context. Fiddes' argument should not be extrapolated to an assertion that disability theology is a mere artifact of a particular worldview; rather, a change in our concept of the world brings to light both presumptions and possibilities previously unexamined.
15 The tension between ideas of God's suffering, human suffering, and incarnation as the "involvement" of God is explored in Herbert McCabe, *God Matters* (London: Mowbray, 1987), 39–51.
16 This idea of the language of risk is explored very helpfully in Brian Brock's discussion of anomalous births and prenatal testing. See Brian Brock, *Wondrously Wounded: Theology, Disability, and the Body of Christ* (Waco, Tex.: Baylor University Press, 2019), 149–50.
17 Moltmann, *The Crucified God*, 277.
18 "My God, my God, why have you forsaken me?" See Matt 27:46; Mark 15:34.
19 Jüngel, *God as the Mystery of the World*, 219.
20 Paul Fiddes, with his affinity for a moral influence understanding of the atonement, adds to this that God's encounter with death in Jesus demonstrates his "participation in our estrangement," which prompts a real change in us, moving us to put our faith in him. See Fiddes, *Creative Suffering of God*, 266–67.
21 The approach of systematic theology has typically been to identify the two categories of moral evil and natural evil and either look for a relationship between each of these, sin

and the fall, or identify some other purpose behind natural evil. However, the discussion here presents a more nuanced argument, suggesting that this binary categorization as an approach to what the atonement addresses is too limited.

22 The term "explanation relativity" comes from work by the sociologist Alan Garfinkel. He set out to explore how we arrive at what we regard as valid explanations of phenomena within his particular field of sociology, but his proposals are equally relevant here. See Alan Garfinkel, *Forms of Explanation—Rethinking the Questions in Social Theory* (New Haven, Conn.: Yale University Press, 1981), 21–33.

23 Fiddes, *Participating in God*, 199.

24 To quote Moltmann, of Jesus: "His mission is fulfilled once he has been abandoned on the cross." See Moltmann, *Crucified God*, 205.

25 This idea of a deeply connected sinfulness that afflicts humanity is explored to great effect by Alistair McFadyen. He does so by deliberately choosing the two difficult cases of the Holocaust and child sexual abuse and asking whether such extreme and destructive behavior can be described and explained using just moral or psychological concepts and language, or whether theological concepts and language are necessary. His suggestion is that going back to St. Augustine's doctrine of original sin and considering the breadth of the idea that Augustine seemed to have in mind brings a way of understanding these phenomena that is not available to moral, psychological, or indeed some other theological approaches. See Alistair McFadyen, *Bound to Sin: Abuse, Holocaust and the Christian Doctrine of Sin* (Cambridge: Cambridge University Press, 2000).

26 McFadyen, *Bound to Sin*, 36.

27 McFadyen also examines the contribution of feminist theology to this discussion of sin and alienation. He finds that it usefully identifies, for example, pride as the pathology of sin in patriarchy. However, he concludes that the feminist critique is coy about the language of God himself. God is experienced in right relations but is not really distinct, so the analysis fails to reach what he considers to be the core of human alienation, being alienation from God. See McFadyen, *Bound to Sin*, 164–65.

28 Brian Brock brings a much-needed focus on human solidarity as one of the radical ideas of the early Christian church, demonstrating how it overturned prevailing ideas of hierarchy and patrimony as foundations of society in the Greek and Roman worlds. He points out that not least among its effects was to open the way for ideas like universal care for the sick and the founding of hospitals open to all people. Brock, *Wondrously Wounded*, 22–37.

29 Alistair McFadyen, *The Call to Personhood: A Christian Theory of the Individual in Social Relationships* (Cambridge: Cambridge University Press, 1990), 38-45.

30 For example, Eiesland, *The Disabled God*, 89–90.

31 A fascinating insight into Hull's experiences and his very practical theological reflections on those experiences is captured in a feature film released in 2016: *Notes on Blindness*, directed by Peter Middleton and James Spinney (Brooklyn, N.Y.: Oscilloscope, 2016).

32 Hull, *In the Beginning*, 1–3.

33 John M. Hull, "The Broken Body in a Broken World," in *Journal of Religion, Disability & Health* 7 (2004): 5–23 (9–11), http://dx.doi.org/10.1300/J095v07n04_02.

34 John Swinton explores these ways of knowing God in a paper where he contrasts a more participative, relational view of faith with his own Reformed background, which emphasized words, reason, and intellectual understanding. His insights come from his experience working as a psychiatric nurse. As he puts it, "Faith has a closer resemblance

to friendship than dogmatic assertion." See John Swinton, "Restoring the Image: Spirituality, Faith and Cognitive Disability," in *Journal of Religion and Health* 36, no.1 (1997): 21–27 (25).

35 Swinton develops these thoughts further in a later article, where he adds insights from the contemplative tradition (knowing God through loving him) and the liberationist tradition (recognizing the presence of God in actions of social justice). See John Swinton, "Known by God," in *The Paradox of Disability: Responses to Jean Vanier and L'Arche Communities from Theology and the Sciences*, ed. Hans S. Reinders (Grand Rapids: Eerdmans, 2010), 140–53.

36 A connection can also be made here with the idea of "body theology." Nancy Eiesland and others have suggested that our bodies and bodily experience should be seen as a source of theological insight. Attractive as that idea is, hitherto it has not moved much beyond an assertion that Jesus' impaired crucified body and the wounds of the cross on his resurrected body reveal a solidarity with human impaired bodies. The concepts discussed here, of the atonement as God's most intimate, once-for-all participation in humanity as it is, which can be apprehended and participated in through affective forms of knowledge, gathered not just intellectually but through the whole experience of the person, would seem to provide a more solid foundation from which that idea of a body theology might be developed further.

37 The doctrine of accommodation is explored in this way in Jill Harshaw, "Finding Accommodation: Spirituality and People with Profound Intellectual Disabilities," in *Journal of Disability and Religion* 20 (2016): 140–53 (143), http://dx.doi.org/10.1080/23312521.2016.1203694. Harshaw provides a particular example of the presumption that people with intellectual impairment are incapable of developing a spiritual life in the following paper: Peter Birchenall and Mary Birchenall, "Caring for Mentally Handicapped People: The Community and the Church," in *Professional Nurse* 1, no. 6 (1986): 150.

38 Harshaw, "Finding Accommodation," 145.

39 John Swinton et al., "Whose Story Am I? Redescribing Profound Intellectual Disability in the Kingdom of God," in *Journal of Religion, Disability and Health* 15 (2011): 5–19 (14), http://dx.doi.org/10.1080/15228967.2011.539337.

40 A point made rather sharply by Stanley Hauerwas: Hauerwas, *Suffering Presence*, 178.

5 THE CROSS AS THE FOUNDATION FOR DISABILITY THEOLOGY

1 Taken from the subtitle of Moltmann, *The Crucified God*.

2 Eiesland, *The Disabled God*, 101.

3 The ecclesial point is also explored by John Swinton in an article about his friend Stephen, who has learning disabilities. Swinton challenges the church to understand Stephen's life with his disabilities as an authentic form of human existence. See John Swinton, "Building a Church for Strangers," in *Journal of Religion, Disability and Health* 4 (2001): 25–63 (48), http://dx.doi.org/10.1300/J095v04n04_03.

4 Nancy Eiesland, again, famously pressed that point of the image of God and God's identification with those with impairments further by asking whether we could envisage a disabled God. See Eiesland, *The Disabled God*, 89.

5 Reinders, *Receiving the Gift of Friendship*, 273–75.

6 Reinders, *Receiving the Gift of Friendship*, 313–14. Reinders touches only briefly on the cross as this public outworking. It is not the focus of his argument.

7 The point is made particularly by Frances Young, as part of her argument that disability reveals, among other things, the corporate nature of Adam, Christ, and the image of God. See Young, *God's Presence*, 174–75.

8 Young, *Making of the Creeds*, 84.

9 Yong, *Bible, Disability, and the Church*, 133.

10 See for example Joel B. Green, *The Gospel of Luke*, The New International Commentary on the New Testament (Grand Rapids: Eerdmans, 1997), 554–63.

11 For example, Paul's exploration of the body of Christ in 1 Cor explicitly includes being baptized into that body (12:13) and sharing in that body at the Eucharist (10:16).

12 For example, the advocacy organization Disability Rights UK, as might be expected, uses language of both rights and participation in its literature. Its vision is "of a society where everyone with lived experience of disability or health conditions can participate equally as full citizens," and it commits to "promote the rights of disabled people in all our work and actions." See https://www.disabilityrightsuk.org/about-us/our-customer-charter. The question here is whether, from a theological point of view, what is sought in the former is really what is secured by the latter.

13 Nancy Eiesland adopts this as her model in her discussion of disability and God. See Eiesland, *The Disabled God*, ch. 3.

14 Reinders, *Receiving the Gift of Friendship*, 283–84.

15 For further discussion of the problems of such language, see Thomas E. Reynolds, "Theology and Disability: Changing the Conversation," in *Journal of Religion, Disability and Health* 16 (2012): 33–48, http://dx.doi.org/10.1080/15228967.2012.645612.

16 Block, *Copious Hosting*, 121.

17 For an exploration of this point about segregation, see Wolf Wolfensberger, "The Good Life for Mentally Retarded Persons," in *Journal of Religion, Disability and Health* 4 (2001): 103–9 (106–7), http://dx.doi.org/10.1300/J095v04n02_07.

18 Brock expands on this in his exegesis of 1 Cor 12. He argues that the gifts of the Holy Spirit only really exist in the dynamic of being shared between members of the fellowship. If that is correct, it is the expectation of giving and receiving to and from all, and the experience of that, that constitutes the church. See Brock, *Wondrously Wounded*, 201–14.

19 Examples of where the celebration of the Eucharist seems to function as this critical test are found in Eiesland, *The Disabled God*, 113; Gillibrand, *Disabled Church, Disabled Society*, 147; and Block, *Copious Hosting*, 115.

20 David T. Mitchell and Sharon L. Snyder, *Narrative Prosthesis: Disability and the Dependencies of Discourse* (Ann Arbor: University of Michigan Press, 2000), 47, www.jstor.org/stable/10.3998/mpub.11523.6.

21 In this discussion, "readers" is used as a summary term to encompass the various ways in which people of diverse embodiment and ability might encounter Scripture. The idea of the reader of Scripture also points to much wider studies and theories of the relationship between text and reader which are not explored further here.

22 Yong, *Bible, Disability, and the Church*, 13. Another example is Kathy Black's work on hermeneutics, looking at a number of instances of disability in the biblical text, how they have tended to be read in the past, and how they might be read in a way that interprets disability positively. See Kathy Black, *A Healing Homiletic: Preaching and Disability* (Nashville: Abingdon, 1996).

23 The "invisibilizing" of a character typically occurs when the person becomes hidden behind ether a supposed spiritual meaning for their disability or behind what the event

says about Jesus or the promises of God. See Warren Carter, "The Blind, Lame and Paralyzed (John 5:3): John's Gospel, Disability Studies, and Postcolonial Perspectives," in *Disability Studies and Biblical Literature*, ed. Candida R. Moss and Jeremy Schipper (New York: Palgrave Macmillan, 2011), 129–50.

24 This is part of the biblical studies aspect of disability-perspective hermeneutics, seeking to understand what presumptions lay behind the way disability appears in the biblical text. A fascinating study of how physicality was thought to reveal character is provided in Mikeal C. Parsons, *Body and Character in Luke and Acts: The Subversion of Physiognomy in Early Christianity* (Grand Rapids: Baker Academic, 2006).

25 Parsons, *Body and Character*, 113–21.

26 Weiss-Block makes the general point that those in the healing narratives, apart from Bartimaeus, are generally not named, which she interprets as reducing them to figures without status and adding to the challenges of disability-perspective hermeneutics. See Block, *Copious Hosting*, 111.

27 Black, *Healing Homiletic*, 75–77.

28 As Hull puts it: "Blindness is not just something that happens to one's eyes; it is something that happens to one's world." See Hull, "Broken Body in a Broken World," 9.

29 Clark-Soles examines the range of ways that Mark's gospel uses disability rhetorically, particularly its use of blindness as a metaphor as in this passage. He points out that use of disabilities by the text in this way raises all the discomforts about exclusion that the disability rights movement has so effectively put its finger on. See Jaime Clark-Soles, "Mark and Disability," *Interpretation: A Journal of Bible and Theology* 70 (2016): 159–71 (161).

30 Hull, *In the Beginning*, 48.

31 Holly Joan Toensing, "Living among the Tombs: Society, Mental Illness and Self-Destruction in Mark 5:1-20," in *This Abled Body: Rethinking Disabilities in Biblical Studies*, ed. Hector Avalos et al. (Atlanta: Society of Biblical Literature, 2007), 131–43 (140–43).

32 The lack of distinction between disease and disability has long been a source of difficulty. The development of the charismatic healing movement pioneered by John Wimber, for example, also did not differentiate. It placed all that might be regarded as a potential target for healing under the general heading of "sickness" and treated it as an outworking of the original deep spiritual sickness of sin. See for example, Wimber and Springer, *Power Healing*, 35.

33 Yong, *Bible, Disability, and the Church*, 53.

34 See, for example, Black, *Healing Homiletic*, 183.

35 There are of course other interpretations of Paul's thorn, suggesting for example that it is a reference to his religious opponents. Those may or may not arise from discomfort with the idea that, having prayed, Paul is seemingly not healed.

36 Returning to Carter's postcolonial reading above, he interprets the healings as a prefiguring of Jesus rolling back imperial power and exposing its false claims to bring health and prosperity, which will happen at the cross. However, that reading again has the issue of treating disability as illustrative and healing as a metaphor for dealing with sin, albeit that it is the sin of the empire, not of the individual, that is dealt with. See Carter, "Blind, Lame and Paralyzed," 145.

37 For example, this was found in Frances Young's comments, noted earlier, about her perception that her son Arthur has such a vocation. It is also echoed in the writing of Jean Vanier, the founder of the L'Arche communities.

6 CONTINUITY OF THE TRADITIONAL MODELS

1 This inability to discern the complexity of sin is more than just an acknowledgment of a lack of awareness. It includes the perception that our actions or attitudes are right, though another may see them as clearly wrong. Situations of discrimination, whether on grounds of race, gender, ability, or other measures would provide examples.

2 There are echoes here of McFadyen's discussion of the complexity of personal and systemic sin in the earlier discussion of the nature of alienation.

3 A preference for placing the emphasis of a sacrifice interpretation of the atonement on the Passover was found earlier in both Paul Fiddes and N. T. Wright. This is not least because the Passion and crucifixion took place at the Passover celebration and because Jesus himself seems to imply the connection in his celebration of the Last Supper. See Fiddes, *Past Event and Present Salvation*, 61; and Wright, *Day the Revolution Began*, 296.

4 This symbolic connection is made explicitly in Heb 13:11-12 as part of that letter's extended interpretation of the cross using ideas of sacrifice and priesthood.

5 N. T. Wright, *The Resurrection of the Son of God* (London: SPCK, 2003), 730.

6 The challenge of avoiding an exemplarist interpretation of the atonement seems always to have been with us. For example, it arises in the much earlier Christian idea of recapitulation that is found particularly in Irenaeus. Following his approach, the victory of the atonement is not only a cosmic battle won through the cross and resurrection. It involves Jesus going over all of the ground on which we (who are "in Adam") have failed and on which Jesus remains faithful and succeeds. In this way Jesus participates in all aspects of being human, and his victory incorporates his human overcoming of a wide variety of (greater and lesser) temptation and suffering. Under a careless reading this can easily slide toward an exemplarist understanding, but Irenaeus' emphasis on Jesus' intimate participation in all aspects of life, temptation, and death brings it closer to what is being suggested here. See Pugh, *Atonement Theories*, 25.

Bibliography

Anselm. *Cur Deus Homo*. In *Basic Writings*, 2nd ed., translated by S. N. Deane. La Salle, Ill.: Open Court, 1974.

Athanasius. *Contra Gentes and De Incarnatione*. Translated by Robert W. Thomson. Oxford: Clarendon Press, 1971.

Aulén, Gustaf. *Christus Victor: An Historical Study of the Three Main Types of the Idea of the Atonement*. Translated by A. G. Herbert. London: SPCK, 1931.

Balcomb, Anthony. "The Metaphysics of Participation: Exploring an Idea Whose Time Has Returned." *Journal of Theology for Southern Africa* 145 (2013): 18–34.

Barbour, Ian G. *Myths, Models and Paradigms*. New York: Harper & Row, 1974.

Barnes, Colin. "Understanding the Social Model of Disability." In *Routledge Handbook of Disability Studies*, edited by N. Watson et al., 12–29. Abingdon: Routledge, 2012.

Bauckham, Richard. "Eschatology." In *The Oxford Handbook of Systematic Theology*, edited by John Webster et al. Oxford: Oxford University Press, 2007. http://dx.doi.org/10.1093/oxfordhb/9780199245765.001.0001.

Bell, Richard H. "Sacrifice and Christology in Paul." *Journal of Theological Studies* 53, no. 1 (2002): 1–27. www.jstor.org/stable/23969330.

Bickenbach, Jerome. "The International Classification of Functioning, Disability and Health and Its Relationship to Disability Studies." In *Routledge Handbook of Disability Studies*, edited by N. Watson et al., 51–66. Abingdon: Routledge, 2012.

Birchenall, Peter, and Mary Birchenall. "Caring for Mentally Handicapped People: The Community and the Church." *Professional Nurse* 1, no. 6 (1986): 148–50.

Black, Kathy. *A Healing Homiletic: Preaching and Disability*. Nashville: Abingdon, 1996.

Black, Max. *Models and Metaphors: Studies in Language and Philosophy*. Ithaca, N.Y.: Cornell University Press, 1962.

Block, Jennie Weiss. *Copious Hosting: A Theology of Access for People with Disabilities*. New York: Continuum, 2002.

Bowers, Faith. *When Weak, Then Strong: Disability in the Life of the Church*. London: Bloomsbury Central Baptist Church, 2008.

———. "Where Ministers Fear to Tread." In *Let Love Be Genuine: Mental Handicap and the Church*, edited by Faith Bowers, 55–63. London: Baptist Union, 1985.

Brock, Brian "Augustine's Incitement to Lament, from the Enarrationes in Psalmos." In *Evoking Lament*, edited by Eva Harasta and Brian Brock, 183–203. London: T&T Clark International, 2009.

———. "Autism, Care, and Christian Hope." *Journal of Religion, Disability and Health* 13, no. 1 (2009): 7–28. https://doi.org/10.1080/15228960802581404.

———. *Christian Ethics in a Technological Age*. Grand Rapids: Eerdmans, 2010.

———. "Disability and the Quest for the Human." In *Disability in the Christian Tradition*, edited by Brian Brock and John Swinton, 1–23. Grand Rapids: Eerdmans, 2012.

———. "How Can We Talk about Disability." Presentation at the Summer Institute on Theology and Disability, 2017. https://www.youtube.com/watch?v=3OonmVpI7fU.

———. "Supererogation and the Riskiness of Human Vulnerability." In *The Paradox of Disability: Responses to Jean Vanier and L'Arche Communities from Theology and the Sciences*, edited by Hans S. Reinders, 127–39. Grand Rapids: Eerdmans, 2010.

———. "Theologizing Inclusion: 1 Corinthians 12 and the Politics of the Body of Christ." *Journal of Religion, Disability and Health* 15 (2011): 351–76. http://dx.doi.org/10.1080/15228967.2011.620389.

———. *Wondrously Wounded: Theology, Disability, and the Body of Christ*. Waco, Tex.: Baylor University Press, 2019.

Brock, Brian, and John Swinton, eds. *Disability in the Christian Tradition: A Reader*. Grand Rapids: Eerdmans, 2012.

Brock, Brian, and Stephanie Brock. "Being Disabled in the New World of Genetic Testing: A Snapshot of Shifting Landscapes." In *Theology, Disability and the New Genetics: Why Science Needs the Church*, edited by John Swinton and Brian Brock, 29–43. London: Continuum, 2007.

Bunch, William H. "Toward a Theology of Inclusion for Those with Disabilities." *Journal of Religion, Disability and Health* 5 (2001): 37–44. http://dx.doi.org/10.1300/J095v05n04_03.

Caird, G. B. *The Language and Imagery of the Bible*. London: Duckworth, 1980.

Carter, Warren. "The Blind, Lame and Paralyzed (John 5:3): John's Gospel, Disability Studies, and Postcolonial Perspectives." In *Disability Studies and Biblical Literature*, edited by Candida R. Moss and Jeremy Schipper, 129–50. New York: Palgrave Macmillan, 2011.

Chalke, Steve, and Alan Mann. *The Lost Message of Jesus*. Grand Rapids: Zondervan, 2003.

Clark-Soles, Jaime. "John, First–Third John, and Revelation." In *The Bible and Disability: A Commentary*, edited by Sarah J. Melcher et al., 333–78. Waco, Tex.: Baylor University Press, 2017.

Clark-Soles, Jaime. "Mark and Disability." *Interpretation: A Journal of Bible and Theology* 70 (2016): 159–71.

Creamer, Deborah Beth. *Disability and Christian Theology: Embodied Limits and Constructive Possibilities*. Oxford: Oxford University Press, 2009.

———. "God Doesn't Treat His Children That Way." *Journal of Religion, Disability and Health* 9, no. 3 (2006): 73–84. https://doi.org/10.1300/J095v09n03_05.

———. "Including All Bodies in the Body of God." *Journal of Religion, Disability and Health* 9, no. 4 (2006): 55–69. https://doi.org/10.1300/J095v09n04_04.

Crisp, Oliver D. "By His Birth We Are Healed: Our Redemption, It Turns Out, Began Long before Calvary." *Christianity Today* 56, no. 3 (2012): 30–34.

———. "Methodological Issues in Approaching the Atonement." In *T&T Clark Companion to Atonement*, edited by Adam J. Johnson, 315–33. London: Bloomsbury T&T Clark, 2017.

Davidson, Ivor J. "Atonement and Incarnation." In *T&T Clark Companion to Atonement*, edited by Adam J. Johnson, 35–56. London: Bloomsbury T&T Clark, 2017.

De Vaux, Roland. *Studies in Old Testament Sacrifice*. Cardiff: University of Wales Press, 1964.

Dillistone, F. W. *The Christian Understanding of Atonement*. Welwyn: James Nisbet, 1968.

Dunhill, John. "Communicative Bodies and Economies of Grace: The Role of Sacrifice in the Christian Understanding of the Body." *Journal of Religion* 83, no. 1 (2003): 79–93.

Easter, Brian. "Sacraments and the Mentally Handicapped." In *Let Love Be Genuine: Mental Handicap and the Church*, edited by Faith Bowers, 64–74. London: Baptist Union, 1985.

Edwards, Denis. *How God Acts: Creation, Redemption, and Special Divine Action*. Minneapolis: Fortress Press, 2010.

Edwards, Steven D. "Definitions of Disability." In *Arguing about Disability: Philosophical Perspectives*, edited by Simo Vehmas and et al., 30–41. Abingdon: Routledge, 2009.

Eiesland, Nancy L. *The Disabled God: Toward a Liberatory Theology of Disability*. Nashville: Abingdon, 1994.

———. "Sacramental Bodies." *Journals of Religion, Disability and Health* 13, nos. 3–4 (2009): 236–46. https://doi.org/10.1080/15228960902931830.

Fast, Mary Schaefer. "A Theology of Disability: Living as a Theologian of the Cross." *Journal of Religion, Disability and Health* 15 (2011): 414–30. http://dx.doi.org/10.1080/15228967.2011.620392.

Fiddes, Paul S. "Creation Out of Love." In *The Work of Love: Creation and Kenosis*, edited by John Polkinghorne, 167–91. London: SPCK, 2001.

———. *The Creative Suffering of God*. New ed. Oxford: Oxford University Press, 1992.

———. *Participating in God: A Pastoral Doctrine of the Trinity*. London: Darton, Longman & Todd, 2000.

———. *Past Event and Present Salvation: The Christian Idea of Atonement*. London: Darton, Longman & Todd, 1989.

Fine, Lawrence. *Physician of the Soul, Healer of the Cosmos: Isaac Luria and His Kabbalistic Fellowship*. Stanford, Calif.: Stanford University Press, 2003.

Gane, Roy E. *Cult and Character: Purification Offerings, Day of Atonement, and Theodicy*. Winona Lake, Ind.: Eisenbrauns, 2005.

Garcia, Mark A. "Union with Christ." In *T&T Clark Companion to Atonement*, edited by Adam J. Johnson, 781–86. London: Bloomsbury T&T Clark, 2017.

Garfinkel, Alan. *Forms of Explanation—Rethinking the Questions in Social Theory*. New Haven, Conn.: Yale University Press, 1981.

Gaventa, William C. *Disability and Spirituality: Recovering Wholeness*. Waco, Tex.: Baylor University Press, 2018.

Gillibrand, John. *Disabled Church—Disabled Society: The Implications of Autism for Philosophy, Theology and Politics*. London: Jessica Kingsley, 2010.

Gorman, Michael J. "Effecting the New Covenant: A (Not So) New, New Testament Model for the Atonement." *Ex Auditu* 26 (2010): 26–59.

———. "Paul's Corporate, Cruciform, Missional Theosis in 2 Corinthians." In *"In Christ" in Paul: Explorations in Paul's Theology of Union and Participation*, edited by Michael J. Thate et al., 181–208. Tübingen: Mohr Siebeck, 2014.

Gould, James Barton. "The Hope of Heavenly Healing of Disability Part 1: Theological Issues." *Journal of Disability and Religion* 20 (2016): 317–34. http://dx.doi.org/10.1080/23312521.2016.1239153.

———. “The Hope of Heavenly Healing of Disability Part 2: Philosophical Issues.” *Journal of Disability and Religion* 21 (2017): 98–116. http://dx.doi.org/10.1080/23312521.2016.1270177.

Graham, Jeannine Michele. “Substitution and Representation.” In *T&T Clark Companion to Atonement*, edited by Adam J. Johnson, 763–68. London: Bloomsbury T&T Clark, 2017.

Green, Joel B. *The Gospel of Luke*. The New International Commentary on the New Testament. Grand Rapids: Eerdmans, 1997.

———. “Theologies of the Atonement in the New Testament.” In *T&T Clark Companion to Atonement*, edited by Adam J. Johnson, 115–34. London: Bloomsbury T&T Clark, 2017.

Green, Joel B., and Mark D. Baker. *Recovering the Scandal of the Cross: Atonement in New Testament and Contemporary Contexts*. Carlisle: Paternoster, 2000.

Guđmundsdóttir, Arnfríđur. “Crucified—So What? Feminist Rereadings of the Cross-Event.” In *T&T Clark Companion to Atonement*, edited by Adam J. Johnson, 335–54. London: Bloomsbury T&T Clark, 2017.

Gunton, Colin E. *The Actuality of Atonement: A Study of Metaphor, Rationality and the Christian Tradition*. London: T&T Clark, 1988.

Harris, Murray J. *The Second Epistle to the Corinthians*. The New International Greek Testament Commentary. Grand Rapids: Eerdmans, 2005.

Harshaw, Jill. “Finding Accommodation: Spirituality and People with Profound Intellectual Disabilities.” *Journal of Disability and Religion* 20 (2016): 140–53. http://dx.doi.org/10.1080/23312521.2016.1203694.

———. *God beyond Words: Christian Theology and the Spiritual Experiences of People with Profound Intellectual Disabilities*. London: Jessica Kingsley, 2016.

Hauerwas, Stanley. “Chapter 7. The Retarded and the Criteria for the Human.” *Journal of Religion, Disability & Health* 8, nos. 3–4 (2005): 127–34. https://doi.org/10.1300/J095v08n03_15.

———. *Suffering Presence: Theological Reflections on Medicine, the Mentally Handicapped, and the Church*. Edinburgh: T&T Clark, 1988.

Hayes, John H. “Atonement in the Book of Leviticus.” *Interpretation: A Journal of Bible and Theology* 20, no. 1 (1998): 5–15. https://doi.org/10.1177/002096439605200102.

Hick, John, and Paul F. Knitter, eds. *The Myth of Christian Uniqueness*. London: SCM Press, 1988.

Hilborn, David. “Atonement, Evangelicalism, and the Evangelical Alliance: The Present Debate in Context.” In *Atonement Debate: Papers from the London Symposium on the Theology of Atonement*, edited by Derek Tidball et al., 15–33. Grand Rapids: Zondervan, 2008.

Hull, John M. “The Broken Body in a Broken World.” *Journal of Religion, Disability and Health* 7 (2004): 5–23. http://dx.doi.org/10.1300/J095v07n04_02.

———. *In the Beginning There Was Darkness*. London: SCM Press, 2001.

———. *On Sight and Insight: A Journey into the World of Blindness*. Oxford: Oneworld, 1997.

———. *Touching the Rock: An Experience of Blindness*. London: SPCK, 2013.

Hull, Richard. “Disability and Freedom.” In *Arguing about Disability: Philosophical Perspectives*, edited by Simo Vehmas et al., 93–104. Abingdon: Routledge, 2009.

Isherwood, Lisa, and Elizabeth Stuart. *Introducing Body Theology*. Sheffield: Sheffield Academic Press, 1998.

Johnson, Adam J. “Atonement: The Shape and State of the Doctrine.” In *T&T Clark Companion to Atonement*, edited by Adam J. Johnson, 1–17. London: Bloomsbury T&T Clark, 2017.

———. “Peter Abelard.” In *T&T Clark Companion to Atonement*, edited by Adam J. Johnson, 357–60. London: Bloomsbury T&T Clark, 2017.

———, ed. *T&T Clark Companion to Atonement*. London: Bloomsbury T&T Clark, 2017.

Johnstone, David. *An Introduction to Disability Studies*. 2nd ed. London: David Fulton, 2001.

Jüngel, Eberhard. *God as the Mystery of the World: On the Foundation of the Theology of the Crucified One in the Dispute between Theism and Atheism*. Edinburgh: T&T Clark, 1983.

———. "Metaphorical Truth." In *Eberhard Jüngel, Theological Essays*, vol. 1, edited by J. B. Webster, 25–71. Edinburgh, T&T Clark, 1989.

Kotsko, Adam. "Exemplarism." In *T&T Clark Companion to Atonement*, edited by Adam J. Johnson, 485–88. London: Bloomsbury T&T Clark, 2017.

MacQuarrie, John. *Principles of Christian Theology*. London: SCM Press, 1966.

Marshall, I. Howard. *Aspects of the Atonement: Cross and Resurrection in the Reconciling of God and Humanity*. Milton Keynes: Authentic Media, 2007.

———. *The Gospel of Luke: A Commentary on the Greek Text*. The New International Greek Testament Commentary. Exeter: Paternoster, 1978.

Matthews, Pia. "Participation and the Profoundly Disabled: 'Being' Engaged—a Theological Approach." *Journal of Religion, Disability and Health* 17 (2013): 426–38. http://dx.doi.org/10.1080/15228967.2013.840971.

McCabe, Herbert. *God, Christ and Us*. Edited by Brian Davies. London: Continuum, 2003.

———. *God Matters*. London: Mowbray, 1987.

———. *God Still Matters*. Edited by Brian Davies. London: Continuum, 2002.

McCloughry, Roy, and Wayne Morris. *Making a World of Difference: Christian Reflections on Disability*. London: SPCK, 2002.

McDonald, H. D. *The New Testament Concept of the Atonement: The Gospel of the Calvary Event*. Cambridge: Lutterworth, 1994.

McFadyen, Alistair. *Bound to Sin: Abuse, Holocaust and the Christian Doctrine of Sin*. Cambridge: Cambridge University Press, 2000.

———. *The Call to Personhood: A Christian Theory of the Individual in Social Relationships*. Cambridge: Cambridge University Press, 1990.

McFague, Sallie. *Metaphorical Theology: Models of God in Religious Language*. London: SCM Press, 1983.

———. *Models of God: Theology for an Ecological Nuclear Age*. London: SCM Press, 1987.

———. *Speaking in Parables: A Study in Metaphor and Theology*. London: SCM Press, 2002.

McGrath, Alister. "The Moral Theory of the Atonement: An Historical and Theological Critique." *Scottish Journal of Theology* 38, no. 2 (1985): 205–20. doi:10.1017/S0036930600041351.

McIntyre, John. *The Shape of Soteriology*. Edinburgh: T&T Clark, 1992.

McLachlan, David. "Minding the Gap—a Theological Examination of the Disconnection between Christian Theologies of Charismatic Healing and Theologies of Disability in a Contemporary Evangelical Context." Unpublished Master of Theology dissertation, University of Manchester, 2015.

Melcher, Sarah J. "With Whom Do the Disabled Associate? Metaphorical Interplay in the Latter Prophets." In *This Abled Body: Rethinking Disabilities in Biblical Studies*, edited by Hector Avalos et al., 115–29. Atlanta: Society of Biblical Literature, 2007.

Middleton, Peter, and James Spinney, dirs. *Notes on Blindness*. Brooklyn, N.Y.: Oscilloscope, 2016.

Milgrom, Jacob. *Leviticus 1–16: A New Translation and Commentary*. Anchor Bible 3. New York: Doubleday, 1991.

Mitchell, David, and Sharon Snyder. "Jesus Thrown Everything Off Balance: Disability and Redemption in Biblical Literature." In *This Abled Body: Rethinking Disabilities in Biblical Studies*, edited by Hector Avalos et al., 173–83. Atlanta: Society of Biblical Literature, 2007.

———. *Narrative Prosthesis: Disability and the Dependencies of Discourse*. Ann Arbor: University of Michigan Press, 2000. www.jstor.org/stable/10.3998/mpub.11523.6.

Moltmann, Jürgen. *The Crucified God: The Cross of Christ as the Foundation and Criticism of Christian Theology*. Translated by R. A. Wilson and John Bowden. London: SCM Press, 1974.

———. *The Future of Creation*. Translated by Margaret Kohl. London: SCM Press, 1979.

———. *God in Creation: An Ecological Doctrine of Creation*. Translated by Margaret Kohl. London: SCM Press, 1985.

———. "God's Kenosis in the Creation and Consummation of the World." In *The Work of Love: Creation and Kenosis*, edited by John Polkinghorne, 137–51. London: SPCK, 2001.

———. *The Trinity and the Kingdom of God: The Doctrine of God*. Translated by Margaret Kohl. London: SCM Press, 1981.

Morris, Wayne. *Theology without Words: Theology in the Deaf Community*. Aldershot: Ashgate, 2008.

———. "Transforming Able-Bodied Normativity: The Wounded Christ and Human Vulnerability." *Irish Theological Quarterly* 78, no. 3 (2013): 231–43. http://itq.sagepub.com/content/78/3/231.full.pdf+html.

Moss, Candida R., and Jeremy Schipper, eds. *Disability Studies and Biblical Literature*. New York: Palgrave Macmillan, 2011.

Moule, C. F. D. *The Origin of Christology*. Cambridge: Cambridge University Press, 1977.

Nelson, James B. *Body Theology*. Louisville: Westminster John Knox, 1992.

O'Connor, Timothy, and Hong Yu Wong. "Emergent Properties." In *The Stanford Encyclopedia of Philosophy*, edited by Edward N. Zalta, Spring 2012 ed. http://plato.stanford.edu/archives/spr2012/entries/properties-emergent.

Oliver, Michael. *The Politics of Disablement*. Critical Texts in Social Work and the Welfare State. Basingstoke: MacMillan, 1990.

———. *Understanding Disability: From Theory to Practice*. 2nd ed. Basingstoke: Palgrave Macmillan, 2009.

Pailin, David A. *A Gentle Touch: From a Theology of Handicap to a Theology of Human Being*. London: SPCK, 1992.

Parsons, Mikeal C. *Body and Character in Luke and Acts: The Subversion of Physiognomy in Early Christianity*. Grand Rapids: Baker Academic, 2006.

Peters, Roger K. "Self-Advocacy through Participation in the Lord's Supper for Persons Who Are Conceptually Non-expressive." *Journal of Religion, Disability and Health* 13 (2009): 297–310. http://dx.doi.org/10.1080/15228960902931913.

Poirier, John C. "Another Look at the 'Man Born Blind' in John 9." *Journal of Disability, Religion and Health* 14, no. 1 (2010): 60–65. https://doi.org/10.1080/15228960903517323.

Polkinghorne, John. "The Corporate Christ." In *Who Is Jesus Christ for Us Today? Pathways to Contemporary Christology*, edited by A. Schuele and G. Thomas, 103–14. Louisville: Westminster John Knox, 2009.

———. "Kenotic Creation and Divine Action." In *The Work of Love: Creation and Kenosis*, edited by John Polkinghorne, 90–106. London: SPCK, 2001.

———, ed. *The Work of Love: Creation and Kenosis*. London SPCK, 2001.

Pugh, Ben. *Atonement Theories: A Way Through the Maze*. Cambridge: James Clarke, 2015.

Reeve, Donna. "Biopolitics and Bare Life: Does the Impaired Body Provide Contemporary Examples of Homo Sacer?" In *Arguing about Disability: Philosophical Perspectives*, edited by Simo Vehmas et al., 203–17. Abingdon: Routledge, 2009.

Reinders, Hans S. *Disability, Providence and Ethics: Bridging Gaps, Transforming Lives*. Waco, Tex.: Baylor University Press, 2014.

———. *Receiving the Gift of Friendship: Profound Disability, Theological Anthropology, and Ethics*. Grand Rapids: Eerdmans, 2008.

———. "Watch the Lilies of the Field: Theological Reflections on Profound Disability and Time." In *The Paradox of Disability: Responses to Jean Vanier and L'Arche Communities from Theology and the Sciences*, edited by Hans S. Reinders, 154–68. Grand Rapids: Eerdmans, 2010.

Reynolds, Thomas E. "Theology and Disability: Changing the Conversation." *Journal of Religion, Disability and Health* 16 (2012): 33–48. http://dx.doi.org/10.1080/15228967.2012.645612.

———. *Vulnerable Communion: A Theology of Disability and Hospitality*. Grand Rapids: Brazos, 2008.

Ricoeur, Paul. *The Rule of Metaphor: The Creation of Meaning in Language*. Translated by Robert Czerny et al. Abingdon: Routledge Classics, 2003.

Rowley, Howard H. *The Meaning of Sacrifice in the Old Testament*. Manchester: John Rylands Library, 1950.

Sansom, M. C. "Laying On of Hands in the Old Testament." *Expository Times* 94, no. 11 (1983): 323–36. http://ext.sagepub.com.manchester.idm.oclc.org/content/94/11/323.

Schmiechen, Peter. *Saving Power: Theories of Atonement and Forms of the Church*. Grand Rapids: Eerdmans, 2005.

Scholem, Gershom G. *Major Trends in Jewish Mysticism*. London: Thames and Hudson, 1955.

Sellers, R. V. *The Council of Chalcedon*. London: SPCK, 1953.

Sewell, Elizabeth. *The Human Metaphor*. Notre Dame, Ind.: University of Notre Dame Press, 1964.

Shakespeare, Tom. *Disability Rights and Wrongs Revisited*. 2nd ed. Abingdon: Routledge, 2014.

Soskice, Janet Martin. *Metaphor and Religious Language*. Oxford: Oxford University Press, 1985.

Stott, John. *The Cross of Christ*. Leicester: InterVarsity, 1986.

Surin, Kenneth. *Theology and the Problem of Evil*. Oxford: Blackwell, 1986.

Sutton, Agneta. *Christian Bioethics: A Guide for the Perplexed*. London: T&T Clark, 2008.

Swinton, John. *Becoming Friends of Time: Disability, Timefullness and Gentle Discipleship*. London: SCM Press, 2017.

———. *Building a Church for Strangers*. Contact Pastoral Monographs 9. Edinburgh: Contact Pastoral Trust, 1999.

———. "Building a Church for Strangers." *Journal of Religion, Disability and Health* 4 (2001): 25–63. http://dx.doi.org/10.1300/J095v04n04_03.

———. "Known by God." In *The Paradox of Disability: Responses to Jean Vanier and L'Arche Communities from Theology and the Sciences*, edited by Hans S. Reinders, 140–53. Grand Rapids: Eerdmans, 2010.

———. *Raging with Compassion: Pastoral Responses to the Problem of Evil*. Grand Rapids: Eerdmans, 2007.

———. "Restoring the Image: Spirituality, Faith and Cognitive Disability." *Journal of Religion and Health* 36, no. 1 (1997): 21–27.

———. "Using Our Bodies Faithfully: Christian Friendship and the Life of Worship." *Journal of Disability and Religion* 19 (2015): 228–42. http://dx.doi.org/10.1080/23312521.2015.1062350.

Swinton, John, et al. "Whose Story Am I? Redescribing Profound Intellectual Disability in the Kingdom of God." *Journal of Religion, Disability and Health* 15 (2011): 5–19. http://dx.doi.org/10.1080/15228967.2011.539337.

Swinton, John, and Harriet Mowat. *Practical Theology and Qualitative Research*. London: SCM Press, 2006.

Tan, Amanda Shao. "The Disabled Christ." *Transformation* 15, no. 4 (1998): 8–14.

Tennent, Timothy C. *Theology in the Context of World Christianity*. Grand Rapids: Zondervan, 2007.

Toensing, Holly Joan. "Living among the Tombs: Society, Mental Illness and Self-Destruction in Mark 5:1-20." In *This Abled Body: Rethinking Disabilities in Biblical Studies*, edited by Hector Avalos et al., 131–43. Atlanta: Society of Biblical Literature, 2007.

Torrance, Alan J. *Persons in Communion: Trinitarian Description and Human Participation*. Edinburgh: T&T Clark, 1996.

United Kingdom. *Disability Discrimination Act 1995* (as amended by the 2005 Act). HMSO, 1995. http://www.legislation.gov.uk/ukpga/1995/50.

United Nations. *Convention on the Rights of Persons with Disabilities*. http://www.un.org/development/desa/disabilities/convention-on-the-rights-of-persons-with-disabilities.html.

Vanhoozer, Kevin J. "From 'Blessed in Christ' to 'Being in Christ': The State of Union and the Place of Participation in Paul's Discourse, New Testament Exegesis, and Systematic Theology Today." In *"In Christ" in Paul: Explorations in Paul's Theology of Union and Participation*, edited by Michael J. Thate et al., 3–36. Tübingen: Mohr Siebeck, 2014.

Vanier, Jean. *Becoming Human*. London: Darton, Longman & Todd, 1999.

———. *Essential Writings*. Edited by Carolyn Whitney-Brown. Maryknoll, N.Y.: Orbis Books, 2008.

———. *Signs of the Times: Seven Paths of Hope for a Troubled World*. London: DLT, 2013.

Vanier, Jean, and John Swinton. "Theology: A Place to Belong—Understanding and Being alongside People Experiencing Mental Health Problems." In *Mental Health: The Inclusive Church Resource*, 53–103. London: Darton, Longman & Todd, 2014.

Vehmas, Simo, Kristjana Kristiansen, and Tom Shakespeare. "The Unavoidable Alliance of Disability Studies and Philosophy." In *Arguing about Disability: Philosophical Perspectives*, edited by Simo Vehmas et al., 1–11. Abingdon: Routledge, 2009.

Vehmas, Simo, and Pekka Mäkelä. "The Ontology of Disability and Impairment: A Discussion of the Natural and Social Features." In *Arguing about Disability: Philosophical Perspectives*, edited by Simo Vehmas et al., 42–56. Abingdon: Routledge, 2009.

Weinandy, Thomas G. *Athanasius: A Theological Introduction*. Farnham: Ashgate, 2007.

Weingard, Richard E. *The Logic of Divine Love: A Critical Analysis of the Soteriology of Peter Abailard*. Oxford: Oxford University Press, 1970.

White, Vernon. *Atonement and Incarnation: An Essay in Universalism and Particularity*. Cambridge: Cambridge University Press, 1991.

Wilder, C. "On Christ and Healing: Eiesland, Tillich, and Disability Theology." *Dialog* 51 (2012): 202–11. doi:10.1111/j.1540-6385.2012.00686.x.

Wiles, Maurice. *The Remaking of Christian Doctrine*. London: SCM Press, 1974.

Wimber, John, and Kevin Springer. *Power Evangelism: Signs and Wonders Today*. London: Hodder and Stoughton, 1985.

———. *Power Healing*. London: Hodder & Stoughton, 1986.

Wolfensberger, Wolf. "The Good Life for Mentally Retarded Persons." *Journal of Religion, Disability and Health* 4 (2001): 103–9. http://dx.doi.org/10.1300/J095v04n02_07.

Wolterstorff, Nicholas. *Justice Rights and Wrongs*. Princeton, N.J.: Princeton University Press, 2008.

World Health Organization. *How to Use the ICF: A Practical Manual Exposure Draft for Comment, October 2013*. Geneva: World Health Organization, 2013. http://www.who.int/classifications/drafticfpracticalmanual2.pdf?ua=1.

———. *International Classification of Diseases (ICD)*. Version 10. Geneva: World Health Organization, 2010. http://www.who.int/classifications/icd/en/.

———. *International Classification of Functioning, Disability and Health (ICF)*. Geneva: World Health Organization, 2001. http://www.who.int/classifications/icf/en/.

———. *International Classification of Impairments, Disabilities and Handicaps*. Geneva: World Health Organization, 1980. http://apps.who.int/iris/bitstream/10665/41003/1/9241541261_eng.pdf.

———. *WHO ICD-11 Revision*. http://www.who.int/classifications/icd/revision/en/.

Wright, David P. "The Gesture of Hand Placement in the Hebrew Bible and in Hittite Literature." *Journal of the American Oriental Society* 106, no. 3 (1986): 433–46. www.jstor.org/stable/602103.

Wright, N. T. *The Day the Revolution Began: Rethinking the Meaning of Jesus' Crucifixion*. London: SPCK, 2016.

———. *Paul and the Faithfulness of God, Parts III and IV*. London: SPCK, 2013.

———. *The Resurrection of the Son of God*. London: SPCK, 2003.

———. *Surprised by Hope*. London: SPCK, 2007.

Yong, Amos. *The Bible, Disability, and the Church: A New Vision of the People of God*. Grand Rapids: Eerdmans, 2011.

———. "Disability from the Margins to the Center: Hospitality and Inclusion in the Church." *Journal of Religion, Disability and Health* 15, no. 4 (2011): 339–50. https://doi.org/10.1080/15228967.2011.620387.

———. *Theology and Down Syndrome*. Waco, Tex.: Baylor University Press, 2007.

Young, Frances M. *Arthur's Call: A Journey of Faith in the Face of Severe Learning Disability*. London: SPCK, 2014.

———. *The Art of Performance: Towards a Theology of Holy Scripture*. London: Darton, Longman & Todd, 1990.

———. *Brokenness and Blessing: Towards a Biblical Spirituality*. London: Darton, Longman & Todd, 2007.

———. *Can These Dry Bones Live?* London: SCM Press, 1982.

———. "A Cloud of Witnesses." In *The Myth of God Incarnate*, edited by John Hick, 13–47. London: SCM, 1977.

———. *Construing the Cross: Type, Sign, Symbol, Word, Action*. London: SPCK, 2016.

———. *Face to Face: A Narrative Essay in the Theology of Suffering*. Edinburgh: T&T Clark, 1990.

———. *God's Presence: A Contemporary Recapitulation of Early Christianity*. Cambridge: Cambridge University Press, 2013.

———. "Incarnation and Atonement: God Suffered and Died." In *Incarnation and Myth: The Debate Continued*, edited by Michael Goulder, 101–3. London: SCM Press, 1979.

———. *The Making of the Creeds*. London: SCM Press, 1991.

———. *Nicea to Chalcedon: A Guide to the Literature and Its Background*. 2nd ed. London: SCM Press, 2010.

———. *Sacrifice and the Death of Christ*. Reprint, London: Xpress Reprints, 1994.

———. *The Theology of the Pastoral Letters*. Cambridge: Cambridge University Press, 1994.

Young, Frances M., and David F. Ford. *Meaning and Truth in 2 Corinthians*. London: SPCK, 1987.

Subject Index

Author Index

Scripture Index

Also Available in the SRTD Series

Formed Together: Mystery, Narrative, and Virtue in Christian Caregiving
Keith Dow

Wondrously Wounded: Theology, Disability, and the Body of Christ
Brian Brock

Disability and Spirituality: Recovering Wholeness
William C. Gaventa

Crippled Grace: Disability, Virtue Ethics, and the Good Life
Shane Clifton

The Bible and Disability: A Commentary
Edited by Sarah J. Melcher, Mikeal C. Parsons, and Amos Yong

Pastoral Care and Intellectual Disability: A Person-Centered Approach
Anna Katherine Shurley

Becoming Friends of Time: Disability, Timefullness, and Gentle Discipleship
John Swinton

Disability and World Religions: An Introduction
Edited by Darla Y. Schumm and Michael Stoltzfus

Madness: American Protestant Responses to Mental Illness
Heather H. Vacek

Disability, Providence, and Ethics: Bridging Gaps, Transforming Lives
Hans S. Reinders

Flannery O'Connor: Writing a Theology of Disabled Humanity
Timothy J. Basselin

Theology and Down Syndrome: Reimagining Disability in Late Modernity
Amos Yong